"Some time back you caused the drowning of the son of Our teacher. I order you to return him." *(p. 54)*

"Kṛṣṇa and Balarāma jumped from the top of the mountain." *(p. 114)*

Kṛṣṇa pulled them strongly, just as a child pulls a toy wooden bull. *(p. 165)*

Balarāma took a club in His hand and, without further talk, struck Rukmī on the head.
(p. 194)

This time, Nārada Muni saw that Lord Kṛṣṇa was engaged as an affectionate father petting His small children. *(p. 245)*

Being kicked by Kṛṣṇa, Ariṣṭāsura rolled over and began to move his legs violently. *(p. 3)*

Akrūra saw Balarāma turned into Śeṣa Nāga and Kṛṣṇa turned into Mahā-Viṣṇu. *(p. 21)*

The florist begged from the Lord that he might remain His eternal servant. *(p. 31)*

Full of feminine bashfulness, Kubjā stood gracefully before Kṛṣṇa. *(p. 81)*

Rukmiṇī was praying to Kṛṣṇa for the life of her brother. *(p. 131)*

The cook found a nice baby within the belly of the fish. *(p. 138)*

Bāṇāsura rushed towards Kṛṣṇa, simultaneously working five hundred bows and two thousand arrows. (p. 203)

Balarāma passed every night with the *gopīs* in the forest of Vṛndāvana. (p. 220)

KṚṢṆA

The Supreme Personality of Godhead

Volume 2

BOOKS by
His Divine Grace A. C. Bhaktivedanta Swami Prabhupāda

Bhagavad-gītā As It Is
Śrīmad-Bhāgavatam, Cantos 1–9 (27 Vols.)
Śrī Caitanya-caritāmṛta (17 Vols.)
Teachings of Lord Caitanya
The Nectar of Devotion
The Nectar of Instruction
Śrī Īśopaniṣad
Easy Journey to Other Planets
Kṛṣṇa Consciousness: The Topmost Yoga System
Kṛṣṇa, the Supreme Personality of Godhead (3 Vols.)
Perfect Questions, Perfect Answers
Transcendental Teachings of Prahlād Mahārāja
Kṛṣṇa, the Reservoir of Pleasure
Life Comes from Life
The Perfection of Yoga
Beyond Birth and Death
On the Way to Kṛṣṇa
Geetār-gan (Bengali)
Rāja-vidyā: The King of Knowledge
Elevation to Kṛṣṇa Consciousness
Kṛṣṇa Consciousness: The Matchless Gift
Back to Godhead Magazine (Founder)

A complete catalog is available upon request

Bhaktivedanta Book Trust
3764 Watseka Avenue
Los Angeles, California 90034

KṚṢṆA

The Supreme Personality of Godhead

A Summary Study of Śrīla Vyāsadeva's *Śrīmad-Bhāgavatam*, Tenth Canto

Volume 2

His Divine Grace
A.C. BHAKTIVEDANTA SWAMI PRABHUPĀDA
Founder-Ācārya of the International Society for Krishna Consciousness

THE BHAKTIVEDANTA BOOK TRUST
New York · Los Angeles · London · Bombay

Readers interested in the subject matter of this book
are invited by the International Society for Krishna Consciousness
to correspond with its Secretary

International Society for Krishna Consciousness
3764 Watseka Avenue
Los Angeles, California 90034

Library of Congress Catalog Card Number: 74-118081
International Standard Book Number for Trilogy: 0-912776-60-9
International Standard Book Number for Volume One: 0-912776-57-9
International Standard Book Number for Volume Two: 0-912776-58-7
International Standard Book Number for Volume Three: 0-912776-59-5

First Printing, 1970: 30,000 copies (2 volumes, hardbound)
Second Printing, 1971: 10,000 copies (2 volumes, hardbound)
Third Printing, 1972: 20,000 copies (2 volumes, hardbound)
Fourth Printing, 1972: 150,000 copies (3 volumes, softbound)
Fifth Printing, 1972: 150,000 copies (3 volumes, softbound)
Sixth Printing, 1972: 300,000 copies (3 volumes, softbound)
Seventh Printing, 1973: 100,000 copies (2 volumes, hardbound)
Eighth Printing, 1973: 900,000 copies (3 volumes, softbound)
Ninth Printing, 1974: 300,000 copies (3 volumes, hardbound)
Tenth Printing, 1976: 300,000 copies (3 volumes, softbound)

Printed in the United States of America

Words from George Harrison

Everybody is looking for KṚṢṆA.

Some don't realize that they are, but they are.

KṚṢṆA is GOD, the Source of all that exists, the Cause of all that is, was, or ever will be.

As GOD is unlimited, HE has many Names.

Allah-Buddha-Jehova-Rama: All are KṚṢṆA, all are ONE.

God is not abstract; He has both the impersonal and the personal aspects to His personality which is SUPREME, ETERNAL, BLISSFUL, and full of KNOWLEDGE. As a single drop of water has the same qualities as an ocean of water, so has our consciousness the qualities of GOD'S consciousness . . . but through our identification and attachment with material energy (physical body, sense pleasures, material possessions, ego, etc.) our true TRANSCENDENTAL CONSCIOUSNESS has been polluted, and like a dirty mirror it is unable to reflect a pure image.

With many lives our association with the TEMPORARY has grown. This impermanent body, a bag of bones and flesh, is mistaken for our true self, and we have accepted this temporary condition to be final.

Through all ages, great SAINTS have remained as living proof that this non-temporary, permanent state of GOD CONSCIOUSNESS can be revived in all living Souls. Each soul is potentially divine.

Kṛṣṇa says in *Bhagavad Gita:* "Steady in the Self, being freed from all material contamination, the yogi achieves the highest perfectional stage of happiness in touch with the Supreme Consciousness." (VI, 28)

YOGA (a scientific method for GOD (SELF) realization) is the process by which we purify our consciousness, stop further pollution, and arrive at the state of Perfection, full KNOWLEDGE, full BLISS.

If there's a God, I want to see Him. It's pointless to believe in something without proof, and Kṛṣṇa Consciousness and meditation are methods where you can actually obtain GOD perception. You can actually see God, and hear Him, play with Him.. It might sound crazy, but He is actually there, actually with you.

There are many yogic Paths—Raja, Jnana, Hatha, Kriya, Karma, Bhakti—which are *all* acclaimed by the MASTERS of each method.

SWAMI BHAKTIVEDANTA is as his title says, a BHAKTI Yogi following the path of DEVOTION. By serving GOD through each thought, word, and DEED, and by chanting of HIS Holy Names, the devotee quickly develops God-consciousness. By chanting

Hare Kṛṣṇa, Hare Kṛṣṇa
Kṛṣṇa Kṛṣṇa, Hare Hare
Hare Rāma, Hare Rāma
Rāma Rāma, Hare Hare

one inevitably arrives at KṚṢṆA Consciousness. (The proof of the pudding is in the eating!)

I request that you take advantage of this book *KṚṢṆA,* and enter into its understanding. I also request that you make an appointment to meet your God now, through the self liberating process of YOGA (UNION) and GIVE PEACE A CHANCE.

ALL YOU NEED IS LOVE (KRISHNA) HARI BOL

George Harrison 31/3/70

Apple Corps Ltd 3 Savile Row London W1 Gerrard 2772/3993 Telex Apcore London

Contents

Foreword

It is a wonder that the average Westerner has never heard of Kṛṣṇa. Every culture has its cherished myths, its heroes, its messiahs and its gods, but Kṛṣṇa transcends our small world of cultural relativities. Knowledge of Kṛṣṇa is a transcultural (or shall we say "transcendental") phenomenon, all-consuming in its relevance and universal in its appeal. Kṛṣṇa is not the product of some fertile religious or poetic imagination appearing within the spiritual mélange of historical Hinduism. Rather, Kṛṣṇa is the Supreme Truth (*paraṁ satyam*), the cause of all causes (*sarva-kāraṇa-kāraṇam*) and, most importantly, the ultimate or supreme person (*puruṣottama*).

The Ultimate Principle is a *Person?* This may discomfit the Westerner seeking refuge from the wrathful bearded old man of Judeo-Christian monotheism. But Śrī Kṛṣṇa, "the Supreme Personality of Godhead," is not like that. He is a blissful, eternal, transcendental youth whose overwhelming bodily beauty, sublime personal attributes and extraordinary activities inspire devotional ecstasy and divine intoxication in those to whom He reveals Himself.

The traditional source of knowledge of Kṛṣṇa, and ultimately of all physical and metaphysical knowledge, is the Vedic and Vedāntic scriptures of ancient and medieval India. It is the divine sage Vyāsadeva who is accredited by orthodox Vedic historiography with exclusive authorship of the original Vedic texts. The Vedic histories recount that after this vastly learned sage completed the huge task of compiling Vedic wisdom, he felt an undefinable dissatisfaction within himself. In the midst of Vyāsa's despondency, his own spiritual preceptor, the illustrious saint Nārada Muni, revealed the root cause of his unhappiness: Vyāsa, while defining, explaining and promoting various paths of material and spiritual upliftment, had neglected to indicate distinctly the ultimate goal of the spiritual quest—realization of pure *bhakti* (selfless devotion) for the Supreme Personality of Godhead, Śrī Kṛṣṇa. Since *kṛṣṇa-bhakti* is inspired by hearing about Kṛṣṇa's sublime transcendental attributes and activities, Nārada advised Vyāsa to compile a literature dedicated to Kṛṣṇa Himself:

> Learned circles have positively concluded that the infallible purpose of advancement of knowledge . . . culminates in the transcendental descriptions of the Lord. . . . Please, therefore, describe the Almighty Lord's activities which you have learned by your vast knowledge of the *Vedas*, for that will satisfy the hankerings of great learned men and at the same time mitigate the miseries of the mass of common people who are always suffering from material pangs. Indeed, there is no other way to get out of such miseries.
>
> (*Śrīmad-Bhāgavatam* 1.5.22, 40)

In pursuance of Nārada's order, Vyāsa, after deep meditation, wrote the glorious *Bhāgavata* (*Śrīmad-Bhāgavatam* or *Bhāgavata Purāṇa*), "the literary incarnation of God."

> This *Śrīmad-Bhāgavatam* is the literary incarnation of God, and it is compiled by Śrīla Vyāsadeva, the incarnation of God. It is meant for the ultimate good of all people, and it is all-successful, all-blissful and all-perfect.
>
> (*Śrīmad-Bhāgavatam* 1.3.40)

A vast and encyclopedic work, the *Bhāgavatam* surveys a broad spectrum of knowledge in metaphysics, ontology, cosmology, epistemology, social dynamics, political science and psychology. Ultimately, it offers the cream of Vedic truth. The nineteenth-century American transcendentalist Ralph Waldo Emerson once exalted the *Bhāgavatam* as a book to be read "on one's knees."

On the summit of this monolithic literature rests the effulgent jewel of its Tenth Canto, dedicated exclusively to delineating the divine attributes and activities of Śrī Kṛṣṇa, performed when He descended to earth in a past age. This work, *Kṛṣṇa, the Supreme Personality of Godhead*, is a fluid summary study of this celebrated Tenth Canto.

Now, the question arises, "Why does Kṛṣṇa descend and from where?" Kṛṣṇa descends from the transcendental world (Vaikuṇṭha), where He eternally resides on His planet, Goloka. In this supraterrestrial abode, Kṛṣṇa perpetually enjoys blissful "pastimes" (*līlā*) in the company of His innumerable pure devotees, who relish a variety of eternal relationships with Him. But whenever civilized religious life degenerates in human society, Kṛṣṇa descends to rectify the situation, as He tells Arjuna in *Bhagavad-gītā* (4.7–8):

> Whenever and wherever there is a decline in religious practice, O descendant of Bharata, and a predominant rise in irreligion—at

> that time I descend Myself. To deliver the pious and to annihilate the miscreants, as well as to reestablish the principles of religion, I advent Myself millennium after millennium.

To ameliorate one such state of affairs, Śrī Kṛṣṇa descended five thousand years ago in the land of Bharata-varṣa (India). This state of affairs, involving the increasing militarism of irreligious and sinister kings, climaxed in the famous Battle of Kurukṣetra, in which Kṛṣṇa played a decisive role. The history of this battle fills the major portion of the great epic *Mahābhārata.*

There is another, even more significant reason for Kṛṣṇa's appearance. Kṛṣṇa descended and displayed His transcendental pastimes in the mundane realm to attract and invite the souls confined within the material world to return to their eternal home in the spiritual world. When He appeared, He fully manifested the spiritual realm, in all its transcendental splendor, on the material plane. Accompanied by His eternal associates, He performed inconceivable, extraordinary pastimes, which, by their overpowering transcendental sublimity, attract the minds of all sentient beings.

It is these pastimes which Vyāsa recorded in the Tenth Canto of the *Bhāgavatam.* It is said that by hearing of such transcendental pastimes one comes into direct spiritual contact with Kṛṣṇa. Such aural connection with Kṛṣṇa purifies the heart, provokes *kṛṣṇa-bhakti* and elevates one to perfection:

> Śrī Kṛṣṇa, the Personality of Godhead, who is the Paramātmā [Supersoul] in everyone's heart and the benefactor of the truthful devotee, cleanses desire for material enjoyment from the heart of the devotee who has developed the urge to hear His messages, which are in themselves virtuous when properly heard and chanted.
>
> Simply by hearing this Vedic literature [*Bhāgavatam*], the feeling for loving devotional service to Lord Kṛṣṇa, the Supreme Personality of Godhead, sprouts up at once to extinguish the fire of lamentation, illusion and fearfulness.
>
> (*Śrīmad-Bhāgavatam* 1.2.17/1.7.7)

Until fairly recent times, characterized by the accelerating influence of Western culture, India's spiritual culture was almost totally obsessed with *kṛṣṇa-līlā.* Even now, episodes from Kṛṣṇa's pastimes are ceaselessly recited, enacted, sung and danced in every available medium of cultural expression. Holy festivals in honor of Lord Kṛṣṇa's birth and activities are observed with great pomp and festivity throughout the year by young and old, educated and illiterate, rich and poor, in all Indian cities and villages. In addition, many of the greatest literary masterpieces of the last several centuries in India—the Sanskrit *Gīta-Govinda* of Jayadeva, the Hindi poems of Bilvamaṅgala (Suradāsa) and Mīrābhāī, the Bengali poems of Vidyāpati and Caṇḍīdāsa, the Sanskrit dramas of Rūpa Gosvāmī—were composed in glorification of Kṛṣṇa as the mischievous and captivating child and as the paramour of the *gopīs* (cowherd maidens).

Kṛṣṇa, the Supreme Personality of Godhead is the most comprehensive exposition of the pastimes of Kṛṣṇa now available in the English-speaking world. Each of the trilogy's ninety stories reveals one episode from the life of Śrī Kṛṣṇa in a highly readable short-story format. *Kṛṣṇa* is the product of the scholarly and devotional effort of His Divine Grace A. C. Bhaktivedanta Swami Prabhupāda, the world's most distinguished teacher of Vedic religious and philosophical thought. Śrīla Prabhupāda is a disciplic descendant of Śrī Caitanya Mahāprabhu, whose *saṅkīrtana* movement of the sixteenth century inspired a massive revival of *kṛṣṇa-bhakti* that has, in turn, played a significant role in molding the religious consciousness of modern India. In this book, *Kṛṣṇa*, Śrīla Prabhupāda provides a flowing commentary that will help the Western reader understand concepts that may be foreign to his own cultural and intellectual milieu. The author's insightful comments, gracefully interwoven with the main fabric of the stories, facilitates the flow of the narrative, supplying important background information where needed.

This important work will be many things to many readers. It will serve as a valuable textbook for students of Asian religions, philosophies and cultures because it offers the kind of penetrating, multidimensional view into Indian culture and thought not usually found in secondary historical and anthropological sources. In *Kṛṣṇa*, students of Indian art, literature, music and dance will discover a fountainhead of themes that for centuries have nourished and enriched the classical Vedic arts. *Kṛṣṇa* will provide students of world literature a rare opportunity to explore one of the classics of Indian devotional literature in a readable and easily accessible English edition. Philosophers and theologians will encounter in *Kṛṣṇa* an inexhaustible source of ideas concerning the ultimate nature of reality and the science of the Absolute Truth. Those who enjoy reading narratives of any kind will find *Kṛṣṇa* a unique and refreshing change of pace from ordinary literature. But from a careful reading of *Kṛṣṇa*, those who will perhaps derive the most are those seeking a factual and scientific basis for spiritual life. The text will lure such a reader from the banal and commonplace and beckon him to take part in a miraculous journey. What he sees at first may strike him as alien and incomprehensible. But, as our pilgrim gradually crosses beyond all ethno- and ego-centric confines, he will find himself entering a transcendental realm beyond space and time, a realm where everything is seen in the light of the Supreme Absolute, who is an eternal transcendental youth, the ultimate object of knowledge and the supreme goal of life.

Introduction

This is a book about Kṛṣṇa, the Supreme Personality of Godhead, by the world's leading authority on this transcendental subject–His Divine Grace A.C. Bhaktivedanta Swami Prabhupāda. In his title to this book, and throughout the work, Śrīla Prabhupāda reminds us that Kṛṣṇa is the Supreme Godhead, the Supreme Being. "Kṛṣṇa is the Godhead," he explains, "because He is all-attractive. From practical experience we can see that one is attractive due to 1) wealth, 2) power, 3) fame, 4) beauty, 5) wisdom, and 6) renunciation. One who is in possession of all six of these opulences at the same time, who possesses them to an unlimited degree, is understood to be the Supreme Personality of Godhead."

Kṛṣṇa is a historical personality who appeared on this earth 5,000 years ago. He stayed on earth for 125 years and played exactly like a human being, but His activities were unparallelled. From the moment of His appearance to the moment of His disappearance, all His activities were extraordinary, and they indicate without a doubt that He is the Supreme Personality of Godhead, the Supreme Lord.

Śrīla Prabhupāda points out the difference between Kṛṣṇa and the modern atheists who try to become God by performing some mystic process. Kṛṣṇa is not the kind of God manufactured in a mystic factory. He never had to do anything to become God because He is God in all circumstances. This book, *Kṛṣṇa,* describes all His activities as a human being. But although Kṛṣṇa plays like a human being, He always maintains His identity as the Supreme Personality of Godhead.

The basis for *Kṛṣṇa* is the Vedic scripture called *Śrīmad-Bhāgavatam,* which is considered the essence of all the Vedic writings, such as the *Vedas* and *Upaniṣads.* It is called the "cream of all Vedic literature."

Śrīmad-Bhāgavatam records the narrations spoken by Śukadeva Gosvāmī to King Parikṣit just before the King's departure from this world. King Parikṣit was the King of the entire world, but he was cursed to die within seven days, and therefore he renounced his throne and went to sit on the bank of the Ganges, fasting until death. At that time he met the great saint Śukadeva Gosvāmī, and he expressed to the Gosvāmī his eagerness to spend his last days hearing about the pastimes of Kṛṣṇa. He assured Sukadeva Gosvāmī, "Hunger and thirst may give trouble to ordinary persons, but the topics of Kṛṣṇa are so nice that one can continue to hear about them without being tired because such hearing situates one in the transcendental position."

When King Parikṣit expressed his untiring desire to hear about Kṛṣṇa, Śukadeva Gosvāmī was very pleased, and he began to speak about Kṛṣṇa's pastimes. He encouraged the King by saying, "Your intelligence is very keen because you are so eager to hear about Kṛṣṇa." He informed the

King that hearing and chanting of the pastimes of Kṛṣṇa are so auspicious that the process purifies the three varieties of men involved; he who recites the transcendental topics of Kṛṣṇa, he who hears such topics, and he who inquires about Kṛṣṇa.

The first volume of *Kṛṣṇa* recounts how Kṛṣṇa appeared as the son of Vasudeva and Devakī, who were imprisoned in the dungeon of the wicked King Kaṁsa. Even from His very appearance Kṛṣṇa showed that He is not an ordinary human being, for He appeared as the majestic four-armed Viṣṇu and then turned Himself into a little baby.

Seeking to protect Him from the envious Kaṁsa, Kṛṣṇa's father escaped from prison and carried his son across the River Yamunā to Gokula, where He became the adopted son of a cowherd man, Nanda Mahārāja, and his wife, Yaśodā.

As the son of Nanda and Yaśodā, Kṛṣṇa performed many pastimes resembling those of an ordinary cowherd boy. Yet He exhibited extraordinary feats demonstrating His power as the Supreme Lord. When Kṛṣṇa was only a few weeks old, a gigantic witch named Pūtanā came to poison the child, but when He sucked Her poisoned breast He also sucked out her life. Similarly, Kṛṣṇa also killed many other demons sent by Kaṁsa. Kṛṣṇa revealed to His mother His identity as God when He showed her all the universes floating within His mouth. He demonstrated His supremacy over all other powerful living entities when He thwarted the wrath of the demigod Indra by lifting Govardhana Hill just as easily as an ordinary child might lift a mushroom. He similarly bewildered the powerful demigod Brahmā. He subdued the poisonous serpent Kāliya by dancing on his many heads, He saved His friends from a raging forest fire, and ultimately He danced with the damsels of Vṛndāvana, the *gopīs,* in the celebrated *rāsa* dance. This brings us to the beginning of Volume Two.

It may further be noted here that one need not have read Volume One of *Kṛṣṇa* to appreciate the narration of Volume Two. The pastimes of Kṛṣṇa are fully transcendental. Wherever one begins, one will find that by reading one page after another, an immense treasure of enjoyment and knowledge in art, science, literature, religion and philosophy will surely be revealed, and ultimately, by reading this book, *Kṛṣṇa,* one's love for the Supreme Personality of Godhead will fructify.

"The Supreme Personality of Godhead is Kṛṣṇa [pronounced KRISHNA]. He has an eternal. blissful, spiritual body. He is the origin of all. He has no other origin, and He is the prime cause of all causes."

Brahma-saṁhitā (5.1)

1 / Kaṁsa Sends Akrūra for Kṛṣṇa

Vṛndāvana was always absorbed in the thought of Kṛṣṇa. Everyone remembered His pastimes and was constantly merged in the ocean of transcendental bliss. But the material world is so contaminated that even in Vṛndāvana the *asuras* or demons tried to disturb the peaceful situation.

One demon named Ariṣṭāsura entered the village like a great bull with a gigantic body and horns, digging up the earth with his hoofs. When the demon entered Vṛndāvana, it appeared that the whole land trembled, as if there were an earthquake. He roared fiercely, and after digging up the earth on the riverside, he entered the village proper. The fearful roaring of the bull was so piercing that some of the pregnant cows and women had miscarriages. Its body was so big, stout and strong that a cloud hovered over its body just as clouds hover over mountains. Ariṣṭāsura entered Vṛndāvana with such a fearful appearance that just on seeing this great demon, all the men and women were afflicted with great fear, and the cows and other animals fled the village.

The situation became very terrible, and all the inhabitants of Vṛndāvana began to cry, "Kṛṣṇa! Kṛṣṇa, please save us!" Kṛṣṇa also saw that the cows were running away, and He immediately replied, "Don't be afraid. Don't be afraid." He then appeared before Ariṣṭāsura and said, "You are the lowest of living entities. Why are you frightening the inhabitants of Gokula? What will you gain by this action? If you have come to challenge My authority, then I am prepared to fight you." In this way, Kṛṣṇa challenged the demon, and the demon became very angry by the words of Kṛṣṇa. Kṛṣṇa stood before the bull, resting His hand on the shoulder of a friend. The bull began to proceed towards Kṛṣṇa in anger. Digging the earth with his hoofs, Ariṣṭāsura lifted his tail, and it appeared that clouds were hovering about the tail. His eyes were reddish and moving in anger. Pointing his horns at Kṛṣṇa, he began to charge Him, just like the thunderbolt of Indra. But Kṛṣṇa immediately caught his horns and tossed him away, just as a gigantic elephant repels a small inimical elephant. Although the demon appeared to be very tired and although he was perspiring, he took courage and got up. Again he charged Kṛṣṇa with great force and anger. While rushing towards Kṛṣṇa, he breathed very heavily. Kṛṣṇa again caught his horns and immediately threw him on the ground, breaking his horns. Kṛṣṇa then began to kick his body, just as one squeezes a wet cloth on the ground. Being thus kicked by Kṛṣṇa, Ariṣṭāsura rolled over and began to move his legs violently. Bleeding and passing stool and urine, his eyes starting from their sockets, he passed to the kingdom of death.

The demigods in the celestial planets began to shower flowers on Kṛṣṇa for His wonderful achievements. Kṛṣṇa was already the life and soul of the inhabitants of Vṛndāvana, and after killing this demon in the shape of a bull, He became the cynosure of all eyes. With Balarāma, He triumphantly entered Vṛndāvana village, and the inhabitants glorified Him and Balarāma with great jubilation. When a person performs some wonderful feat, his kinsmen and relatives and friends naturally become jubilant.

It was after this incident that the great sage Nārada disclosed the secret of Kṛṣṇa. Nārada Muni is generally known as *devadarśana,* which means that he can be seen only by demigods or persons on the same level with the demigods. But Nārada visited Kaṁsa, who was not at all on the level of the demigods, and yet Kaṁsa saw him. Of course Kaṁsa also saw Kṛṣṇa, what to speak of Nārada Muni, but generally one must have purified eyes to see the Lord and His devotees. Of course, by association with a pure devotee, one can derive an imperceptible benefit, which is called *ajñatasukṛti.* He cannot understand how he is making progress, yet he makes progress by seeing the devotee of the Lord. Nārada Muni's mission was to finish things quickly. Kṛṣṇa appeared to kill the demons, and Kaṁsa was the chief among them. Nārada wanted to expedite things; therefore, he immediately approached Kaṁsa with all the real information. "You are to be killed by the eighth son of Vasudeva," Nārada told Kaṁsa. "That eighth son is Kṛṣṇa. You were misled by Vasudeva into believing that the eighth issue of Vasudeva was a daughter. Actually, the daughter was born of Yaśodā, the wife of Nanda Mahārāja, and Vasudeva exchanged the daughter, so you were misled. Kṛṣṇa is the son of Vasudeva, as is Balarāma. Being afraid of your atrocious nature, Vasudeva has tactfully hidden Them in Vṛndāvana, out of your sight." Nārada further informed Kaṁsa, "Kṛṣṇa and Balarāma have been living incognito in the care of Nanda Mahārāja. All the *asuras,* your companions who were sent to Vṛndāvana to kill different children, were all killed by Kṛṣṇa and Balarāma."

As soon as Kaṁsa got this information from Nārada Muni, he took out his sharpened sword and prepared to kill Vasudeva for his duplicity. But Nārada pacified him. "You are not to be killed by Vasudeva," he said. "Why are you so anxious to kill him? Better try to kill Kṛṣṇa and Balarāma." But in order to satisfy his wrath, Kaṁsa arrested Vasudeva and his wife and shackled them in iron chains. Acting on the new information, Kaṁsa immediately called for the Keśī demon and asked him to go to Vṛndāvana immediately to fetch Balarāma and Kṛṣṇa. In actuality, Kaṁsa asked Keśī to go to Vṛndāvana to be killed by Kṛṣṇa and Balarāma and thus get salvation. Then Kaṁsa called for the expert elephant trainers, Cāṇūra, Muṣṭika, Śala, Tośala, etc., and he told them, "My dear friends, try to hear me attentively. At Nanda Mahārāja's place in Vṛndāvana there are two brothers, Kṛṣṇa and Balarāma. They are actually two sons of Vasudeva. As you know, I have been destined to be killed by Kṛṣṇa; there is a prophecy to this effect. Now I am requesting you to arrange for a wrestling match. People from different parts of the country will come to see the festival. I will arrange to get those two boys here, and you will try to kill Them in the wrestling arena."

Wrestling matches are still enjoyed by the indigenous people in the northern part of India, and it appears from the statements of *Śrīmad-Bhāgavatam* that 5,000 years ago wrestling was popular. Kaṁsa planned to arrange such a wrestling competition and to invite people to visit. He also told the trainers of the elephants, "Be sure to bring the elephant named Kuvalayāpīḍa and keep him at the gate of the wrestling camp. Try to capture Kṛṣṇa and Balarāma on Their arrival and kill Them."

Kaṁsa also advised his friends to arrange to worship Lord Śiva by offering animal sacrifices and performing the sacrifice called *Dhanur-yajña* and the sacrifice performed on the fourteenth day of the moon known as *Caturdaśī.* This date falls three days after *Ekādaśī,* and it is set aside for the worship of Lord Śiva. One of the plenary portions of Lord Śiva is called Kālabhairava. This form of Lord Śiva is worshiped by the demons who offer skinned animals before him. The process is still current in India in a place called Vaidyanātha-dhāma where the demons offer animal sacrifices to the deity of Kālabhairava. Kaṁsa belonged to this demonic group. He was also an expert diplomat, and so he quickly arranged for his demon friends to kill Kṛṣṇa and Balarāma.

He then called for Akrūra, one of the descendants in the family of Yadu in which Kṛṣṇa was born as the son of Vasudeva. When Akrūra came to see Kaṁsa, Kaṁsa very politely shook hands with him and said, "My dear Akrūra, actually I've no better friend than you in the Bhoja and Yadu dynasties. You are the most munificent person, so as a friend I am begging charity from you. Actually I have taken shelter of you exactly as King Indra takes shelter of Lord Viṣṇu. I request you to go immediately to Vṛndāvana and find the two boys named Kṛṣṇa and Balarāma. They are sons of Nanda Mahārāja. Take this nice chariot, especially prepared for the boys, and bring Them here immediately. That is my request to you. Now, my plan is to kill these two boys. As soon as They come in the gate, there will be a giant elephant named Kuvalayāpīḍa awaiting, and possibly he will be able to kill Them. But if somehow or other They escape, They will next meet the wrestlers and will be killed by them. That is my plan. And after killing these two boys, I shall kill Vasudeva and Nanda, who are supporters of the Vṛṣṇi and Bhoja dynasties. I shall also kill my father Ugrasena and his brother Devaka, because they are actually my enemies and are hindrances to my diplomacy and politics. Thus I shall get rid of all my enemies. Jarāsandha is my father-in-law, and I have a great monkey friend named Dvivida. With their help it will be easy to kill all the kings on the surface of the world who support the demigods. This is my plan. In this way I shall be free from all opposition, and it will be very pleasant to rule the world without obstruction. You may know also that Śambara, Narakāsura and Bāṇāsura are my intimate friends, and when I begin this war against the kings who support the demigods, they will help me considerably. Surely I shall be rid of all my enemies. Please go immediately to Vṛndāvana and encourage the boys to come here to see the beauty of Mathurā and take pleasure in the wrestling competition."

After hearing this plan of Kaṁsa's, Akrūra replied, "My dear King, your plan is very excellently made to counteract the hindrances to your diplomatic activities. But you should maintain some discretion, or your plans will not be fruitful. After all, man proposes, God disposes. We may make very great plans, but unless they are sanctioned by the supreme authority, they will fail. Everyone in this material world knows that the supernatural power is the ultimate disposer of everything. One may make a very great plan with his fertile brain, but he must know that he will become subjected to the fruits, misery and happiness. But I have nothing to say against your proposal. As a friend, I shall carry out your order and bring Kṛṣṇa and Balarāma here, as you desire."

After instructing his friends in various ways, Kaṁsa retired, and Akrūra went to Vṛndāvana.

Thus ends the Bhaktivedanta purport of the Second Volume, First Chapter of Kṛṣṇa, *"Kaṁsa Sends Akrūra for Kṛṣṇa."*

2 / Killing the Keśī Demon and Vyomāsura

After being instructed by Kaṁsa, the demon Keśī assumed the form of a terrible horse. He entered the area of Vṛndāvana, his great mane flying and his hooves digging up the earth. He began to whinny and terrify the whole world. Kṛṣṇa saw that the demon was terrifying all the residents of Vṛndāvana with his whinnying and his tail wheeling in the sky like a big cloud. Kṛṣṇa could understand that the horse was challenging Him to fight. The Lord accepted his challenge and stood before the Keśī demon. As He called him to fight, the horse began to proceed towards Kṛṣṇa, making a horrible sound like a roaring lion. Keśī rushed toward the Lord with great speed and tried to trample Him with his legs, which were strong, forceful, and as hard as stone. Kṛṣṇa, however, immediately caught hold of his legs and thus baffled him. Being somewhat angry, Kṛṣṇa began to move around the horse dextrously. After a few rounds, He threw him a hundred yards away, just as Garuḍa throws a big snake. Thrown by Kṛṣṇa, the horse immediately passed out, but after a little while he regained consciousness and with great anger and force rushed toward Kṛṣṇa again, this time with his mouth open. As soon as Keśī reached Him, Kṛṣṇa pushed His left hand within the horse's mouth. The horse felt great pain because the hand of Kṛṣṇa felt to him like a hot iron rod. Immediately his teeth fell out. Kṛṣṇa's hand within the mouth of the horse at once began to inflate, and Keśī's throat choked up. As the great horse began to suffocate, perspiration appeared on his body, and he began to throw his legs hither and thither. As his last breath came, his eyeballs bulged in their sockets, and he passed stool and urine simultaneously. Thus the vital force of his life expired. When the horse was dead, his mouth became loose and Kṛṣṇa could extract His hand without difficulty. He did not feel any surprise that the Keśī demon was killed so easily, but the demigods were amazed, and out of their great appreciation they offered Kṛṣṇa greetings by showering flowers.

After this incident, Nārada Muni, the greatest of all devotees, came to see Kṛṣṇa in a solitary place and began to talk with Him. "My dear Lord Kṛṣṇa," he said, "You are the unlimited Supersoul, the supreme controller of all mystic powers, the Lord of the whole universe, the all-pervading Personality of Godhead. You are the resting place of the cosmic manifestation, the master of all the devotees and the Lord of everyone. My dear Lord, as the Supersoul of all living entities, You remain concealed within their hearts exactly as fire remains concealed in every piece of fuel. You are the witness of all the activities of the living entities, and You are the supreme controller within their hearts. You are self-sufficient; before the creation, you existed, and by Your energy You have created the whole material universe. According to Your perfect plan, this material world is created by the interaction of the modes of nature, and by You they are maintained and annihilated. Although You are unaffected by all these activities, You are the supreme controller eternally. My dear Lord, You have advented Yourself on the surface of this world just to kill all the so-called kings who are actually demons. These hobgoblins are cheating people in the dress of the princely order. You have advented Yourself to fulfill Your own statement that You come within this material world just to protect the principles of religion and annihilate unwanted miscreants. My dear Lord, I am therefore sure that the day after tomorrow I shall see demons like Cāṇūra, Muṣṭika and the other wrestlers and elephants, as well as Kaṁsa himself, killed by You. And I shall see this with my own eyes. After this, I hope I shall be able to see the killing of other demons like Śaṅkha, Yavana, Mura, and Narakāsura. I shall also see how You take away the *pārijāta* flower from the kingdom of heaven, and how You defeat the king of heaven himself.

"My dear Lord," Nārada Muni continued, "I shall then be able to see how You marry princesses, the daughters of chivalrous kings, by paying the price of *kṣatriya* strength." (Whenever a *kṣatriya* wants to marry a very beautiful and qualified princess of a great king, he must fight his competitors and emerge victorious. Then he is given the hand of the princess in charity.)

"I shall also see how You save King Nṛga from a hellish condition," said Nārada Muni. "This You shall enact in Dvārakā. I shall also be able to see how You get Your wife and the Syamantaka jewel and how You save the son of a *brāhmaṇa* from death after he has already been transferred to another planet. After this, I will be able to see You kill the Pauṇḍraka demon and burn to ashes the kingdom of Kāśī. I will see how You kill the King of Cedi and Dantavakra in great fights, on behalf of Mahārāja

Yudhiṣṭhira. Besides all this, it will be possible for me to see many other chivalrous activities while You remain in Dvārakā. And all these activities performed by Your grace will be sung by great poets for all time. And at the battle of Kurukṣetra You will take part as the chariot driver of Your friend Arjuna, and as the invincible death incarnation, eternal time, You will vanquish all belligerents assembled there. I shall see a large number of military forces killed in that battlefield. My Lord, let me offer my respectful obeisances unto Your lotus feet. You are situated completely in the transcendental position in perfect knowledge and bliss. You are complete in Yourself and are beyond all desires. By exhibiting Your internal potency, You have set up the influence of *māyā.* Your unlimited potency cannot even be measured by anyone. My dear Lord, You are the supreme controller. You are under Your own internal potency, and it is simply vain to think that You are dependent on any of Your creations.

"You have taken birth in the Yadu dynasty, or the Vṛṣṇi dynasty. Your advent on the surface of the earth in Your original form of eternal blissful knowledge is Your own pastime. You are not dependent on anything but Yourself; therefore I offer my respectful obeisances unto Your lotus feet."

Nārada Muni wanted to impress upon people in general that Kṛṣṇa is fully independent. His activities, such as His appearance in the family of Yadu or His friendship with Arjuna, do not necessarily oblige Him to act to enjoy their results. They are all pastimes, and for Him they are all play. But for us they are actual, tangible facts.

After offering his respectful obeisances to Lord Kṛṣṇa, Nārada Muni took permission and left. After He had killed the Keśī demon, Kṛṣṇa returned to tending the cows with His friends in the forest as though nothing had happened. Thus Kṛṣṇa is eternally engaged in His transcendental activities in Vṛndāvana with His friends, the cowherd boys and *gopīs,* but sometimes He exhibits the extraordinary prowess of the Supreme Personality of Godhead by killing different types of demons.

Later that morning Kṛṣṇa went to play with His cowherd boy friends on the top of the Govardhana Hill. They were imitating the play of thieves and police. Some of the boys became police constables, and some became thieves, and some took the role of lambs. While they were thus enjoying their childhood pastimes, a demon known by the name of Vyomāsura, "the demon who flies in the sky," appeared on the scene. He was the son of another great demon named Maya. These demons can perform wonderful magic. Vyomāsura took the part of a cowherd boy playing as thief and stole many boys who were playing the parts of lambs. One after another he took away almost all the boys and put them in the caves of the mountain and sealed the mouths of the caves with stones. Kṛṣṇa could understand the trick the demon was playing; therefore He caught hold of him exactly as a lion catches hold of a lamb. The demon tried to expand himself like a hill to escape arrest, but Kṛṣṇa did not allow him to get out of His clutches. He was immediately thrown on the ground with great force and killed, just as an animal is killed in the slaughter-house. After killing the Vyoma demon, Lord Kṛṣṇa released all His friends from the caves of the mountain. He was then praised by His friends and by the demigods for these wonderful acts. He again returned to Vṛndāvana with His cows and friends.

Thus ends the Bhaktivedanta purport of the Second Volume, Second Chapter of Kṛṣṇa, *"Killing the Keśī Demon and Vyomāsura."*

3 / Akrūra's Arrival in Vṛndāvana

Nārada Muni did not mention Kṛṣṇa's killing Vyomāsura, which means that he was killed on the same day as the Keśī demon. The Keśī demon was killed in the early morning, and after that the boys went to tend the cows on Govardhana Hill, and it was there that Vyomāsura was killed. Both demons were killed in the morning. Akrūra was requested by Kaṁsa to arrive in Vṛndāvana by evening. After receiving instruction from Kaṁsa, Akrūra started the next morning via chariot for Vṛndāvana. Because Akrūra himself was a great devotee of the Lord, while going to Vṛndāvana he began to praise the Lord. Devotees are always absorbed in thoughts of Kṛṣṇa, and Akrūra was constantly thinking of Lord Kṛṣṇa's lotus eyes.

He did not know what sort of pious activities he must have done to gain an opportunity to go see Lord Kṛṣṇa. Akrūra thought that if Kṛṣṇa willed, he would be able to see Him. Akrūra considered himself most fortunate that he was going to see Kṛṣṇa, whom great mystic *yogīs* desire to see. He was confident that on that day all the sinful reactions of his past life would be finished and his fortunate human form of life would be successful. Akrūra also considered that he was very much favored by Kaṁsa, who was sending him to bring back Kṛṣṇa and Balarāma and thus enabling him to see the Lord. Akrūra continued to consider that formerly great sages and saintly persons were liberated from the material world simply by seeing the shining nails of the lotus feet of Kṛṣṇa.

"That Supreme Personality of Godhead has now come just like an ordinary human being, and it is my great fortune to be able to see Him face to face," Akrūra thought. He was thrilled with expectations of seeing the very lotus feet which are worshiped by great demigods like Brahmā, Nārada, and Lord Śiva, which traverse the ground of Vṛndāvana and which touch the breasts of the *gopīs* covered with tinges of *kuṅkuma.* He thought, "I am so fortunate that I will be able to see those very lotus feet on this day, and certainly I shall be able to see the beautiful face of Kṛṣṇa, which is marked on the forehead and the nose with *tilaka.* And I shall also see His smile and His curling black hair. I can be sure of this opportunity because I see that today the deer are passing on my right side. Today it will be possible for me to actually see the beauty of the spiritual kingdom of Viṣṇuloka because Kṛṣṇa is the Supreme Viṣṇu, and He has advented Himself out of His own good will. He is the reservoir of all beauty; therefore my eyes will be filled today."

Akrūra knew beyond doubt that Lord Kṛṣṇa is the Supreme Viṣṇu. Lord Viṣṇu glances over the material energy, and thus the cosmic manifestation comes into being. And although Lord Viṣṇu is the creator of this material world, He is free, by His own energy, from the influence of material energy. By His internal potency He can pierce the darkness of material energy. Similarly, Kṛṣṇa the original Viṣṇu, by expansion of His internal potency, created the inhabitants of Vṛndāvana. In the *Brahma-saṁhitā* it is also confirmed that the paraphernalia and the abode of Kṛṣṇa are expansions of His internal potency. The same internal potency is exhibited on earth as Vṛndāvana, where Kṛṣṇa enjoys Himself with His parents and in the company of His friends, the cowherd boys and *gopīs.* By the statement of Akrūra, it is clear that, since Kṛṣṇa is transcendental to the modes of material nature, the inhabitants of Vṛndāvana, who are engaged in loving service of the Lord, are also transcendental.

Akrūra also considered the necessity of the transcendental pastimes of the Lord. He thought that the transcendental activities, instructions, qualities and pastimes of Kṛṣṇa are all for the good fortune of people in general. The people can remain constantly in Kṛṣṇa consciousness by discussing the Lord's transcendental form, qualities, pastimes, and paraphernalia. By doing so, the whole universe can actually live auspiciously and advance peacefully. But without Kṛṣṇa consciousness, civilization is but a decoration for a dead body. A dead body may be decorated very nicely, but without consciousness such decorations are useless. Human society without Kṛṣṇa consciousness is useless and lifeless.

Akrūra thought, "That Supreme Personality of Godhead, Kṛṣṇa, has now appeared as one of the descendants of the Yadu dynasty. The principles of religion are His enacted laws. Those who are abiding by such laws are the demigods, and those who are not abiding are demons. He has advented Himself to give protection to the demigods, who are very obedient to the laws of the Supreme Lord. The demigods and the devotees of the Lord take pleasure in abiding by the laws of Kṛṣṇa, and Kṛṣṇa takes pleasure in giving them all sorts of protection. These activities of Kṛṣṇa,

His protection of the devotees and killing the demons, as confirmed in the *Bhagavad-gītā*, are always good for men to hear and narrate. The glorious activities of the Lord will ever increasingly be chanted by the devotees and demigods.

"Kṛṣṇa, the Supreme Personality of Godhead, is the spiritual master of all spiritual masters; He is the deliverer of all fallen souls and the proprietor of the three worlds. Anyone is able to see Him by eyes smeared with love of Godhead. Today I shall be able to see the Supreme Personality of Godhead, who by His transcendental beauty has attracted the goddess of fortune to live with Him perpetually. As soon as I arrive in Vṛndāvana, I will get down from this chariot and fall prostrate to offer my obeisances to the Supreme Lord, the master of material nature and all living entities. The lotus feet of Kṛṣṇa are always worshiped by great mystic *yogīs*, so I shall also worship His lotus feet and become one of His friends in Vṛndāvana like the cowherd boys. When I bow down before Lord Kṛṣṇa in that way, certainly He will place His fearless lotus hand on my head. His hand is offered to all conditioned souls who take shelter under His lotus feet Kṛṣṇa is the ultimate goal of life for all people who fear material existence, and certainly when I see Him He will give me the shelter of His lotus feet. I am aspiring for the touch of His lotus-like hands on my head."

In this way Akrūra expected blessings from the hand of Kṛṣṇa. He knew that Indra, who is the king of heaven and the master of the three worlds—the upper, middle, and lower planetary systems—was blessed by the Lord simply for his offering a little water which Kṛṣṇa accepted. Similarly, Bali Mahārāja gave only three feet of land in charity to Vāmanadeva, and he also offered a little water which Lord Vāmanadeva accepted, and thereby Bali Mahārāja attained the position of Indra. When the *gopīs* were dancing with Kṛṣṇa in the *rāsa* dance, they became fatigued, and Kṛṣṇa smeared His hand, which is as fragrant as a lotus flower, over the pearl-like drops of perspiration on the faces of the *gopīs*, and immediately they became refreshed. Thus Akrūra was expecting benediction from that supreme hand of Kṛṣṇa. Kṛṣṇa's hand is capable of bestowing benediction to all kinds of men if they take to Kṛṣṇa consciousness. If one wants material happiness like the king of heaven, he can derive that benediction from the hand of Kṛṣṇa; if one wants liberation from the pangs of material existence, he can also get benediction from the hand of Kṛṣṇa; and if one in pure transcendental love for Kṛṣṇa wants personal association and the touch of His transcendental body, he can also gain benediction from His hand.

Akrūra was afraid, however, of being deputed by Kaṁsa, the enemy of Kṛṣṇa. He thought, "I am going to see Kṛṣṇa as a messenger of the enemy."

And at the same time, he thought, "Kṛṣṇa is in each and everyone's heart as the Supersoul, so He must know my heart." Although Akrūra was trusted by the enemy of Kṛṣṇa, his heart was clear. He was a pure devotee of Kṛṣṇa. He risked Kaṁsa's wrath just to meet Kṛṣṇa. He was certain that although he was going as a representative of Kaṁsa, Kṛṣṇa would not accept him as an enemy. "Even though I am on a sinful mission, being deputed by Kaṁsa, when I approach the Supreme Personality of Godhead, I shall stand before Him with all humility and folded hands. Surely, He will be pleased with my devotional attitude, and maybe He will smile lovingly and look upon me and thereby free me from all kinds of sinful reaction. I shall then be on the platform of transcendental bliss and knowledge. Since Kṛṣṇa knows my heart, certainly when I approach Him, He will embrace me. I am not only one of the members of the Yadu dynasty, but I am an unalloyed pure devotee. By His merciful embrace, my body, my heart and soul will be completely cleansed of the actions and reactions of my past life. When our bodies touch, I will immediately stand up with folded hands, with all humility. Certainly Kṛṣṇa and Balarāma will call me, 'Akrūra, uncle,' and at that time my whole life will be glorious. Unless one is recognized by the Supreme Personality of Godhead, his life cannot be successful."

It is clearly stated here that one should try to be recognized by the Supreme Personality of Godhead by one's service and devotion, without which the human form of life is condemned. As stated in the *Bhagavad-gītā,* the Supreme Lord, Personality of Godhead, is equal to everyone. He has no friends and no enemies. But He is inclined to a devotee who renders Him service with devotional love. The *Bhagavad-gītā* also declares that the Supreme Lord is responsive to the devotional service rendered by the devotee. Akrūra thought that Kṛṣṇa was like the desire tree in the heavenly planets which gives fruit according to the desire of the worshiper. The Supreme Personality of Godhead is also the source of everything. A devotee must know how to render service unto Him and thus be recognized by Him. In the *Caitanya-caritāmṛta* it is therefore explained that one should serve both the spiritual master and Kṛṣṇa simultaneously and in that way make progress in Kṛṣṇa consciousness. Service rendered to Kṛṣṇa under the direction of the spiritual master is bona fide service because the spiritual master is the manifested representative of Kṛṣṇa. Śrī Viśvanātha Cakravartī Ṭhākur says that when one satisfies the spiritual master, he satisfies the Supreme Lord. It is exactly like service in a government office. One has to work under the supervision of the departmental head. If the supervisor of the department is satisfied with the service of a particular person, a promotion and increase in pay will automatically come.

Akrūra then thought, "When Kṛṣṇa and Balarāma are pleased with my prayers, certainly They will take my hand, receive me within Their homes and offer me all kinds of respectable hospitalities, and They will surely ask me of the activities of Kaṁsa and his friends."

In this way, Akrūra, who was the son of Śvaphalka, meditated on Śrī Kṛṣṇa on his journey from Mathurā. He reached Vṛndāvana by the end of the day. Akrūra passed the whole journey without knowing how long it took. When he reached Vṛndāvana, the sun was setting. As soon as he entered the boundary of Vṛndāvana, he saw the footprints of the cows and Lord Kṛṣṇa's footprints, impressed with the signs of His sole, the flag, trident, thunderbolt and lotus flower. Upon seeing the footprints of Kṛṣṇa, Akrūra immediately jumped down from the chariot, out of respect. He became overwhelmed with all the symptoms of ecstasy; he wept, and his body trembled. Out of extreme jubilation upon seeing the dust touched by the lotus feet of Kṛṣṇa, Akrūra fell flat on his face and began to roll on the ground.

Akrūra's journey to Vṛndāvana is exemplary. One who intends to visit Vṛndāvana should follow the ideal footsteps of Akrūra and always think of the pastimes and activities of the Lord. As soon as one reaches the boundary of Vṛndāvana, he should immediately smear the dust of Vṛndāvana over his body without thinking of his material position and prestige. Narottamadāsa Ṭhākur has sung in his celebrated song, *Viṣaya-chāṛiyā kave śuddha have mana:* "When my mind will be purified after leaving the contamination of material sense enjoyment, I shall be able to visit Vṛndāvana." Actually, one cannot go to Vṛndāvana by purchasing a ticket. The process of going to Vṛndāvana is shown by Akrūra.

When Akrūra entered Vṛndāvana, he saw Kṛṣṇa and Balarāma engaged in supervising the milking of the cows. Kṛṣṇa was dressed in yellow garments and Balarāma in bluish. Akrūra also saw that Kṛṣṇa's eyes were exactly like the beautifully grown lotus flower of the autumn season. He saw both Kṛṣṇa and Balarāma in the spring of Their youth. Although both were similar in bodily features, Kṛṣṇa was blackish in complexion, whereas Balarāma was whitish. Both were the shelter of the goddess of fortune. They had well-constructed bodies, beautiful hands and pleasing faces, and They were as strong as elephants. Now, after seeing Their footprints, Akrūra actually saw Kṛṣṇa and Balarāma, face to face. Although They were the most influential personalities, They were glancing at him with smiling faces. Akrūra could understand that both Kṛṣṇa and Balarāma had returned from tending cows in the forest; They had taken Their baths and were dressed with fresh clothing and garlanded with flowers and necklaces made of valuable jewels. Their bodies were smeared with the pulp of sandalwood. Akrūra greatly appreciated the aroma of flowers and sandalwood and Their bodily presence. He considered himself very fortunate to see Kṛṣṇa, the Supreme Personality of Godhead, and His plenary expansion, Balarāma, face to face, for he knew that They were the original personalities of the creation.

As stated in the *Brahma-saṁhitā,* Kṛṣṇa is the original Personality of Godhead and the cause of all causes. Akrūra could understand that the Supreme Personality of Godhead appeared personally for the welfare of His creation, to reestablish the principles of religion and to annihilate the demons. With Their bodily effulgence, the brothers were dissipating all the darkness of the world, as if They were mountains of sapphire and silver. Without hesitating, Akrūra immediately got down from his chariot and fell flat, just like a rod, before Kṛṣṇa and Balarāma. Upon touching the lotus feet of the Supreme Personality of Godhead, he became overwhelmed with transcendental bliss; his voice choked up and he could not speak. Due to Kṛṣṇa's transcendental presence, incessant torrents of tears fell from his eyes. He remained stunned in ecstasy, as if devoid of all powers to see and speak. Lord Kṛṣṇa, who is very kind to His devotees, raised Akrūra with His hand and embraced him. It appeared that Lord Kṛṣṇa was very pleased with Akrūra. Balarāma also embraced Akrūra. Taking him by the hand, Kṛṣṇa and Balarāma brought him to Their sitting room where They offered him a very nice sitting place and water for washing his feet. They also worshiped him with suitable presentations of honey and other ingredients. When Akrūra was thus comfortably seated, both Kṛṣṇa and Balarāma offered Him a cow in charity and then brought very palatable dishes of eatables, and Akrūra accepted them. When Akrūra finished eating, Balarāma gave him betel nut and spices, as well as pulp of sandalwood, just to make him more pleased and comfortable. The Vedic system of receiving a guest was completely observed by Lord Kṛṣṇa Himself to teach all others how to receive a guest at home. It is a Vedic injunction that even if a guest is an enemy, he should be received so well that he does not apprehend any danger from the host. If the host is a poor man, he should at least offer a straw mat as a sitting place and a glass of water to drink. Kṛṣṇa and Balarāma welcomed Akrūra just befitting his exalted position.

After Akrūra was thus properly received and seated, Nanda Mahārāja, the foster father of Kṛṣṇa, said, "My dear Akrūra, what shall I inquire from you? I know that you are being protected by Kaṁsa, who is most cruel and demoniac. His protection is just like the slaughterhouse keeper's protection of animals he will kill in the future. Kaṁsa is so selfish that he has killed the sons of his own sister, so how can I honestly believe that he is protecting the citizens of Mathurā?" This statement is most significant. If the political or executive heads of the state are simply interested in themselves, they can never look after the welfare of the citizens.

As Nanda Mahārāja spoke to Akrūra with pleasing words, Akrūra forgot all the fatigue of his day's journey from Mathurā to Vṛndāvana.

Thus ends the Bhaktivedanta purport of the Second Volume, Third Chapter of* Kṛṣṇa, *"Akrūra's Arrival in Vṛndāvana."

4 / Akrūra's Return Journey and His Visiting of Viṣṇuloka Within the Yamunā River

Akrūra was warmly received by Lord Kṛṣṇa and Nanda Mahārāja and offered a resting place for the night. In the meantime, the two brothers Balarāma and Kṛṣṇa went to take Their supper. Akrūra sat on his bed and began to reflect that all the desires which he had anticipated while coming from Mathurā to Vṛndāvana had been fulfilled. Lord Kṛṣṇa is the husband of the goddess of fortune; being pleased with His pure devotee, He can offer whatever the devotee desires. But the pure devotee does not ask anything from the Lord for his personal benefit.

After taking Their supper, Kṛṣṇa and Balarāma came to bid goodnight to Akrūra. Kṛṣṇa asked about His maternal uncle, Kaṁsa, "How is he dealing with his friends?" And He asked, "How are my relatives?" He also inquired into Kaṁsa's plans. The Supreme Personality of Godhead then informed Akrūra that his presence was very much welcome. He inquired from him whether all his relatives and friends were well and free from all kinds of ailments. Kṛṣṇa stated that He was very sorry that His maternal uncle Kaṁsa was the head of the kingdom; He said that Kaṁsa was the greatest anachronism in the whole system of government and that they could not expect any welfare for the citizens while he ruled. Then Kṛṣṇa said, "My father has undergone much tribulation simply from My being his son. For this reason also he has lost many other sons. I think Myself so fortunate that you have come as My friend and relative. My good friend Akrūra, please tell me the purpose of your coming to Vṛndāvana."

After this inquiry, Akrūra, who belonged to the dynasty of Yadu, explained the recent events in Mathurā, including Kaṁsa's attempt to kill Vasudeva, the father of Kṛṣṇa. He related the things which happened after the disclosure by Nārada that Kṛṣṇa was the son of Vasudeva. Sitting by Him in the house of Nanda Mahārāja, Akrūra narrated all the stories regarding Kaṁsa. He told how Nārada met Kaṁsa and how he himself was deputed by Kaṁsa to come to Vṛndāvana. Akrūra explained to Kṛṣṇa that

Nārada had told Kaṁsa all about Kṛṣṇa's being transferred from Mathurā to Vṛndāvana just after His birth and about His killing all the demons sent by Kaṁsa. Akrūra then explained to Kṛṣṇa the purpose of his coming to Vṛndāvana: to take him back to Mathurā. After hearing of these arrangements, Balarāma and Kṛṣṇa, who are very expert in killing opponents, mildly laughed at the plans of Kaṁsa.

They asked Nanda Mahārāja to invite all the cowherd boys to go to Mathurā to participate in the ceremony known as *Dhanur-yajña.* Kaṁsa wanted them all to go there to participate in the function. On Kṛṣṇa's word, Nanda Mahārāja at once called for the cowherd boys and asked them to collect all kinds of milk preparations and milk to present in the ceremony. He also sent instructions to the police chief of Vṛndāvana to tell all the inhabitants about Kaṁsa's great Dhanur-yajña function and invite them to join. Nanda Mahārāja informed the cowherd boys that they would start the next morning. They therefore arranged for the cows and bulls to carry them all to Mathurā.

When the *gopīs* saw that Akrūra had come to take Kṛṣṇa and Balarāma away to Mathurā, they became overwhelmed with anxiety. Some of them became so aggrieved that their faces turned black, and they began to breathe warmly and had palpitations of the heart. They discovered that their hair and dress immediately loosened. Hearing the news that Kṛṣṇa and Balarāma were leaving for Mathurā, others who were engaged in household duties stopped working as if they had forgotten everything, like a person who is called forth to die and leave this world at once. Others immediately fainted due to separation from Kṛṣṇa. Remembering His attractive smile and His talks with them, the *gopīs* became overwhelmed with grief. They all remembered the characteristics of the Personality of Godhead, how He moved within the area of Vṛndāvana and how, with joking words, He attracted all their hearts. Thinking of Kṛṣṇa and of their imminent separation from Him, the *gopīs* assembled together with heavy beating hearts. Completely absorbed in thought of Kṛṣṇa, tears fell from their eyes. They began to converse as follows.

"O Providence, you are so cruel! It appears that you do not know how to show mercy to others. By your arrangement, friends contact one another, but without fulfilling their desires you separate them. This is exactly like children's play that has no meaning. It is very abominable that you arrange to show us beautiful Kṛṣṇa, whose bluish curling hair beautifies His broad forehead and sharp nose, who is always smiling to minimize all contention in this material world, and then arrange to separate Him from us. O Providence, You are so cruel! But most astonishingly You appear now as 'Akrūra,' which means 'not cruel.' In the beginning we appreciated Your workmanship in giving us these eyes to see the beautiful face of Kṛṣṇa, but now, just like a foolish creature, You are trying to take out our eyes so we may not see Kṛṣṇa here again. Kṛṣṇa, the son of Nanda Mahārāja, is also very cruel! He must always have new friends; He does not like to keep friendship for a long time with anyone. We *gopīs* of Vṛndāvana, having left our homes, friends, and relatives, have become Kṛṣṇa's maidservants, but He is neglecting us and going away. He does not even look upon us, although we are completely surrendered unto Him. Now all the young girls in Mathurā will have the opportunity. They are expecting Kṛṣṇa's arrival, and they will enjoy His sweet smiling face and will drink its honey. Although we know that Kṛṣṇa is very steady and determined, we are threatened that as soon as He sees the beautiful faces of the young girls in Mathurā, He will forget Himself. We fear He will become controlled by them and will forget us, for we are simple village girls. He will no longer be kind to us. We therefore do not expect Kṛṣṇa to return to Vṛndāvana. He will not leave the company of the girls in Mathurā."

The *gopīs* began to imagine the great functions in the city of Mathurā. Kṛṣṇa would pass through the streets, and the ladies and young girls of the city would see Him from the balconies of their respective houses. Mathurā City contained different communities, known then as Daśārha, Bhoja, Andhaka and Sātvata. All these communities were different branches of the same family in which Kṛṣṇa appeared, namely the Yadu dynasty. They were also expecting the arrival of Kṛṣṇa. It had already been ascertained that Kṛṣṇa, who is the rest of the goddess of fortune and reservoir of all pleasure and transcendental qualities, was going to visit Mathurā City.

The *gopīs* then began to condemn the activities of Akrūra. They stated that he was taking Kṛṣṇa, who was more dear than the dearest to them and who was the pleasure of their eyes. He was being taken from their sight without their being informed or solaced by Akrūra. Akrūra should not have been so merciless but should have taken compassion on them. The *gopīs* went on to say: "The most astonishing feature is that Kṛṣṇa, the son of Nanda, without consideration, has already seated Himself on the chariot. From this it appears that Kṛṣṇa is not very intelligent. Yet He may be very intelligent—but He is not very civilized. Not only Kṛṣṇa, but all the cowherd men are so callous that they are already yoking the bulls and calves for the journey to Mathurā. The elderly persons in Vṛndāvana are also merciless; they do not take our plight into consideration and stop Kṛṣṇa's journey to Mathurā. Even the demigods are very unkind to us; they are not impeding His going to Mathurā."

The *gopīs* prayed to the demigods to create some natural disturbance, such as a hurricane, storm or heavy rainfall, so that Kṛṣṇa could not go to Mathurā. They then began to consider: "Despite our elderly parents and guardians, we shall personally stop Kṛṣṇa from going to Mathurā. We have no other alternative than to take this direct action. Everyone has gone against us to take away Kṛṣṇa from our sight. Without Him we cannot live for a moment." The *gopīs* thus decided to obstruct the passage through which the chariot of Kṛṣṇa was supposed to pass. They began to talk among themselves: "We have passed a very long night—which seemed only a moment—engaged in the *rāsa* dance with Kṛṣṇa. We were looking at His sweet smile and were embracing and talking. Now, how shall we live even for a moment if He goes away from us? At the end of the day, in the evening, along with His elder brother Balarāma, Kṛṣṇa would return home with His friends. His face would be smeared with the dust raised by the hooves of the cows, and He would smile and play on His flute and look upon us so kindly. How shall we be able to forget Him? How shall we be able to forget Kṛṣṇa, who is our life and soul? He has already taken away our hearts in so many ways throughout our days and nights, and if He goes away, there is no possibility of our continuing to live." Thinking like this, the *gopīs* became more and more griefstricken at Kṛṣṇa's leaving Vṛndāvana. They could not check their minds, and they began to cry loudly, calling the different names of Kṛṣṇa, "O dear Dāmodara! Dear Mādhava!"

The *gopīs* cried all night before the departure of Kṛṣṇa. As soon as the sun rose, Akrūra finished his morning bath, got on the chariot and began to start for Mathurā with Kṛṣṇa and Balarāma. Nanda Mahārāja and the cowherd men got up on bullock carts, after loading them with milk preparations, such as yogurt, milk, and ghee, filled in big earthen pots, and began to follow the chariot of Kṛṣṇa and Balarāma. In spite of Kṛṣṇa's asking them not to obstruct their way, all the *gopīs* surrounded the chariot and stood up to see Kṛṣṇa with pitiable eyes. Kṛṣṇa was very much affected upon seeing the plight of the *gopīs*, but His duty was to start for Mathurā, for this was foretold by Nārada. Kṛṣṇa, therefore, consoled the *gopīs*. He told them that they should not be aggrieved; He was coming back very soon after finishing His business. But they could not be persuaded to disperse. The chariot, however, began to head west, and as it proceeded, the minds of the *gopīs* followed it as far as possible. They watched the flag on the chariot as long as it was visible; finally they could only see the dust of the chariot in the distance. The *gopīs* did not move from their places but stood until the chariot could not be seen at all. They remained standing still, as if they were painted pictures. All the *gopīs* decided that Kṛṣṇa was not returning immediately, and with greatly disappointed hearts, they returned to their respective homes. Being greatly disturbed by the absence of Kṛṣṇa, they simply thought all day and night about His pastimes and thus derived some consolation.

The Lord, accompanied by Akrūra and Balarāma, drove the chariot with great speed towards the bank of the Yamunā. Simply by taking a bath in the Yamunā, anyone can diminish the reaction of his sinful activities. Both Kṛṣṇa and Balarāma took Their baths in the river and washed Their faces. After drinking the transparent crystal clear water of the Yamunā, They took Their seats again on the chariot. The chariot was standing underneath the shade of big trees, and both brothers sat down there. Akrūra then took Their permission to also take bath in the Yamunā. According to Vedic ritual, after taking bath in the river, one should stand at least half-submerged and murmur the *Gāyatrī mantra.* While he was standing in the river, Akrūra suddenly saw both Balarāma and Kṛṣṇa within the water. He was surprised to see Them there because he was confident that They were sitting on the chariot. Confused, he immediately came out of the water and went to see where the boys were, and he was very surprised to see that They were sitting on the chariot as before. When he saw Them on the chariot, he began to wonder whether he saw Them in the water. He therefore went back to the river. This time he saw not only Balarāma and Kṛṣṇa there, but many of the demigods and all the Siddhas, Cāraṇas, and Gandharvas. They were all standing before the Lord, who was lying down. He also saw the Śeṣa Nāga with thousands of hoods. Lord Śeṣa Nāga was covered with bluish garments, and His necks were all white. The white necks of Śeṣa Nāga appeared exactly like snowcapped mountains. On the curved lap of Śeṣa Nāga, Akrūra saw Kṛṣṇa sitting very soberly, with four hands. His eyes were like the reddish petals of the lotus flower.

In other words, after returning, Akrūra saw Balarāma turned into Śeṣa Nāga and Kṛṣṇa turned into Mahā-Viṣṇu. He saw the fourhanded Supreme Personality of Godhead, smiling very beautifully. He was very pleasing to all and was looking towards everyone. He appeared beautiful with His raised nose, broad forehead, spread-up ears and reddish lips. His arms, reaching to the knees, were very strongly built. His shoulders were high, His chest very broad and shaped like the conchshell. His navel was very deep, and His abdomen was marked with three lines. His waist was broad and big, resembling the hips of a woman, and His thighs resembled the trunks of elephants. The other parts of His legs, the joints and lower extremities, were all very beautiful, the nails of His feet were dazzling, and His toes were as beautiful as the petals of the lotus flower. His helmet was decorated with very valuable jewels. There was a nice belt around the waist, and He wore a sacred thread across His broad chest. Bangles were on His hands and armlets on the upper portion of His arms. He wore bells on His ankles. He possessed dazzling beauty, and His palms were like the lotus flower. He was still more beautiful with different emblems of the Viṣṇu-mūrti, the conchshell, club, disc and lotus flower, which He held in His four hands. His chest was marked with the particular signs of Viṣṇu, and He wore fresh flower garlands. All in all, He was very beautiful to look at. Akrūra also saw His Lordship surrounded by intimate associates like the four Kumāras, Sanaka, Sanātana, Sananda and Sanatkumāra, and other associates like Sunanda and Nanda, as well as demigods like Brahmā and Lord Śiva. The nine great learned sages were there, and devotees like Prahlāda and Nārada were engaged in offering prayers to the Lord with clean hearts and pure words. After seeing the transcendental Personality of Godhead, Akrūra immediately became overwhelmed with great devotion, and all over his body there was transcendental shivering. Although for the moment he was bewildered, he retained his clear consciousness and bowed down his head before the Lord. With folded hands and faltering voice, he began to offer prayers to the Lord.

Thus ends the Bhaktivedanta purport of the Second Volume, Fourth Chapter of Kṛṣṇa, ***"Akrūra's Return Journey and His Visiting of Viṣṇuloka Within the Yamunā River."***

5 / Prayers by Akrūra

Akrūra offered his prayers as follows: "My dear Lord, I here pay my respectful obeisances unto You because You are the supreme cause of all causes and the original inexhaustible Personality, Nārāyaṇa. From Your navel a lotus flower grows, and from that lotus, Brahmā, the creator of this universe, is born. Since Brahmā is the cause of this universe, You are the cause of all causes. All the elements of this cosmic manifestation—earth, water, fire, air, ether, ego and the total material energy, as well as nature, the marginal energy, the living entities, mind, senses, the sense objects and the demigods who control the affairs of the cosmos—are all produced from Your body. You are the Supersoul of everything, but no one knows Your transcendental form. Everyone within this material world is influenced by the modes of material nature. Demigods like Lord Brahmā, being covered by the influence of material nature, do not exactly know Your transcendental existence beyond the cosmic manifestation of the three modes of material nature. Great sages and mystics worship You as the Supreme Personality of Godhead, the original cause of all living entities, all cosmic manifestation and all demigods. They worship You as all-inclusive. Some of the learned *brāhmaṇas* also worship You by observing the ritualistic ceremony of the *Ṛg-veda.* They offer different kinds of sacrifices in the names of different gods. And there are others also who are fond of worshiping transcendental knowledge. They are very peaceful and wish to give up all kinds of material activities. They engage themselves in the philosophical search for You, known as *jñāna-yoga.*

"There are devotees also known as *Bhāgavatas* who worship You as the Supreme Personality of Godhead. After being properly initiated in the method of *Pāñcarātra,* they decorate their bodies with *tilaka* and engage in worshiping Your different forms of Viṣṇu *mūrti.* There are others also, known as Śaivites, followers of the different *ācāryas*, who worship You in the form of Lord Śiva."

It is stated in the *Bhagavad-gītā* that worship of demigods is also indirectly worship of the Supreme Lord. But such worship is not orthodox, because the worshipable Lord is the Supreme Personality of Godhead, Nārāyaṇa. Demigods such as Brahmā and Śiva are incarnations of the material qualities, which are also emanations from the body of Nārāyaṇa. Actually, there was no one existing before the creation except Nārāyaṇa, the Supreme Personality of Godhead. The worship of a demigod is not on the level with worship of Nārāyaṇa.

Akrūra said, "Although the minds of those who are devotees of the demigods are fixed on a particular demigod, because You are the Supersoul of all living entities, including the demigods, worship of demigods indirectly goes to You. Sometimes, after flowing down from the mountains during the rainy season, small rivers fail to reach the sea; some reach the sea and some do not. Similarly, the worshipers of the demigods may or may not reach You. There is no guarantee. Their success depends on the strength of their worship."

According to Vedic principle, when a worshiper worships a particular demigod, he also conducts some ritual for Nārāyaṇa, *Yajñeśvara,* for it is mentioned in *Bhagavad-gītā* that demigods cannot fulfill the desires of their worshipers without the sanction of Nārāyaṇa, or Kṛṣṇa. The exact words used in the *Bhagavad-gītā* are *mayaiva vihitān hi tān,* which means that the demigods can award some benediction after being authorized by the Supreme Lord. When the demigod worshiper comes to his senses, he can reason as follows: "The demigod can offer benediction only after being empowered by the Supreme Lord, so why not worship the Supreme Lord directly?" Worshipers of the demigods may come to the Supreme Personality of Godhead, but others, who take the demigod as all in all, cannot reach the ultimate goal.

Akrūra continued to pray: "My dear Lord, the whole world is filled with the three material modes of nature, namely, goodness, passion and ignorance. Everyone within this material world is covered by these modes, from Lord Brahmā down to the immovable plants and trees. My dear Lord, I offer my respectful obeisances unto You, because You are beyond the influence of the three modes. Except for You, everyone is being carried away by the waves of these modes. My dear Lord, fire is Your mouth, the earth is Your feet, the sun is Your eye, the sky is Your navel, and the directions are Your ears. Space is Your head, the demigods are Your arms, the oceans and seas are Your abdomen, and the winds and air are Your strength and vitality. All the plants and herbs are the hair on Your body; the clouds are Your hair, the mountains are Your bones and nails, the days and nights are the twinkling of Your eyelids; Prajāpati (the progenitor) is

Your genitals, and the rains are Your semina.

"My dear Lord, all living entities, including different grades of demigods, different grades of overlords, kings and other living entities, are supposed to be resting in You. As part and parcel of the big unit, one cannot know You by experimental knowledge. One can simply understand Your transcendental existence as the great ocean in which different grades of living entities are included, or as the fruit *kadamba* out of which small mosquitoes come. My dear Lord, whatever eternal forms and incarnations You accept and which appear in this world are meant for relieving the living entities from their ignorance, illusion and lamentation. All people, therefore, can appreciate the incarnations and pastimes of Your Lordship and eternally glorify Your activities. No one can estimate how many forms and incarnations You have, nor can anyone estimate the number of universes that are existing within You.

"Let me therefore offer my respectful obeisances unto the incarnation of fish, who appeared in devastation, although Your Lordship is the cause of all causes. Let me offer my respectful obeisances unto the Hayagrīva incarnation who killed the two demons, Madhu and Kaiṭabha; let me offer my respectful obeisances unto You who appeared as the gigantic tortoise and held up the great mountain Mandara, and who appeared as the boar who rescued the earth planet which had fallen into the water of Garbhodaka. Let me offer my respectful obeisances unto Your Lordship, who appeared as Nṛsiṁhadeva, who delivered all kinds of devotees from the fearful condition of atheistic atrocities. Let me offer my respectful obeisances unto You who appeared as Vāmanadeva and covered the three worlds simply by expanding Your lotus feet. Let me offer my respectful obeisances unto You who appeared as the Lord of the Bhṛgus in order to kill all the infidel administrators of the world. And let me offer my respectful obeisances unto You who appeared as Lord Rāma to kill demons like Rāvaṇa. You are worshiped by all devotees as the chief of the Raghu dynasty, Lord Rāmacandra. Let me offer my respectful obeisances unto You who appeared as Lord Vāsudeva, Lord Saṅkarṣaṇa, Lord Pradyumna and Lord Aniruddha. Let me offer my respectful obeisances unto You, who appeared as Lord Buddha in order to bewilder the atheistic and demoniac. And let me offer my respectful obeisances unto You, who appeared as Kalki in order to chastise the so-called royal order degraded to the abominable condition of the *mlecchas*, who are below the jurisdiction of Vedic regulative principles.

"My dear Lord, everyone within this material world is conditioned by Your illusory energy. Under the impression of false identification and false possession, everyone is transmigrating from one body to another in the path of fruitive activities and their reactions. My dear Lord, I am also no exception to these conditioned souls. I am falsely thinking myself happy in possessing my home, wife, children, state, property and effects. In this way I am acting as if in a dreamland because none of these are permanent. I am a fool to be always absorbed in such thoughts, accepting them as permanent and true. My dear Lord, due to my false identification, I have accepted everything which is nonpermanent, such as this material body, which is not spiritual and is the source of all kinds of miserable conditions. Being bewildered by such concepts of life, I am always absorbed in thoughts of duality, and I have forgotten You who are the reservoir of all transcendental pleasure. I am bereft of Your transcendental association and am just like a foolish creature who goes in search of water in the desert, leaving the water spot which is covered by water-nourished vegetables. The conditioned souls want to quench their thirst, but they do not know where to find water. They give up the spot where there is actually a reservoir of water and run into the desert where there is no water. My dear Lord, I am completely incapable of controlling my mind, which is now driven by the unbridled senses and is attracted by fruitive activities and their results. My dear Lord, Your lotus feet cannot be appreciated by any person in the conditional stage of material existence, but somehow or other I have come near Your lotus feet, and I consider this to be Your causeless mercy upon me. You can act in any way because You are the supreme controller. I can thus understand that when a person becomes eligible to be delivered from the path of repeated birth and death, it is only by Your causeless mercy that he further progresses to become attached to Your causeless devotional service."

Akrūra fell down before the Lord and said, "My dear Lord, Your transcendental eternal form is full of knowledge. Simply by concentrating one's mind upon Your form, one can understand in full knowledge everything that be, because You are the original source of all knowledge. You are the supreme powerful, possessing all kinds of energies. You are the Supreme Brahman and the Supreme Person, supreme controller and master of the material energies. I offer my respectful obeisances unto You because You are Vāsudeva, the resting place of all creation. You are the all-pervading Supreme Personality of Godhead, and You are also the Supreme Soul residing in everyone's heart and giving direction to act. Now, my Lord, I am completely surrendered unto You. Please give me Your protection."

Thus ends the Bhaktivedanta purport of the Second Volume, Fifth Chapter of* Kṛṣṇa, *"Prayers by Akrūra."

6 / Kṛṣṇa Enters Mathurā

While Akrūra was offering his prayers to the Supreme Personality of Godhead, the Lord disappeared from the water, exactly as an expert dramatic actor changes his dress and assumes his original feature. After the Viṣṇu-mūrti disappeared, Akrūra got out of the water. Finishing the rest of his ritualistic performance, he went near the chariot of Balarāma and Kṛṣṇa and was struck with wonder. Kṛṣṇa asked whether he had seen something wonderful within the water or in space. Akrūra said, "My dear Lord, all wonderful things that are happening within this world, either in the sky or in the water or on the land, are factually appearing in Your universal form. So when I have seen You, what wonderful things have I not seen?" This statement confirms the Vedic version that one who knows Kṛṣṇa knows everything, and one who has seen Kṛṣṇa has seen everything, regardless of how wonderful a thing may be. "My dear Lord," Akrūra continued, "there cannot be anything more wonderful than Your transcendental form. When I have seen Your transcendental form, what is there left to see?"

After saying this, Akrūra immediately started the chariot. By the end of the day, they had almost reached the precincts of Mathurā. When passing from Vṛndāvana to Mathurā, all passersby along the way who saw Kṛṣṇa and Balarāma could not help but look at Them again and again. In the meantime, the other inhabitants of Vṛndāvana, headed by Nanda and Upananda, had already reached Mathurā by going through forests and rivers, and they were awaiting the arrival of Kṛṣṇa and Balarāma. Upon reaching the entrance to Mathurā, Kṛṣṇa and Balarāma got down from the chariot and shook hands with Akrūra. Kṛṣṇa informed Akrūra, "You may go home now because We shall enter Mathurā along with Our associates." Akrūra replied, "My dear Lord, I cannot go to Mathurā alone, leaving You aside. I am Your surrendered servant. Please do not try to avoid me. Please, come along with me, with Your elder brother and cowherd boy friends, and sanctify my house. My dear Lord, if You come, my home will be sanctified by the dust of Your lotus feet. The water emanating from the perspiration of Your lotus feet, namely the Ganges, purifies everyone, including the forefathers, the fire-god and all other demigods. King Bali Mahārāja has become famous simply by washing Your lotus feet, and all his relatives have achieved the heavenly planet due to his contact with the Ganges water. Bali Mahārāja himself enjoyed all material opulences and later on was elevated to the highest exalted position of liberation. The Ganges water not only sanctifies the three worlds but is carried on the head of Lord Śiva. O Supreme Lord of all lords! O master of the universe! I offer my respectful obeisances unto You."

On hearing this, the Supreme Personality of Godhead, Kṛṣṇa, replied, "Akrūra, I shall surely come to your home with My elder brother Balarāma, but only after killing all the demons who are envious of the Yadu dynasty. In this way I shall please all My relatives." Akrūra became a little disappointed by these words of the Supreme Personality of Godhead, but he could not disregard the order. He therefore entered Mathurā and informed Kaṁsa about the arrival of Kṛṣṇa, and then he entered his own home.

After the departure of Akrūra, Lord Kṛṣṇa, Balarāma and the cowherd boys entered Mathurā to see the city. They observed that the gate of Mathurā was made of first-class marble, very well constructed, and the doors were made of pure gold. There were gorgeous gardens all around, and the whole city was encircled by cannons so that no enemy could enter very easily. They saw that all the crossings of the roads were decorated with gold. And there were many rich men's houses, all appearing symmetrical, as if constructed by one engineer. The houses were decorated with costly jewels, and each and every house had nice compounds of trees, fruits and flowers. The gardens, corridors and verandas of the houses were decorated with silk cloth and embroidery work in jewels and pearls. In front of the balcony windows were pigeons and peacocks walking and cooing. All the grain dealers' shops within the city were decorated with different kinds of flowers and garlands, newly grown grass and blossoming roses. The central doors of the houses were decorated with water pots filled with water, and a mixture of water and yogurt was sprinkled all around. There were flowers decorated with burning lamps of different sizes over the doors, and there were also decorations of fresh mango leaves and silk festoons on all the doors of the houses.

When the news spread that Kṛṣṇa, Balarāma and the cowherd boys were within Mathurā City, all the inhabitants gathered, and the ladies and girls immediately went up to the roofs of the houses to see Them. They had been awaiting the arrival of Kṛṣṇa and Balarāma with great anxiety, and in their extreme eagerness to see Kṛṣṇa and Balarāma, the ladies did not dress themselves very properly. Some of them placed their dress in the wrong place. Some annointed their eyes on one side only, and some wore ankle bells only on one leg or only one earring. Thus in great haste, not even decorated properly, they came to see Kṛṣṇa from the roofs. Some of them had been taking their lunch, but as soon as they heard that Kṛṣṇa and Balarāma were in the city, they left their eating and ran to the roof. Some of them were in the bathroom, taking their baths, but without properly finishing their baths, they came to see Kṛṣṇa and Balarāma. Passing by very slowly and smiling, Lord Kṛṣṇa immediately stole their hearts. He who is the husband of the goddess of fortune passed through the street like an elephant. For a very long time the women of Mathurā had heard about Kṛṣṇa and Balarāma and Their uncommon characteristics, and they were very much attracted and eager to see Them. Now when they actually saw Kṛṣṇa and Balarāma passing on the street and saw Them sweetly smiling, the ladies' joy reached the point of ecstasy. When they actually saw Them with their eyes, they took Kṛṣṇa and Balarāma within their hearts and began to embrace Them to their fullest desire. Their hairs stood up in ecstasy. They had heard of Kṛṣṇa, but they had never seen Him, and now their longing was relieved. After going up on the roofs of the palaces of Mathurā, the ladies began to shower flowers upon Kṛṣṇa and Balarāma. When the brothers were passing through the streets, all the *brāhmaṇas* in the neighborhood also went out with sandalwood and flowers and respectfully welcomed Them to the city. All the residents of Mathurā began to talk among themselves about the elevated and pious activities of the people of Vṛndāvana. The residents of Mathurā were surprised at the pious activities the cowherd men in Vṛndāvana must have performed in their previous lives to be able to see Kṛṣṇa and Balarāma daily as cowherd boys.

While Kṛṣṇa and Balarāma were passing in this way, They saw a washerman and dyer of clothing. Kṛṣṇa was pleased to ask him for some nice clothing. He also promised that if the washerman would deliver the nicest dyed cloth to Him, he would be very happy, and all good fortune would be his. Kṛṣṇa was neither beggar nor was He in need of clothing, but by this request He indicated that everyone should be ready to offer to Kṛṣṇa whatever He wants. That is the purpose of Kṛṣṇa consciousness.

Unfortunately, this washerman was a servant of Kaṁsa and therefore could not appreciate the demand of Lord Kṛṣṇa, the Supreme Personality of Godhead. This is the effect of bad association. He could have immediately delivered the clothing to the Supreme Personality of Godhead, who promised him all good fortune, but being a servant of Kaṁsa, the sinful demon could not accept the offer. Instead of being pleased, he was very angry and refused the Lord's request saying, "How is it that You are asking clothing which is meant for the king?" The washerman then began to instruct Kṛṣṇa and Balarāma: "My dear boys, in the future don't be so impudent as to ask for things which belong to the king. Otherwise, You will be punished by the government men. They will arrest You and punish You, and You will be in difficulty. I have practical experience of this fact. Anyone who unlawfully wants to use the king's property is very severely punished."

On hearing this, Lord Kṛṣṇa, the son of Devakī, became very angry at the washerman, and striking him with the upper portion of His hand, He separated the man's head from his body. The washerman fell down dead on the ground. In this way Lord Kṛṣṇa confirmed the statement that every limb of His body is capable of doing everything He likes. Without a sword, but simply with His hand, he cut off the head of the washerman. This is proof that the Supreme Lord is omnipotent. If He wants to do something, He can do it without extraneous help.

After this ghastly incident, the employees of the washerman immediately dispersed, leaving the clothing. Kṛṣṇa and Balarāma took possession of it and dressed according to Their choice; the rest of the clothes were offered to the cowherd boys, who also used them as they desired. What they did not use remained there. They then continued to proceed. In the meantime, a devotee-tailor took the opportunity of service and prepared some nice clothes from the cloth for Kṛṣṇa and Balarāma. Thus being very nicely attired, Kṛṣṇa and Balarāma looked like elephants dressed with colored clothings on the full moon day of the dark moon. Kṛṣṇa was very much pleased with the tailor and gave him the benediction of *sārūpya-mukti*, which means that after leaving his body, he would be liberated and would attain a body exactly like fourhanded Nārāyaṇa's in the Vaikuṇṭha planets. He also granted him that as long as he would live he would earn sufficient opulence to be able to enjoy sense gratification. By this incident Kṛṣṇa proved that those who are Kṛṣṇa conscious devotees will not be lacking material enjoyment or sense gratification. They will have sufficient opportunity for such things, but after leaving this life they will be allowed to enter the spiritual planets of Vaikuṇṭhaloka or Kṛṣṇaloka, Goloka Vṛndāvana.

After dressing nicely, Kṛṣṇa and Balarāma went to a florist of the name Sudāmā. As soon as they reached the precinct of his house, the florist immediately came out and with great devotion fell down on his face to offer his respectful obeisances. He offered a nice seat to Kṛṣṇa and Balarāma and asked his assistant to bring out flowers and betel nuts smeared with pulp of *candana.* The florist's welcome greatly satisfied the Lord.

The florist very humbly and submissively offered his prayers to the Lord, saying, "My dear Lord, because You have come to my place, I think all my forefathers and all my worshipable superiors are pleased and delivered. My dear Lord, You are the supreme cause of all causes of this cosmic manifestation, but for the benefit of the residents of this earthly planet, You have appeared with Your plenary portion to give protection to Your devotees and annihilate the demons. You are equally disposed as the friend of all living entities; You are the Supersoul, and You do not discriminate between friend and enemy. Yet You are pleased to give Your devotees the special result of their devotional activities. My Lord, I am praying that You please tell me whatever You wish me to do, because I am Your eternal servant. If You will allow me to do something, it will be a great favor to me." The florist, Sudāmā, was greatly pleased within his heart by seeing Kṛṣṇa and Balarāma in his place, and thus, as his choicest desire, he made two exquisite garlands of various flowers and presented them to the Lord. Both Kṛṣṇa and Balarāma were very pleased with his sincere service, and Kṛṣṇa offered the florist His salutation and benediction, which He is always prepared to bestow upon the surrendered souls. When the florist was offered benediction, he begged from the Lord that he might remain His eternal servant in devotional service and by such service do good to all living creatures. By this, it is clear that a devotee of the Lord in Kṛṣṇa consciousness should not be simply satisfied by his own advancement in devotional service; he must be willing to work for the welfare of all others. This example was followed by the six Gosvāmīs of Vṛndāvana. It is therefore stated in their prayer, *lokānāṁ hitakāriṇau:* Vaiṣṇavas, or devotees of the Lord, are not selfish. Whatever benefit they derive from the Supreme Personality of Godhead as benediction they want to distribute to all other persons. That is the greatest of all humanitarian activities. Being satisfied with the florist, Lord Kṛṣṇa not only gave him benediction for whatever he wanted, but over and above that, He offered him all material opulences, family prosperity, long duration of life, and whatever else his heart desired within the material world.

Thus ends the Bhaktivedanta purport of the Second Volume, Sixth Chapter of Kṛṣṇa, *"Kṛṣṇa Enters Mathurā."*

7 / The Breaking of the Bow in the Sacrificial Arena

After leaving the florist's place, Kṛṣṇa and Balarāma saw a hunchbacked young woman carrying a dish of sandalwood pulp through the streets. Since Kṛṣṇa is the reservoir of all pleasure, He wanted to make all His companions joyous by cutting a joke with the hunchbacked woman. Kṛṣṇa addressed her, "O tall young woman, who are you? Tell Me, for whom are you carrying this sandalwood pulp in your hand? I think you should offer this sandalwood to Me, and if you do so I am sure you will be fortunate." Kṛṣṇa is the Supreme Personality of Godhead, and He knew everything about the hunchback. By His inquiry He indicated that there was no use in serving a demon; one had better serve Kṛṣṇa and Balarāma and get rid of the result of sins.

The woman replied to Kṛṣṇa, "My dear Śyāmasundara, dear beautiful dark boy, You may know that I am engaged as maidservant of Kaṁsa. I am supplying him pulp of sandalwood daily. The king is very pleased with me for supplying this nice thing, but now I see that there is no one who can better be served by this pulp of sandalwood than You two brothers." Being captivated by the beautiful features of Kṛṣṇa and Balarāma, Their talking, Their smiling, Their glancing and other activities, the hunchbacked woman began to smear the pulp of sandalwood over Their bodies with great satisfaction and devotion. The two transcendental beggars, Kṛṣṇa and Balarāma, were naturally beautiful and had beautiful complexions, and They were nicely dressed in colorful garments. The upper portions of Their bodies were already very attractive, and when the hunchbacked woman smeared Their bodies with sandalwood pulp, They looked even more beautiful. Kṛṣṇa was very pleased by this service, and He began to consider how to reward her. In other words, in order to draw the attention of the Lord, the Kṛṣṇa conscious devotee has to serve Him in great love and devotion. Kṛṣṇa cannot be pleased by any action other than transcendental loving service unto Him. Thinking like this, Lord Kṛṣṇa pressed the feet of the hunchbacked woman with His toes and, capturing her cheeks with His fingers, gave her a jerk in order to make her straight. At once the hunchbacked woman looked like a beautiful straight girl, with broad hips, thin waist and very nice, well shaped breasts. Since Kṛṣṇa was pleased with the service of the hunchbacked woman, and since she was touched by Kṛṣṇa's hands, she became the most beautiful girl among women. This incident shows that by serving Kṛṣṇa the devotee immediately becomes elevated to the most exalted position. In all respects, devotional service is so potent that anyone who takes to it becomes qualified with all godly qualities. Kṛṣṇa was attracted to the hunchbacked woman not for her beauty but for her service; as soon as she rendered service, she immediately became the most beautiful woman. A Kṛṣṇa conscious person does not have to be qualified or beautiful; after becoming Kṛṣṇa conscious and rendering service unto Kṛṣṇa, he becomes very qualified and beautiful.

When the woman was turned by Kṛṣṇa's favor into an exquisitely beautiful young girl, she naturally felt very much obliged to Kṛṣṇa, and she was also attracted by His beauty. Without hesitation, she caught the rear part of His cloth and began to snatch it. She smiled flirtatiously and admitted that she was agitated by lusty desires. She forgot that she was on the street and before the elder brother of Kṛṣṇa and His friends.

She frankly proposed to Kṛṣṇa: "My dear hero, I cannot leave You in this way. You must come to my place. I am already very much attracted to Your beauty, so I must receive You well, for You are the best among males. You must also be very kind upon me." In plain words she proposed that Kṛṣṇa come to her home and satisfy her lusty desires. Kṛṣṇa, of course, felt a little bit embarassed in front of His elder brother, Balarāma, but He knew that the girl was simple and attracted; therefore He simply smiled at her words. Looking towards His cowherd boy friends, he replied to the girl, "My dear beautiful girl, I am very much pleased by your invitation, and I must come to your home after finishing My other business here. Such a beautiful girl like you is the only means of solace for a person like Me, for I am away from home and not married. Certainly, as a suitable girl friend, you can give us relief from all kinds of mental agitation." Kṛṣṇa satisfied the girl in this way with sweet words. Leaving her there, He began to proceed down the street of the marketplace where the citizens were prepared to receive Him with various kinds of presentations, especially betel nuts, flowers and sandalwood.

The mercantile men in the market worshiped Kṛṣṇa and Balarāma with great respect. When Kṛṣṇa was passing through the street, all the women in the surrounding houses came to see Him, and some of the younger ones almost fainted, being captivated by His beauty. Their hair and tight dresses loosened, and they forgot where they were standing.

Kṛṣṇa next inquired from the citizens as to the location of the place of sacrifice. Kaṁsa had arranged for the sacrifice called *Dhanur-yajña*, and to designate this particular sacrifice he had placed a big bow near the sacrificial altar. The bow was very big and wonderful and resembled the rainbow in the sky. Within the sacrificial arena, this bow was protected by many constables and watchmen engaged by King Kaṁsa. As Kṛṣṇa and Balarāma approached the bow, they were warned not to go nearer, but Kṛṣṇa ignored this warning. He forcibly went up and immediately took the big bow in His left hand. After stringing the bow in the presence of the crowd, He drew it and broke it at the middle into two parts, exactly as an elephant breaks sugar cane in the field. Everyone present appreciated Kṛṣṇa's power. The sound of the bow cracking filled both sky and land and was heard by Kaṁsa. When Kaṁsa heard what had happened, he began to fear for his life. The caretaker of the bow, who was standing by watching, became very angry. He ordered his men to take up weapons, and he began to rush towards Kṛṣṇa, shouting, "Arrest Him! Kill Him! Kill Him!" Kṛṣṇa and Balarāma were surrounded. When They saw the threatening motions of the guards, they became angry, and taking up the two pieces of the broken bow, They began to beat off all the caretaker's men. While this turmoil was going on, Kaṁsa sent a small group of troops to assist the caretakers, but both Kṛṣṇa and Balarāma fought with them also and killed them.

After this, Kṛṣṇa did not proceed further into the sacrificial arena but went out the gate and proceeded towards Their resting camp. Along the way, He visited various places in Mathurā City with great delight. Seeing the activities and wonderful prowess of Kṛṣṇa, all the citizens of Mathurā began to consider the two brothers to be demigods who had come down to Mathurā, and they all looked upon Them with great astonishment. The two brothers strolled carefree in the street, not caring for the law and order of Kaṁsa.

When evening came, Kṛṣṇa and Balarāma, with Their cowherd boy friends, went to the outskirts of the city where all their cars were assembled. Thus Kṛṣṇa and Balarāma gave some preliminary hints of Their arrival to Kaṁsa, and he could understand what severe type of danger was awaiting him the next day in the sacrificial arena.

When Kṛṣṇa and Balarāma were going from Vṛndāvana to Mathurā, the inhabitants of Vṛndāvana had imagined the great fortune of the citizens of Mathurā in being able to see the wonderful beauty of Kṛṣṇa, who is worshiped by His pure devotees as well as the goddess of fortune. The fantasies of the residents of Vṛndāvana were actually realized, for the citizens of Mathurā became fully satisfied by seeing Kṛṣṇa.

When Kṛṣṇa returned to His camp, He was taken care of by servants who washed His lotus feet, gave Him a nice seat and offered Him milk and palatable dishes of foodstuffs. After taking supper and thinking of the next day's program, He very peacefully began to take rest. Thus He passed the night there.

On the other side, when Kaṁsa came to understand about the breaking of his wonderful bow and the killing of the caretaker and soldiers by Kṛṣṇa, he could partially realize the power of the Supreme Personality of Godhead. He could realize that the eighth son of Devakī had appeared and that now his death was imminent. Thinking of his imminent death, he could not rest the entire night. He began to have many inauspicious visions, and he could understand that both Kṛṣṇa and Balarāma, who had approached the precincts of the city, were his messengers of death. Kaṁsa began to see various kinds of inauspicious signs, both awake and dreaming. When he looked in the mirror he could not see his head, although the head was actually present. He could see the luminaries in the sky in double, although there was only one set factually. He began to see holes in his shadow, and he could hear a high buzzing sound within his ears. All the trees before him appeared to be made of gold, and he could not see his own footprints in dust or muddy clay. In dream he saw various kinds of ghosts being carried in a carriage drawn by donkeys. He also dreamed that someone gave him poison, and he was drinking it. He dreamed also that he was going naked with a garland of flowers and was smearing oil all over his body. Thus, as Kaṁsa saw various signs of death both awake and sleeping, he could understand that death was certain, and thus in great anxiety he could not rest that night. Just after the night expired, he busily arranged for the wrestling match.

The wrestling arena was nicely cleansed and decorated with flags, festoons and flowers, and the match was announced by the beating of kettledrums. The platform appeared very beautiful due to streamers and flags. Different types of galleries were arranged for respectable persons—kings, *brāhmaṇas* and *kṣatriyas.* The various kings had reserved thrones, and others had arranged seats also. Kaṁsa finally arrived, accompanied by various ministers and secretaries, and he sat on the raised platform especially meant for him. Unfortunately, although he was sitting in the center of all governing executive heads, his heart was palpitating in fear of death. Cruel death evidently does not care even for a person as powerful as Kaṁsa.

When death comes, it does not care for anyone's exalted position.

When everything was complete, the wrestlers, who were to exhibit their skills before the assembly, walked into the arena. They were decorated with bright ornaments and dress. Some of the famous wrestlers were Cāṇūra, Muṣṭika, Śala, Kūṭa and Tośala. Being enlivened by the musical concert, they passed through with great alacrity. All the respectable cowherd men who came from Vṛndāvana, headed by Nanda, were also welcomed by Kaṁsa. After presenting Kaṁsa with the milk products they had brought with them, the cowherd men also took their respective seats by the side of the king, on a platform especially meant for them.

Thus ends the Bhaktivedanta purport of the Second Volume, Seventh Chapter of* Kṛṣṇa, *"The Breaking of the Bow in the Sacrificial Arena."

8 / The Killing of the Elephant Kuvalayāpīḍa

After taking their baths and finishing all other morning duties, Kṛṣṇa and Balarāma could hear the beating of the kettledrums in the wrestling camp. They immediately prepared Themselves to proceed to the spot to see the fun. When Kṛṣṇa and Balarāma reached the gate of the wrestling camp, They saw a big elephant of the name Kuvalayāpīḍa being tended by a caretaker. The caretaker was deliberately blocking Their entrance by keeping the elephant in front of the gateway. Kṛṣṇa could understand the purpose of the caretaker, and He prepared Himself by tightening His dress before combatting the elephant. He began to address the caretaker in a very grave voice, as resounding as a cloud: "You miscreant caretaker, give way and let Me pass through the gate. If you block My way, I shall send you and your elephant to the house of death personified."

The caretaker, being thus insulted by Kṛṣṇa, became very angry, and in order to challenge Kṛṣṇa, as was previously planned, he provoked the elephant to attack. The elephant then moved before Kṛṣṇa like inevitable death. It rushed towards Him and tried to catch Him with its trunk, but Kṛṣṇa very dexterously moved behind the elephant. Being able to see only to the end of its nose, the elephant could not see Kṛṣṇa hiding behind its legs, but it tried to capture Him with its trunk. Kṛṣṇa again very quickly escaped capture, and He again ran behind the elephant and caught its tail. Holding the elephant by its tail, Kṛṣṇa began to pull it, and with very great strength He dragged it for at least twenty-five yards, just as Garuḍa drags an insignificant snake. Kṛṣṇa pulled the elephant from this side to that, from right to left, just as He used to pull the tail of a calf in His childhood. After this, Kṛṣṇa went in front of the elephant and gave it a strong slap. He then slipped away from the elephant's view and ran to its back. Then, falling down on the ground, Kṛṣṇa placed Himself in front of the elephant's two legs and caused it to trip and fall. Kṛṣṇa immediately got up, but the elephant, thinking that He was still lying down, tried to push an ivory tusk through the body of Kṛṣṇa by forcibly stabbing it into the ground. Although the elephant was harassed and angry, the caretaker riding on its head tried to provoke it further. The elephant then rushed madly towards Kṛṣṇa. As soon as it came within reach, Kṛṣṇa caught hold of the trunk and pulled the elephant down. When the elephant and caretaker fell, Kṛṣṇa jumped up on the elephant's back and broke it and killed the caretaker also. After killing the elephant, Kṛṣṇa took an ivory tusk on His shoulder. Decorated with drops of perspiration and sprinkled with the blood of the elephant, He felt very blissful, and thus He began to proceed towards the wrestling camp. Lord Balarāma took the other tusk of the elephant on His shoulder. Accompanied by Their cowherd boy friends, They entered the arena.

When Kṛṣṇa entered the wrestling arena with Balarāma and Their friends, He appeared differently to different people according to their different relationships *(rasas)* with Him. Kṛṣṇa is the reservoir of all pleasure and all kinds of *rasas*, both favorable and unfavorable. He appeared to the wrestlers exactly like a thunderbolt. To the people in general He appeared as the most beautiful personality. To the females He appeared to be the most attractive male, Cupid personified, and thus increased their lust. The cowherd men who were present there looked upon Kṛṣṇa as their own kinsman, coming from the same village of Vṛndāvana. The *kṣatriya* kings who were present saw Him as the strongest ruler. To the parents of Kṛṣṇa, Nanda and Yaśodā, He appeared to be the most loving child. To Kaṁsa, the king of the Bhoja dynasty, He appeared to be death personified. To the unintelligent, He appeared to be an incapable personality. To the *yogīs* present, He appeared to be the Supersoul. To the members of the Vṛṣṇi dynasty He appeared to be the most celebrated descendant. Thus appreciated differently by different kinds of men present, Kṛṣṇa entered the wrestling arena with Balarāma and His cowherd boy friends. Having heard that Kṛṣṇa had already killed the elephant, Kuvalayāpīḍa, Kaṁsa knew beyond doubt that Kṛṣṇa was formidable. He thus became very much afraid of Him. Kṛṣṇa and Balarāma had long hands. They were beautifully dressed, and They were attractive to all the people assembled there. They were dressed as if They were going to act on a dramatic stage, and They drew the attention of all people.

The citizens of Mathurā City who saw Kṛṣṇa, the Supreme Personality of Godhead, became very pleased and began to look on His face with insatiable glances, as if they were drinking the nectar of heaven. Seeing Kṛṣṇa gave them so much pleasure that it appeared that they were not only drinking the nectar of seeing His face, but were smelling the aroma and licking up the taste of His body and were embracing Him and Balarāma with their arms. They began to talk among themselves about the two transcendental brothers. For a long time they had heard of the beauty and activities of Kṛṣṇa and Balarāma, but now they were personally seeing Them face to face. They thought that Kṛṣṇa and Balarāma were two plenary incarnations of the Supreme Personality of Godhead, Nārāyaṇa, who had appeared in Vṛndāvana.

The citizens of Mathurā began to recite Kṛṣṇa's pastimes, His birth as the son of Vasudeva, His being taken into the care of Nanda Mahārāja and his wife in Gokula, and all those events leading to His coming to Mathurā. They spoke of the killing of the demon Pūtanā, as well as the killing of Tṛṇāvarta, who came as a whirlwind. They also recalled the deliverance of the twin brothers from within the *yamala arjuna* trees. The citizens of Mathurā spoke among themselves: Śaṅkhāsura, Keśī, Dhenukāsura and many other demons were killed by Kṛṣṇa and Balarāma in Vṛndāvana. Kṛṣṇa also saved all the cowherd men of Vṛndāvana from devastating fire. He chastised the Kāliya snake in the water of Yamunā, and He curbed the false pride of the heavenly king, Indra. Kṛṣṇa held up the great Govardhana Hill in one hand for seven continuous days and saved all the people of Gokula from incessant rain, hurricane and windstorm." They also began to remember other enlivening activities: "The damsels of Vṛndāvana were so pleased by seeing Kṛṣṇa's beauty and participating in His activities that they forgot the purpose of material existence. By seeing and thinking of Kṛṣṇa, they forgot all sorts of material fatigue." The Mathurā citizens discussed the dynasty of Yadu, saying that because of Kṛṣṇa's appearance in this dynasty, the Yadus would remain the most celebrated family in the whole universe. While they were thus talking about the activities of Kṛṣṇa and Balarāma, they heard the vibrations of different bands announcing the wrestling match.

The famous wrestler Cāṇūra then began to talk with Kṛṣṇa and Balarāma. "My dear Kṛṣṇa and Balarāma," he said, "we have heard about Your past activities. You are great heroes, and therefore the king has called you. We have heard that Your arms are very strong. The king and all the people present here desire to see a display of Your wrestling abilities. A citizen should be obedient and please the mind of the ruling king; acting in that way, the citizen attains all kinds of good fortune. One who does not care to act obediently is made unhappy because of the king's anger. You are cowherd boys, and we have heard that while tending Your cows in the forest, You enjoy wrestling with each other. We wish, therefore, for You to join with us in wrestling so that all the people present here, along with the king, will be pleased."

Kṛṣṇa immediately understood the purpose of Cāṇūra's statements, and He prepared to wrestle with him. But according to the time and circumstances, He spoke as follows: "You are the subject of the King of Bhoja, and you live in the jungle. We are also indirectly his subjects, and we try to please him as far as possible. This offer of wrestling is a great favor of his, but the fact is that We are simply boys. We sometimes play in the forest of Vṛndāvana with our friends who are our own age. We think that to combat persons of equal age and strength is good for us, but to fight great wrestlers like you would not be good for the audience. It would contradict their religious principles." Kṛṣṇa thus indicated that the celebrated, strong wrestlers should not challenge Kṛṣṇa and Balarāma to fight.

In reply to this, Cāṇūra said, "My dear Kṛṣṇa, we can understand that You are neither a child nor a young man. You are transcendental to everyone, as is Your big brother, Balarāma. You have already killed the elephant Kuvalayāpīḍa, who was capable of fighting and defeating other elephants. You have killed him in a wonderful way. Because of Your strength, it behooves You to compete with the stronger wrestlers amongst us. I therefore wish to wrestle with You, and Your elder brother, Balarāma, will wrestle with Muṣṭika."

Thus ends the Bhaktivedanta purport of the Second Volume, Eighth Chapter of* Kṛṣṇa, *"The Killing of the Elephant Kuvalayāpīḍa."

9 / The Killing of Kaṁsa

After Kaṁsa's wrestlers expressed their determination, the Supreme Personality of Godhead, the killer of Madhu, confronted Cāṇūra, and Lord Balarāma, the son of Rohiṇī, confronted Muṣṭika. Kṛṣṇa and Cāṇūra and then Balarāma and Muṣṭika locked themselves hand to hand, leg to leg, and each began to press against the other with a view to come out victorious. They joined palm to palm, calf to calf, head to head, chest to chest and began to strike each other. The fighting increased as they pushed one another from one place to another. One captured another and threw him down on the ground, and another rushed from the back to the front of another and tried to overcome him with a hold. The fighting increased step by step. There was picking up, the dragging and pushing, and then the legs and hands were locked together. All the arts of wrestling were perfectly exhibited by the parties, as each tried his best to defeat his opponent.

But the audience in the wrestling arena was not very satisfied because the combatants did not appear to be equally matched. They considered Kṛṣṇa and Balarāma to be mere boys before the wrestlers Cāṇūra and Muṣṭika, who were huge men as solid as stone. Being compassionate and favoring Kṛṣṇa and Balarāma, many members of the audience began to talk as follows. "Dear friends, there is danger here." Another said, "Even in front of the king this wrestling is going on between incompatible sides." The audience had lost their sense of enjoyment. They could not encourage the fighting between the strong and the weak. "Muṣṭika and Cāṇūra are just like thunderbolts, as strong as great mountains, and Kṛṣṇa and Balarāma are two delicate boys of very tender age. The principle of justice has already left this assembly. Persons who are aware of the civilized principles of justice will not remain to watch this unfair match. Those taking part in this wrestling match are not very much enlightened; therefore whether they speak or remain silent, they are being subjected to the reactions of sinful activities." "But my dear friends," another in the assembly spoke out, "just look at the face of Kṛṣṇa. There are drops of perspiration on His face from chasing His enemy, and His face appears like the lotus flower with drops of water. And do you see how the face of Lord Balarāma has turned especially beautiful? There is a reddish hue on His white face because He is engaged in a strong wrestling match with Muṣṭika."

Ladies in the assembly also addressed one another. "Dear friends, just imagine how fortunate the land of Vṛndāvana is where the Supreme Personality of Godhead Himself is present, always decorated with flower garlands and engaged in tending cows along with His brother, Lord Balarāma. He is always accompanied by His cowherd boy friends, and He plays His transcendental flute. The residents of Vṛndāvana are fortunate to be able to constantly see the lotus feet of Kṛṣṇa and Balarāma, which are worshiped by great demigods like Lord Śiva and Brahmā and the goddess of fortune. We cannot estimate how many pious activities were executed by the damsels of Vrajabhūmi so that they were able to enjoy the Supreme Personality of Godhead and look on the unparalleled beauty of His transcendental body. The beauty of the Lord is beyond compare. No one is higher or equal to Him in beauty of complexion or bodily luster. Kṛṣṇa and Balarāma are the reservoir of all kinds of opulence—namely wealth, strength, beauty, fame, knowledge and renunciation. The *gopīs* are so fortunate that they can see and think of Kṛṣṇa twenty-four hours a day, beginning from their milking the cows or husking the paddy or churning the butter in the morning. While engaged in cleaning their houses and washing their floors, they are always absorbed in the thought of Kṛṣṇa."

The *gopīs* give a perfect example of how one can execute Kṛṣṇa consciousness even if he is in different types of material engagement. By constantly being absorbed in the thought of Kṛṣṇa, one cannot be affected by the contamination of material activities. The *gopīs* are, therefore, perfectly in trance, *samādhi,* the highest perfectional stage of mystic power. In the *Bhagavad-gītā,* it is confirmed that one who is constantly thinking of Kṛṣṇa is a first-class *yogī* among all kinds of *yogīs.* "My dear friends," one lady told another, "we must accept the *gopīs'* activities to be the highest form of piety; otherwise, how could they have achieved the opportunity of seeing Kṛṣṇa both morning and evening when He goes to the pasturing ground with His cows and cowherd boy friends and returns in the evening? They frequently see Him playing on His flute and smiling very brilliantly."

When Lord Kṛṣṇa, the Supersoul of every living being, understood that the ladies in the assembly were anxious for Him, He decided not to continue wrestling but to kill the wrestlers immediately. The parents of Kṛṣṇa and Balarāma, namely Nanda Mahārāja, Yaśodā, Vasudeva and Devakī, were also very anxious because they did not know the unlimited strength of their children. Lord Balarāma was fighting with the wrestler Muṣṭika in the same way that Kṛṣṇa, the Supreme Personality of Godhead, was fighting and wrestling with Cāṇūra. Lord Kṛṣṇa appeared to be cruel to Cāṇūra, and He immediately struck him thrice with His fist. The great wrestler was jolted, to the astonishment of the audience. Cāṇūra then took his last chance and attacked Kṛṣṇa, just as one hawk swoops upon another. Folding his two hands, he began to strike the chest of Kṛṣṇa, but Lord Kṛṣṇa was not even slightly disturbed, no more than an elephant that is hit by a flower garland. Kṛṣṇa quickly caught the two hands of Cāṇūra and began to wheel him around, and simply by this centrifugal action, Cāṇūra lost his life. Kṛṣṇa then threw him to the ground. Cāṇūra fell just like the flag of Indra, and all his nicely decorated ornaments were scattered hither and thither.

Muṣṭika also struck Balarāma, and Balarāma returned the stroke with great force. Muṣṭika began to tremble, and blood and vomit flowed from his mouth. Distressed, he gave up his vital force and fell down just as a tree falls down in a hurricane. After the two wrestlers were killed, a wrestler named Kūṭa came forward. Lord Balarāma immediately caught him in His left hand and killed him nonchalantly. Another wrestler of the name Śala came forward, and Kṛṣṇa immediately kicked him and cracked his head. Another wrestler named Tośala came forward and was killed in the same way. Thus all the great wrestlers were killed by Kṛṣṇa and Balarāma, and the remaining wrestlers began to flee from the assembly out of fear for their lives. All the cowherd boy friends of Kṛṣṇa and Balarāma approached Them and congratulated Them with great pleasure. While drums beat and they talked of the victory, the leg bells on the feet of Kṛṣṇa and Balarāma tinkled.

All people gathered there began to clap in great ecstasy, and no one could estimate the bounds of their pleasure. The *brāhmaṇas* present began to praise Kṛṣṇa and Balarāma ecstatically. Only Kaṁsa was morose; he neither clapped nor offered benediction to Kṛṣṇa. Kaṁsa resented the drums' being beaten for Kṛṣṇa's victory, and he was very sorry that the wrestlers had been killed and had fled the assembly. He therefore immediately ordered the drum playing to stop and began to address his friends as follows: "I order that these two sons of Vasudeva be immediately driven out of Mathurā. The cowherd boys who have come with Them should be plundered and all their riches taken away. Nanda Mahārāja should immediately be arrested and killed for his cunning behavior, and the rascal Vasudeva should also be killed without delay. Also my father, Ugrasena, who has always supported my enemies against my will, should be killed."

When Kaṁsa spoke in this way, Lord Kṛṣṇa became very angry with him, and within a second He jumped over the high guards of King Kaṁsa. Kaṁsa was prepared for Kṛṣṇa's attack, for he knew from the beginning that He was to be the cause of his death. He immediately unsheathed his sword and prepared to answer the challenge of Kṛṣṇa with sword and shield. As Kaṁsa wielded his sword up and down, hither and thither, Lord Kṛṣṇa, the supreme powerful Lord, caught hold of him with great force. The Supreme Personality of Godhead, who is the shelter of the complete creation and from whose lotus navel the whole creation is manifested, immediately knocked the crown from the head of Kaṁsa and grabbed his long hair in His hand. He then dragged Kaṁsa from his seat to the wrestling dais and threw him down. Then Kṛṣṇa at once straddled his chest and began to strike him over and over again. Simply from the strokes of His fist, Kaṁsa lost his vital force.

In order to assure His parents that Kaṁsa was dead, Lord Kṛṣṇa dragged him just as a lion drags an elephant after killing it. On sight of this, there was a great roaring sound from all sides, as some spectators expressed their jubilation and others cried in lamentation. From the day Kaṁsa heard that he would be killed by the eighth son of Devakī, he was always thinking of Kṛṣṇa twenty-four hours a day without any stoppage—even while he was eating, while he was walking, while he was breathing—and naturally he got the blessing of liberation. In the *Bhagavad-gītā* it is stated, *sadā tad-bhāva-bhāvitaḥ:* a person gets his next life according to the thoughts in which he is always absorbed. Kaṁsa was thinking of Kṛṣṇa with His wheel, which means Nārāyaṇa who holds a wheel, conchshell, lotus flower and club.

According to the opinion of authorities, Kaṁsa attained *sārūpya-mukti* after death, that is to say he attained the same form as Nārāyaṇa (Viṣṇu). On the Vaikuṇṭha planets all the inhabitants have the same bodily features as Nārāyaṇa. After his death, Kaṁsa attained liberation and was promoted to Vaikuṇṭhaloka. From this instance we can understand that even a person who thinks of the Supreme Personality of Godhead as an enemy gets liberation and a place in a Vaikuṇṭha planet, so what to speak of the pure devotees who are always absorbed in favorable thoughts of Kṛṣṇa? Even an enemy who is killed by Kṛṣṇa gets liberation and is placed in the impersonal *brahmajyoti.* Since the Supreme Personality of Godhead is all good, anyone thinking of Him, either as enemy or as friend, gets liberation. But the liberation of the devotee and the liberation of the enemy are not the same. The enemy generally gets the liberation of *sāyujya,* and sometimes he gets *sārūpya* liberation.

Kaṁsa had eight brothers, headed by Kaṅka. All of them were younger than he, and when they learned that their elder brother had been killed, they combined together and rushed towards Kṛṣṇa in great anger to kill Him. Kaṁsa and his brothers were all Kṛṣṇa's maternal uncles. They were all brothers of Kṛṣṇa's mother, Devakī. When Kṛṣṇa killed Kaṁsa He killed His maternal uncle, which is against the regulation of Vedic injunction. Although Kṛṣṇa is independent of all Vedic injunction, He violates the Vedic injunction only in inevitable cases. Kaṁsa could not be killed by anyone but Kṛṣṇa; therefore Kṛṣṇa was obliged to kill him. As far as Kaṁsa's eight brothers were concerned, Balarāma took charge of killing them. Balarāma's mother, Rohiṇī, although the wife of Vasudeva, was not the sister of Kaṁsa; therefore Balarāma took charge of killing all of Kaṁsa's eight brothers. He immediately took up an available weapon (most probably the elephant's tusk which He carried) and killed the eight brothers one after another, just as a lion kills a flock of deer. Kṛṣṇa and Balarāma thus verified the statement that the Supreme Personality of Godhead appears to give protection to the pious and to kill the impious demons who are always enemies of the demigods.

The demigods from the higher planetary systems began to shower flowers, congratulating Kṛṣṇa and Balarāma. Among the demigods were powerful personalities like Lord Brahmā and Śiva, and all joined together in showing their jubilation over Kaṁsa's death. There was beating of drums and showering of flowers from the heavenly planets, and the wives of the demigods began to dance in ecstasy.

The wives of Kaṁsa and his eight brothers became aggrieved on account of their husbands' sudden deaths, and all of them were striking their foreheads and shedding torrents of tears. They were crying very loudly and embracing the bodies of their husbands. The wives of Kaṁsa and his brothers began to lament, addressing the dead bodies: "Our dear husbands, you are so kind and are the protectors of your dependents. Now, after your death, we are also dead, along with your homes and children. We are no longer looking very auspicious. On account of your death, the auspicious functions which were to take place, such as the sacrifice of the bow, have all been spoiled. Our dear husbands, you treated persons ill who were faultless, and as a result you have been killed. This is inevitable because a person who torments an innocent person must be punished by the laws of nature. We know that Lord Kṛṣṇa is the Supreme Personality of Godhead. He is the supreme master of everything and the supreme enjoyer of everything, and therefore anyone who neglects His authority can never be happy, and ultimately, as you have, he meets death."

Since Kṛṣṇa was kind and affectionate to His aunts, He began to give them solace as far as was possible. The ritualistic ceremonies after death were then conducted under the personal supervision of Kṛṣṇa because He happened to be the nephew of all the dead princes. After finishing this business, Kṛṣṇa and Balarāma immediately released Their father and mother, Vasudeva and Devakī who had been imprisoned by Kaṁsa. Kṛṣṇa and Balarāma fell at Their parents' feet and offered them prayers. Vasudeva and Devakī had suffered so much trouble because Kṛṣṇa was their son; it was because of Kṛṣṇa that Kaṁsa was always giving them trouble. Devakī and Vasudeva were fully conscious of Kṛṣṇa's exalted position as the Supreme Personality of Godhead; therefore, although Kṛṣṇa touched their feet and offered obeisances and prayers to them, they did not embrace Him, but simply stood up to hear the Supreme Personality of Godhead. Although Kṛṣṇa was born as their son, Vasudeva and Devakī were always conscious of His position.

Thus ends the Bhaktivedanta purport of the Second Volume, Ninth Chapter of* Kṛṣṇa, *"The Killing of Kaṁsa."

10 / Kṛṣṇa Recovers the Son of His Teacher

When Lord Kṛṣṇa saw that Vasudeva and Devakī were remaining standing in a reverential attitude, He immediately expanded His influence of *yogamāyā* so that they could treat Him and Balarāma as children. As in the material world the relationship existing between father and mother and children can be established amongst different living entities by the influence of the illusory energy, so, by the influence of *yogamāyā,* the devotee can establish a relationship in which the Supreme Personality of Godhead is his child. After creating this situation by His *yogamāyā,* Kṛṣṇa, appearing with His elder brother Balarāma as the most illustrious sons in the dynasty of the Sātvatas, very submissively and respectfully addressed Vasudeva and Devakī: "My dear father and mother, although you have always been very anxious for the protection of Our lives, you could not enjoy the pleasure of having Us as your babies, as your growing boys and as your adolescent youths." Kṛṣṇa indirectly praised the fatherhood of Nanda Mahārāja and motherhood of Yaśodā as most glorious because although He and Balarāma were not their born sons, Nanda and Yaśodā actually enjoyed Their childhood pastimes. By nature's own arrangement, the childhood of the embodied living being is enjoyed by the parents. Even in the animal kingdom the parents are found to be affectionate to the cubs. Being captivated by the activities of their children, they take much care for their well-being. As for Vasudeva and Devakī, they were always very anxious for the protection of their sons, Kṛṣṇa and Balarāma. That is why Kṛṣṇa, after His appearance, was immediately transferred to another's house. Balarāma was also transferred from Devakī's womb to Rohiṇī's womb.

Vasudeva and Devakī were full of anxieties for Kṛṣṇa's and Balarāma's protection, and they could not enjoy Their childhood pastimes. Kṛṣṇa said, "Unfortunately, being ordered by Our fate, We could not be raised by Our own parents to enjoy childhood pleasures at home. My dear father and mother, a man has a debt to pay to his parents, from whom he gets this body which can bestow upon him all the benefits of material existence. According to the Vedic injunction, this human form of life enables one to perform all kinds of religious activities, fulfill all kinds of desires and acquire all kinds of wealth. And only in this human form is there every possibility that one can get liberation from material existence. This body is produced by the combined efforts of the father and mother. Every human being should be obliged to his parents and understand that he cannot repay his debt to them. If, after growing up, a son does not try to satisfy his parents by his actions or by an endowment of riches, he is surely punished after death by the superintendent of death and made to eat his own flesh. If a person is able to care for or give protection to old parents, children, the spiritual master, *brāhmaṇas* and other dependents, but does not do so, he is considered to be already dead, although he is supposedly breathing. My dear father and mother, you have always been very anxious for Our protection, but unfortunately We could not render any service unto you. Up to date We have simply wasted Our time; We could not serve you for reasons beyond Our control. Mother and father, please excuse Us for Our sinful action."

When the Supreme Personality of Godhead was speaking as an innocent boy in very sweet words, both Vasudeva and Devakī became captivated by parental affection and embraced Them with great pleasure. They were amazed and could not speak or answer the words of Kṛṣṇa, but simply embraced Him and Balarāma in great affection and remained silent, shedding incessant tears.

Thus consoling His father and mother, the Supreme Personality of Godhead, appearing as the beloved son of Devakī, approached His grandfather Ugrasena and announced that Ugrasena would now be the King of the Yadu kingdom. Kaṁsa had been forcibly ruling over the kingdom of Yadu, in spite of the presence of his father, whom he had arrested. But after the death of Kaṁsa, Kaṁsa's father was released and announced to be the King of the Yadu kingdom. It appears that in those days, in the western part of India, there were many small kingdoms, and they were ruled by the Yadu dynasty, Andhaka dynasty, Vṛṣṇi dynasty and Bhoja dynasty. Mahārāja Ugrasena belonged to the Bhoja dynasty; therefore Kṛṣṇa indirectly declared that the king of the Bhoja dynasty would be emperor of the other small kingdoms. He willingly asked Mahārāja Ugrasena to rule over Them because They were his subjects. The word *prajā* is used both for the progeny and for the citizens, so Kṛṣṇa belonged to the *prajā*, both as a grandson to Mahārāja Ugrasena and as a member of the Yadu dynasty. He voluntarily accepted the rule of Mahārāja Ugrasena. He informed Ugrasena: "Being cursed by the Yayāti, the kings of the Yadu dynasty will not rise against the throne. It will be Our pleasure to serve you as your servants. Our full cooperation with you will make your position more exalted and secure so that the kings of other dynasties will not hesitate to pay their respective revenues. Protected by Us, you will be honored even by the demigods from the heavenly planets. My dear grandfather, out of fear of My late uncle Kaṁsa, all the kings belonging to the Yadu dynasty, Vṛṣṇi dynasty, Andhaka dynasty, Madhu dynasty, Daśārha dynasty and Kukura dynasty were very anxious and disturbed. Now you can pacify them all and give them assurance of security. The whole kingdom will be peaceful."

All the kings in the neighboring area had left their homes in fear of Kaṁsa and were living in distant parts of the country. Now, after the death of Kaṁsa and the reinstatement of Ugrasena as king, the neighboring kings were given all kinds of presentations and comforts. Then they returned to their respective homes. After this nice political arrangement, the citizens of Mathurā were pleased to live in Mathurā, being protected by the strong arms of Kṛṣṇa and Balarāma. On account of good government in the presence of Kṛṣṇa and Balarāma, the inhabitants of Mathurā felt complete satisfaction in the fulfillment of all their material desires and necessities, and because they saw Kṛṣṇa and Balarāma daily, eye to eye, they soon forgot all material miseries completely. As soon as they saw Kṛṣṇa and Balarāma coming out on the street, very nicely dressed and smiling and looking here and there, the citizens were immediately filled with loving ecstasies, simply by seeing the personal presence of Mukunda. *Mukunda* refers to one who can award liberation and transcendental bliss. Kṛṣṇa's presence acted as such a vitalizing tonic that not only the younger generation, but even the old men of Mathurā became fully invigorated with youthful energy and strength by regularly seeing Him.

Nanda Mahārāja and Yaśodā were also living in Mathurā because Kṛṣṇa and Balarāma were there, but after some time they wanted to go back to Vṛndāvana. Kṛṣṇa and Balarāma went before them and very feelingly and affectionately embraced Nanda and Yaśodā, and Kṛṣṇa began to speak as follows: "My dear father and mother, although I was born of Vasudeva and Devakī, you have been Our real father and mother, because from Our very birth and childhood, you raised Us with great affection and love. Your affectionate love for Us was more than anyone can offer one's own children. You are actually Our father and mother, because you raised Us as your own children at a time when We were just like orphans. For certain reasons We were rejected by Our father and mother, and you protected Us. My dear father and mother, I know you will be feeling separation by returning to Vṛndāvana and leaving Us here, but please rest assured that I shall be coming back to Vṛndāvana just after giving some satisfaction to My real father and mother, Vasudeva and Devakī, My grandfather, and other relatives and family members." Kṛṣṇa and Balarāma satisfied Nanda and Yaśodā by sweet words and by presentation of various clothing, ornaments and properly made utensils. They satisfied them, along with their friends and neighbors who had come with them from Vṛndāvana to Mathurā, as fully as possible. On account of his excessive parental affection for Balarāma and Kṛṣṇa, Nanda Mahārāja felt tears in his eyes, and he embraced Them and started with the cowherd men for Vṛndāvana.

After this, Vasudeva had his son initiated by sacred thread as the token of second birth, which is essential for the higher castes of human society. Vasudeva called for his family priest and learned *brāhmaṇas,* and the sacred thread ceremony of Kṛṣṇa and Balarāma was duly performed. During this ceremony, Vasudeva gave various ornaments in charity to the *brāhmaṇas* and endowed them with cows decorated with silken cloths and golden ornaments. Previously, during the birth of Kṛṣṇa and Balarāma, Vasudeva had wanted to give cows in charity to the *brāhmaṇas,* but being imprisoned by Kaṁsa, he was able to do so only within his mind. With the death of Kaṁsa the actual cows were given to the *brāhmaṇas.* Then Balarāma and Kṛṣṇa were duly initiated with the sacred thread ceremony, and They repeated the chanting of the *Gāyatrī mantra.* The *Gāyatrī mantra* is offered to the disciples after the sacred thread ceremony, and Balarāma and Kṛṣṇa properly discharged the duties of chanting this *mantra.* Anyone who executes the chanting of this *mantra* has to abide by certain principles and vows. Although Balarāma and Kṛṣṇa were both transcendental personalities, They strictly followed the regulative principles. Both were initiated by Their family priest Gargācārya, usually known as Gargamuni, the *ācārya* of the Yadu dynasty. According to Vedic culture, every respectable person has an *ācārya,* or spiritual master. One is not considered to be a perfectly cultured man without being initiated and trained by an *ācārya.* It is said, therefore, that one who has approached an *ācārya* is actually in perfect knowledge. Lord Kṛṣṇa and Balarāma were the Supreme Personality of Godhead, the master of all education and knowledge. There was no need for Them to accept a spiritual master or *ācārya,* yet for the instruction of ordinary men, They also accepted a spiritual master for advancement in spiritual knowledge.

It is customary, after being initiated in the *Gāyatrī mantra,* for one to live away from home for some time under the care of the *ācārya* in order to be trained in spiritual life. During this period one has to work under the spiritual master as an ordinary menial servant. There are many rules and regulations for a *brahmacārī* living under the care of an *ācārya,* and both Lord Kṛṣṇa and Balarāma strictly followed those regulative principles while living under the instruction of their spiritual master, Sāndīpani Muni, in his place in northern India. According to scriptural injunctions, a spiritual master should be respected and be regarded on an equal level with the Supreme Personality of Godhead. Both Kṛṣṇa and Balarāma exactly followed those principles with great devotion and underwent the regulations of *brahmacarya,* and thus They satisfied Their spiritual master, who instructed Them in Vedic knowledge. Being very satisfied, Sāndīpani Muni instructed Them in all the intricacies of Vedic wisdom as well as in supplementary literatures such as the *Upaniṣads.* Because Kṛṣṇa and Balarāma happened to be *kṣatriyas,* They were specifically trained in military science, politics and mathematics. In politics there are six departments of knowledge—how to make peace, how to fight, how to pacify, how to divide and rule, how to give shelter, etc. All these items were fully explained and instructed to Kṛṣṇa and Balarāma.

The ocean is the source of water in a river. The cloud is created by the evaporation of ocean water, and the same water is distributed as rain all over the surface of the earth and then returns toward the ocean in rivers. So Kṛṣṇa and Balarāma, the Supreme Personality of Godhead, are the source of all kinds of knowledge, but because They were playing like ordinary human boys, They set the example so that everyone would receive knowledge from the right source. Thus They agreed to take knowledge from a spiritual master.

After hearing only once from the teacher, Kṛṣṇa and Balarāma learned all the arts and sciences. In sixty-four days and sixty-four nights They learned all the necessary arts and sciences that are required in human society. During daytime They took lessons on a subject from the teacher, and by nightfall, after having heard from the teacher, They were expert in that department of knowledge.

First of all They learned how to sing, how to compose songs and how to recognize the different tunes; They learned the favorable and unfavorable accents and meters, how to sing different kinds of rhythms and melodies, and how to follow them by beating different kinds of drums. They learned how to dance with rhythm, melody and different songs.

They learned how to write dramas, and They learned the various types of paintings, beginning from different village arts up to the highest perfectional stage. They also learned how to paint *tilaka* on the face and make different kinds of dots on the forehead and cheeks. Then They learned the art of painting on the floor with liquid paste of rice and flour; such paintings are very popular at auspicious ceremonies performed at household affairs or in the temple. They learned how to make a resting place with flowers and how to decorate clothing and leaves with colorful paintings. They also learned how to set different valuable jewels in ornaments. They learned the art of ringing water pots. Water pots are filled with water to a certain measurement so that when one beats on the pots, different tunes are produced, and when the pots are beaten together they produce a melodious sound. They also learned how to throw water in the rivers or the lakes while taking a bath among friends. They also learned how to decorate with flowers. This art of decorating can still be seen in various temples of Vṛndāvana during the summer season. It is called *phulabāḍi*. The dais, the throne, the walls and the ceiling are all fully decorated, and a small, aromatic fountain of flowers is fixed in the center. Because of these floral decorations, the people, fatigued from the heat of the summer season, become refreshed.

Kṛṣṇa and Balarāma learned the art of dressing hair in various styles and fixing a helmet in different positions on the head. They also learned how to perform on the theatrical stage, how to decorate dramatic actors with flower ornaments over the ear, and how to sprinkle sandalwood pulp and water to produce a nice fragrance. They also learned the art of performing magical feats. Within the magical field there is an art called *bahurūpī* by which a person dresses himself in such a way that when he approaches a friend he cannot be recognized. They also learned how to make beverages which are required at various times, and They studied syrups and tastes and the effects of intoxication. They learned how to manipulate thin threads for dancing puppets, and They learned how to string wires on musical instruments, such as the *vīṇā*, sitar and tampura, to produce melodious sound. Then They learned puzzles and how to set and solve them. They learned the art of reading books from which even a foolish student can very quickly learn to read the alphabet and comprehend writing. Then They learned how to rehearse and act out a drama. They also studied the art of solving crossword puzzles, filling up the missing space and making complete words.

They also learned how to draw pictographic literature. In some countries in the world, pictographic literature is still current. A story is represented by pictures; for instance, a man and a house are pictured to represent a man going home. Kṛṣṇa and Balarāma also learned the art of architecture—how to construct residential buildings. They learned to recognize valuable jewels by studying the luster and the quality of their colors. Then They learned the art of setting jewels with gold and silver. They also learned how to study soil to find minerals. This study of soil is now a greatly specialized science, but formerly it was common knowledge even for the ordinary man. They learned to study herbs and plants and to extract medicine from the elements. By studying the different species of plants, They learned how to crossbreed plants and get different types of fruits. They learned how to train and engage lambs and cocks in fighting for sporting purposes. They then learned how to teach parrots to speak and answer the questions of human beings.

They learned practical psychology—how to influence another's mind and thus induce another to act according to one's own desire. Sometimes this is called hypnotism. They learned how to wash hair, dye it in different colors and curl it in different ways. They learned the art of telling what is written in someone's book without actually seeing it. They learned to tell what is contained in another's fist. Sometimes children imitate this art, although not very accurately. One child keeps something within his fist and asks his friend, "Can you tell what is within?" and the friend gives some suggestion, although He actually cannot tell. But there is an art by which one can understand and actually tell what is held within the fist.

Kṛṣṇa and Balarāma learned how to speak and understand the languages of various countries. They learned not only the languages of human beings. Kṛṣṇa could also speak even with animals and birds. Evidence of this is found in Vaiṣṇava literature compiled by the Gosvāmīs. Then They learned how to make carriages and airplanes from flowers. It is said in the *Rāmāyaṇa* that after defeating Rāvaṇa, Rāmacandra was carried from Laṅkā to Bhāratavarṣa on a plane of flowers called *puṣpa-ratha.* Kṛṣṇa then learned the art of foretelling events by seeing signs. In a book called *Khanār vacana,* the various types of signs and omens are described. If, when one is going out, one sees someone with a bucket full of water, that is a very good sign. But if one sees someone with an empty bucket, it is not a very good sign. Similarly, if one sees cow's milk along with a calf, it is a good sign. The result of understanding these signs is that one can foretell events, and Kṛṣṇa learned the science. Kṛṣṇa also learned the art of composing *mātṛkā.* A *mātṛkā* is a crossword section with three letters in a line; counting any three from any side, it will count nine. The *mātṛkās* are of different kinds and are for different purposes.

Kṛṣṇa learned the art of cutting valuable stones such as diamonds, and

He learned the art of questioning and answering by immediately composing poetry within His mind. He learned the science of the action and reaction of physical combinations and permutations. He learned the art of a psychiatrist, who can understand the psychic movements of another person. He learned how to satisfy one's desires. Desires are very difficult to fulfill; but if one desires something which is unreasonable and can never be fulfilled, the desire can be subdued and satisfied, and that is an art. By this art one can also subdue sex impulses when they are aroused, as they are even in *brahmacārī* life. By this art one can make even an enemy his friend or transfer the direct action of a physical element to other things.

Lord Kṛṣṇa and Balarāma, the reservoir of all knowledge of arts and sciences, exhibited Their perfect understanding when They offered to serve Their teacher by awarding him anything he desired. This offering by the student to the teacher or spiritual master is called *guru-dakṣiṇā*. It is essential that a student satisfy the teacher in return for any learning received, either material or spiritual. When Kṛṣṇa and Balarāma offered Their service in this way, the teacher, Sāndīpani Muni, thought it wise to ask Them for something extraordinary, something which no common student could offer. He therefore consulted with his wife about what to ask from Them. They had already seen the extraordinary potencies of Kṛṣṇa and Balarāma and could understand that the two boys were the Supreme Personality of Godhead. They decided to ask for the return of their son, who had drowned in the ocean on the bank of Prabhāsakṣetra.

When Kṛṣṇa and Balarāma heard from Their teacher about the death of his son on the bank of Prabhāsakṣetra, They immediately started for the ocean on Their chariot. Reaching the beach, They asked the controlling deity of the ocean to return the son of Their teacher. The ocean deity immediately appeared before the Lord and offered Him all respectful obeisances with great humility.

The Lord said, "Some time back you caused the drowning of the son of Our teacher. I order you to return him."

The ocean deity replied, "The boy was not actually taken by me, but was captured by a demon named Pañcajana. This great demon generally remains deep in the water in the shape of a conchshell. The son of Your teacher might be within the belly of the demon, having been devoured by him."

On hearing this, Kṛṣṇa dove deep into the water and caught hold of the demon Pañcajana. He killed him on the spot, but could not find the son of His teacher within his belly. Therefore He took the demon's dead body (in the shape of a conchshell) and returned to His chariot on the beach of

Prabhāsakṣetra. From there He started for Saṁyamanī, the residence of Yamarāja, the superintendent of death. Accompanied by His elder brother Balarāma, who is also known as Halāyudha, Kṛṣṇa arrived there and blew on His conchshell.

Hearing the vibration, Yamarāja appeared and received Śrī Kṛṣṇa with all respectful obeisances. Yamarāja could understand who Kṛṣṇa and Balarāma were, and therefore he immediately offered his humble service to the Lord. Kṛṣṇa had appeared on the surface of the earth as an ordinary human being, but actually Kṛṣṇa and Balarāma are the Supersoul living within the heart of every living entity. They are Viṣṇu Himself, but were playing just like ordinary human boys. As Yamarāja offered his services to the Lord, Śrī Kṛṣṇa asked him to return His teacher's son, who had come to him as a result of his work. "Considering My ruling as supreme," said Kṛṣṇa, "you should immediately return the son of My teacher."

Yamarāja returned the boy to the Supreme Personality of Godhead, and Kṛṣṇa and Balarāma brought him to his father. The brothers asked if Their teacher had anything more to ask from Them, but he replied, "My dear sons, You have done enough for me. I am now completely satisfied. What further want can there be for a man who has disciples like You? My dear boys, You can go home now. These glorious acts of Yours will always be renowned all over the world. You are above all blessing, yet it is my duty to bless You. I give You the benediction that whatever You speak will remain as eternally fresh as the instruction of the *Vedas.* Your teachings will not only be honored within this universe or in this millennium, but in all places and ages and will remain increasingly new and important." Due to this benediction from His teacher, Lord Kṛṣṇa's *Bhagavad-gītā* is ever increasingly fresh and is not only renowned within this universe, but in other planets and in other universes also.

Being ordered by Their teacher, Kṛṣṇa and Balarāma immediately returned home on Their chariots. They traveled at great speeds like the wind and made sounds like the crashing of clouds. All the residents of Mathurā, who had not seen Kṛṣṇa and Balarāma for a long time, were very pleased to see Them again. They felt joyful, like a person who has regained his lost property.

Thus ends the Bhaktivedanta purport of the Second Volume, Tenth Chapter of* Kṛṣṇa, *"Kṛṣṇa Recovers the Son of His Teacher."

11 / Uddhava Visits Vṛndāvana

Nanda Mahārāja returned to Vṛndāvana without Kṛṣṇa and Balarāma. He was accompanied only by the cowherd boys and men. It was certainly a very pathetic scene for the *gopīs*, mother Yaśodā, Śrīmatī Rādhārāṇī and all the inhabitants and residents of Vṛndāvana. Many devotees have tried to make adjustments to Kṛṣṇa's being away from Vṛndāvana because according to expert opinion, Kṛṣṇa, the original Supreme Personality of Godhead, never goes even a step out of Vṛndāvana. He always remains there. The explanation of expert devotees is that Kṛṣṇa was actually not absent from Vṛndāvana; He came back with Nanda Mahārāja as promised.

When He was going to Mathurā on the chariot driven by Akrūra and the *gopīs* were practically blocking the way, Kṛṣṇa assured them that He was coming back just after finishing His business in Mathurā. He told them not to be overwhelmed, and in this way He pacified them. But when He did not come back with Nanda Mahārāja, it appeared that He either cheated them or could not keep His promise. Expert devotees, however, have decided that Kṛṣṇa was neither a cheater nor a breaker of promises. Kṛṣṇa, in His original identity, returned with Nanda Mahārāja and stayed with the *gopīs* and mother Yaśodā in His *bhava* expansion. Kṛṣṇa and Balarāma remained in Mathurā, not in Their original forms, but in Their expansions as Vāsudeva and Saṅkarṣaṇa. The real Kṛṣṇa and Balarāma were in Vṛndāvana in Their *bhava* manifestation, whereas in Mathurā They appeared in the *prabhava* and *vaibhava* expansions. This is the expert opinion of advanced devotees of Kṛṣṇa. But when Nanda Mahārāja was preparing to return to Vṛndāvana, there was discussion among him, Kṛṣṇa and Balarāma as to how the boys could live in separation from Nanda. The conclusion to separate was reached by mutual agreement.

Vasudeva and Devakī happened to be Kṛṣṇa and Balarāma's real parents. They wanted to keep Them now because of the death of Kaṁsa. While

Kaṁsa was alive, They were kept under the protection of Nanda Mahārāja in Vṛndāvana. Now, naturally, the father and mother of Kṛṣṇa and Balarāma wanted Them to remain with them, specifically for the reformatory function of purification, the sacred thread ceremony. They also wanted to give Them a proper education, for this is the duty of the father. Another consideration was that all the friends of Kaṁsa outside Mathurā were planning to attack Mathurā. For that reason also Kṛṣṇa's presence was required. Kṛṣṇa did not want Vṛndāvana to be disturbed by enemies like Dantavakra and Jarāsandha. If Kṛṣṇa were to go to Vṛndāvana, these enemies would not only attack Mathurā, but would go on to Vṛndāvana, and the peaceful inhabitants of Vṛndāvana would be disturbed. Kṛṣṇa therefore decided to remain in Mathurā, and Nanda Mahārāja went back to Vṛndāvana. Although the inhabitants of Vṛndāvana were feeling separation from Kṛṣṇa, Kṛṣṇa was always present with them by His *līlā*, or pastimes, and this made them ecstatic.

Since Kṛṣṇa had departed from Vṛndāvana to Mathurā, the inhabitants of Vṛndāvana, especially mother Yaśodā, Nanda Mahārāja, Śrīmatī Rādhārāṇī, the *gopīs* and the cowherd boys, were simply thinking of Kṛṣṇa at every step. They were thinking, "Kṛṣṇa was playing in this way. Kṛṣṇa was blowing His flute. Kṛṣṇa was joking with us, and Kṛṣṇa was embracing us." This is called *līlā-smaraṇa,* and it is the process of association with Kṛṣṇa most recommended by great devotees; even Lord Caitanya enjoyed *līlā-smaraṇa* association of Kṛṣṇa when He was at Purī. Those who are in the most exalted position of devotional service and ecstasy can live with Kṛṣṇa always by remembering His pastimes. Śrīla Viśvanātha Cakravartī Ṭhākur has given us a transcendental literature entitled ***Kṛṣṇa-bhāvanāmṛta,*** which is full with Kṛṣṇa's pastimes. Devotees can remain absorbed in Kṛṣṇa-thought by reading such books. Any book of Kṛṣṇa *līlā*, even this book, ***Kṛṣṇa***, and our *Teachings of Lord Caitanya*, is actually solace for devotees who are feeling the separation of Kṛṣṇa.

That Kṛṣṇa and Balarāma did not come to Vṛndāvana can be adjusted as follows: They did not break Their promise to return to Vṛndāvana, nor were They absent, but Their presence was necessary in Mathurā.

In the meantime, Uddhava, a cousin-brother of Kṛṣṇa, came to see Kṛṣṇa from Dvārakā. He was the son of Vasudeva's brother and was almost the same age as Kṛṣṇa. His bodily features resembled Kṛṣṇa's almost exactly. After returning from His teacher's home, Kṛṣṇa was pleased to see Uddhava, who happened to be His dearmost friend. He wanted to send him to Vṛndāvana with a message to the residents to pacify their deep feeling of separation.

As stated in the *Bhagavad-gītā, ye yathā māṁ prapadyante:* Kṛṣṇa is very responsive. He responds in proportion to the devotee's advancement in devotional service. The *gopīs* were thinking of Kṛṣṇa in separation twenty-four hours a day. Kṛṣṇa was also always thinking of the *gopīs,* mother Yaśodā, Nanda Mahārāja and the residents of Vṛndāvana, although He appeared to be away from them. He could understand how they were transcendentally aggrieved, and so He immediately wanted to send Uddhava to give them a message of solace.

Uddhava is described as the most exalted personality in the Vṛṣṇi dynasty, almost equal to Kṛṣṇa. He was a great friend, and on account of being the direct student of Bṛhaspati, the teacher and priest of the heavenly planets, he was very intelligent and sharp in decision. From the intellectual standpoint, he was highly qualified. Kṛṣṇa, being a very loving friend of Uddhava, wanted to send him to Vṛndāvana just to study the highly elevated ecstatic devotional service practiced there. Even if one is highly elevated in material education and is even the disciple of Bṛhaspati, he still has to learn from the *gopīs* and the residents of Vṛndāvana how to love Kṛṣṇa to the highest degree. Sending Uddhava to Vṛndāvana with a message to the residents of Vṛndāvana to pacify them was Kṛṣṇa's special favor to Uddhava.

Lord Kṛṣṇa's name is Hari, which means one who takes away all the distress from the surrendered souls. Lord Caitanya states that there cannot be, at any time, a worship as exalted as that realized by the *gopīs.* Being very anxious about the *gopīs'* grief, Kṛṣṇa talked with Uddhava and politely requested him to go to Vṛndāvana. Shaking Uddhava's hand with His own hands, He said, "My dear gentle friend Uddhava, please go immediately to Vṛndāvana and try to pacify My father and mother, Nanda Mahārāja and Yaśodādevī, and the *gopīs.* They are very much griefstricken, as if suffering from great ailments. Go and give them a message. I hope their ailments will be partially relieved. The *gopīs* are always absorbed in thoughts of Me. They have dedicated body, desire, life and soul to Me. I am anxious not only for the *gopīs,* but for anyone who sacrifices society, friendship, love and personal comforts for Me. It is My duty to protect such exalted devotees. The *gopīs* are the most dear. They are always thinking of Me in such a way that they remain overwhelmed and almost dead in anxiety due to separation from Me. They are keeping alive simply by thinking that I am returning to them very soon."

Requested by Lord Kṛṣṇa, Uddhava immediately left on his chariot and carried the message to Gokula. He approached Vṛndāvana at sunset, when the cows were returning home from the pasturing ground. Uddhava and his chariot were covered by the dust raised by the hooves of the cows. He saw bulls running after cows for mating; other cows, with overladened milkbags, were running after the calves to fill them with milk. Uddhava saw that the entire land of Vṛndāvana was filled with white cows and their calves. Cows were running here and there all over Gokula, and he could hear the sound of milking. Every residential house in Vṛndāvana was decorated for the worship of the sun-god and the fire-god and for the reception of guests, cows, *brāhmaṇas* and demigods. Every home was illuminated with light and incense arranged for sanctification. All over Vṛndāvana there were nice flower garlands, flying birds and the humming sound of the bees. The lakes were filled with lotus flowers and with ducks and swans.

Uddhava entered the house of Nanda Mahārāja and was received as a representative of Vāsudeva. Nanda Mahārāja offered him a place and sat down with him to ask about messages from Kṛṣṇa, Balarāma and other family members in Mathurā. He could understand that Uddhava was a very confidential friend of Kṛṣṇa and therefore must have come with good messages. "My dear Uddhava, how is my friend Vasudeva enjoying life? He is now released from the prison of Kaṁsa, and he is now with his friends and his children, Kṛṣṇa and Balarāma. So he must be very happy. Tell me about him and his welfare. We are also very happy that Kaṁsa, the most sinful demon, is now killed. He was always envious of the family of the Yadus, his friends and relatives. Now because of his sinful activities, he is dead and gone, along with all his brothers.

"Please let us now know whether Kṛṣṇa is remembering His father and mother and His friends and companions in Vṛndāvana. Does He like to remember His cows, His *gopīs,* His Govardhana Hill, His pasturing ground in Vṛndāvana? Or has He forgotten all these now? Is there any possibility of His coming back to His friends and relatives so that we can again see His beautiful face with its raised nose and lotus-like eyes? We remember how He saved us from the forest fire, how He saved us from the great snake Kāliya in the Yamunā, how He saved us from so many other demons, and we simply think how much we are obliged to Him for giving us protection in so many dangerous situations. My dear Uddhava, when we think of Kṛṣṇa's beautiful face and eyes and His different activities here in Vṛndāvana, we become so overwhelmed that all our activities cease. We simply think of Kṛṣṇa, how He used to smile and how He looked upon us. When we go to the banks of the Yamunā and other lakes of Vṛndāvana or near Govardhana Hill or the pasturing field, we see that the impressions of Kṛṣṇa's footprints are still on the surface of the earth. We remember Him playing in those places, because He was constantly visiting them. When His appearance within our minds becomes manifest, we immediately become absorbed in thought of Him.

"We think, therefore, that Kṛṣṇa and Balarāma may be chief demigods in heaven who have appeared before us like ordinary boys in order to execute particular duties on earth. This was also foretold by Gargamuni when making Kṛṣṇa's horoscope. If Kṛṣṇa were not a great personality, how could He have killed Kaṁsa, who possessed the strength of 10,000 elephants? Besides Kaṁsa, there were very strong wrestlers, as well as the giant elephant, Kuvalayāpīḍa. All these animals and demons were killed by Him just as a lion kills an ordinary animal. How wonderful it is that Kṛṣṇa took in one hand the big, heavy bow made of three joined palm trees and broke it very quickly. How wonderful it is that continually for seven days He held up Govardhana Hill in one hand. How wonderful it is that He has killed all the demons, like Pralambāsura, Dhenukāsura, Ariṣṭāsura, Tṛṇāvarta and Bakāsura. They were so strong that even the demigods in the heavenly planets were afraid of them, but Kṛṣṇa killed them as easily as anything."

While describing the uncommon activities of Kṛṣṇa before Uddhava, Nanda Mahārāja gradually became overwhelmed and could not speak anymore. As for mother Yaśodā, she sat by the side of her husband and heard the pastimes of Kṛṣṇa without speaking. She was simply crying incessantly, and milk was pouring from her breasts. When Uddhava saw Mahārāja Nanda and Yaśodā so extraordinarily overwhelmed with thoughts of Kṛṣṇa, the Supreme Personality of Godhead, and when he experienced their extraordinary affection for Him, he also became overwhelmed and began to speak as follows. "My dear mother Yaśodā and Nanda Mahārāja, you are most respectable among human beings because no one but you can meditate in such transcendental ecstasy."

Both Balarāma and Kṛṣṇa are the original Personalities of Godhead from whom the cosmic manifestation is emanating. They are chief among all personalities. Both of Them are the effective cause of this material creation. Material nature is conducted by the *puruṣa* incarnations, who are all acting under Kṛṣṇa and Balarāma. By Their partial representation They enter in the hearts of all living entities. They are the source of all knowledge and all forgetfulness also. This is confirmed in the *Bhagavad-gītā*, Fifteenth Chapter: "I am present in everyone's heart, and I cause one to remember and to forget. I am the original compiler of the *Vedānta*, and I am the actual knower of the *Vedas*." If, at the time of death, a person can fix his pure mind upon Kṛṣṇa even for a moment, he becomes eligible to give up this material body and appear in his original spiritual body, just as the sun rises with all illumination. Passing from his life in this way, he immediately enters into the spiritual kingdom, Vaikuṇṭha. This is the result of Kṛṣṇa conscious practice.

If we practice Kṛṣṇa consciousness in this present body while we are in a healthy condition and in good mind, simply by chanting the holy *mahā-mantra,* Hare Kṛṣṇa, we will have every possibility of fixing our mind upon Kṛṣṇa at the time of death. If that is done, then our life becomes successful without any doubt. Similarly, if we keep our mind always absorbed in fruitive activities for material enjoyment, then naturally at the time of death we shall think of such activities and again be forced to enter into a material, conditioned body to suffer the threefold miseries of material existence. Therefore, to remain always absorbed in Kṛṣṇa consciousness was the standard of the inhabitants of Vṛndāvana, as exhibited by Mahārāja Nanda, Yaśodā and the *gopīs.* If we can simply follow their footsteps, even to a minute proportion, our lives will surely become successful, and we will enter into the spiritual kingdom, Vaikuṇṭha.

"My dear mother Yaśodā and Nanda Mahārāja," Uddhava continued, "you have thus fixed your minds wholly and solely upon that Supreme Personality of Godhead, Nārāyaṇa, in His transcendental form, the cause of impersonal Brahman. The Brahman effulgence is only the bodily ray of Nārāyaṇa, and because you are always absorbed in ecstatic thought of Kṛṣṇa and Balarāma, what activity remains to be performed by you? I have brought a message from Kṛṣṇa to the effect that He will soon come back to Vṛndāvana and satisfy you both by His personal presence. Kṛṣṇa promised that He would come back to Vṛndāvana after finishing His business in Mathurā. This promise He will surely fulfill. I therefore request you both, who are the best among all fortunates, to be not aggrieved on account of Kṛṣṇa's absence.

"You are already perceiving His presence twenty-four hours a day, and yet He will come and see you very soon. Actually He is present everywhere and in everyone's heart, just as fire is present in wood. Since Kṛṣṇa is the Supersoul, no one is His enemy, no one is His friend, no one is equal to Him, and no one is lower or higher than Him. Actually He has no father, mother, brother or relative, nor does He require society, friendship and love. He does not have a material body; He never appears or takes birth as an ordinary human being. He does not appear in higher or lower species of life like ordinary living entities, who are forced to take birth on account of their previous activities. He appears by His internal potency just to give protection to His devotee. He is never influenced by the modes of material nature, but when He appears within this material world, it seems that He acts like an ordinary living entity under the spell of the modes of material nature. In fact, He is the overseer of this material creation and is not affected by the material modes of nature. He creates, maintains and dissolves the whole cosmic manifestation. We wrongly think of Kṛṣṇa and Balarāma as ordinary human beings. We are like dizzy men who see the whole world wheeling around them. The Personality of Godhead is no one's son; He is actually everyone's father, mother and supreme controller. There is no doubt of this. Whatever is being experienced, whatever is already in existence, whatever is not in existence, whatever will be in existence in the future, whatever is the smallest and whatever is the biggest have no separate existence outside the Supreme Personality of Godhead. Everything is resting in Him, but He is out of touch with everything manifested."

Nanda and Uddhava thus passed the whole night in discussing Kṛṣṇa. In the morning, the *gopīs* prepared for morning *ārātrika* by lighting their lamps and sprinkling butter mixed with yogurt. After finishing their *maṅgala-ārātrika,* they engaged themselves in churning butter from yogurt. While the *gopīs* were thus engaged, the lamps reflected on their ornaments became still more illuminated. The churning rod, their arms, their earrings, their bangles, their breasts—everything moved, and the *kuṅkuma* powder gave their faces a saffron luster comparable to the rising sun. While churning, they also sang the glories of Kṛṣṇa. The two sound vibrations mixed together, ascended to the sky and sanctified the whole atmosphere. After sunrise the *gopīs* came as usual to offer their respects to Nanda Mahārāja and Yaśodā, but when they saw the golden chariot of Uddhava at the door, they began to inquire among themselves. What was that chariot, and to whom did it belong? Some of them inquired whether Akrūra, who had taken away Kṛṣṇa, had again returned. They were not very pleased with Akrūra because, being engaged in the service of Kaṁsa, he took Kṛṣṇa away to the city of Mathurā. All the *gopīs* conjectured that Akrūra might have come again to fulfill another cruel plan. But they thought, "We are now dead bodies without our supreme master, Kṛṣṇa. What further act can he perpetrate on these dead bodies?" While they were talking in this way, Uddhava finished his morning ablutions, prayers and chanting and came before them.

Thus ends the Bhaktivedanta purport of the Second Volume, Eleventh Chapter of* Kṛṣṇa, *"Uddhava Visits Vṛndāvana."

12 / Delivery of the Message of Kṛṣṇa to the Gopīs

When the *gopīs* saw Uddhava, they observed that his features almost exactly resembled the features of Kṛṣṇa, and they could understand that he was a great devotee of Kṛṣṇa's. His hands were very long, and his arms were just like the petals of the lotus flower. He was dressed in yellow colored garments and wore a garland of lotus flowers. His face was very beautiful. Having achieved the liberation of *sārūpya* and having the same bodily features as the Lord, Uddhava looked almost like Kṛṣṇa. In Kṛṣṇa's absence, the *gopīs* had been coming dutifully to visit mother Yaśodā's house early in the morning. They knew that Nanda Mahārāja and mother Yaśodā were always griefstricken, and they had made it their first duty to come and pay their respects to the most exalted elderly personalities of Vṛndāvana. Seeing the friends of Kṛṣṇa, Nanda and Yaśodā would remember Kṛṣṇa Himself and be satisfied, and the *gopīs* also would be pleased by seeing Nanda and Yaśodā.

When the *gopīs* saw that Uddhava was representing Kṛṣṇa even in his bodily features, they thought that he must be a soul completely surrendered unto the Supreme Personality of Godhead. They began to contemplate, "Who is this boy who looks just like Kṛṣṇa? He has the same eyes like lotus petals, the same raised nose and beautiful face, and he is smiling in the same way. In all respects he is resembling Kṛṣṇa, Śyāmasundara, the beautiful dark boy. He is even dressed exactly like Kṛṣṇa. Where has this boy come from? Who is the fortunate girl who has him for her husband?" Thus they talked among themselves. They were very anxious to know about him, and because they were simply unsophisticated village girls, they surrounded Uddhava.

When the *gopīs* understood that Uddhava had a message from Kṛṣṇa, they became very happy and called him to a secluded place to sit down. They wanted to talk with him very freely and did not want to be embarrassed before unknown persons. They began to welcome him with polite words, in great submissiveness. "We know that you are a most confidential associate of Kṛṣṇa and that He has therefore sent you to Vṛndāvana to give solace to His father and mother. We can understand that family affection is very strong. Even great sages who have taken to the renounced order of life cannot give up family members. Kṛṣṇa has therefore sent you to His father and mother; otherwise He has no further business in Vṛndāvana. He is now in town. What does He have to know about Vṛndāvana Village or the cows' pasturing grounds? These things are not at all useful for Kṛṣṇa because He is now a man in the city.

"Surely He has nothing to do with persons who do not happen to be His family members. Why should one bother about those who are outside the family, especially and specifically those who are attached as the wives of others. Kṛṣṇa is interested in them as long as there is a need of gratification, like the bumblebees who have interest in the flowers as long as they want to take the honey out of them. It is very natural and psychological that a prostitute does not care for her paramour as soon as he loses his money. Similarly, when the citizens find that a government is incapable of giving them full protection, they leave the country. A student, after finishing his education, gives up his relationship with the teacher and the school. A rich man, after taking his reward from his worshiper, gives him up. When the fruit season is over, the birds are no longer interested in the tree. Just after eating in the house of a lord, the guest gives up his relationship with the host. After a forest fire, when there is a scarcity of green grass, the deer and other animals give up the forest. And so a man, after enjoying his girl friend, gives up his connection with her." In this way, all the *gopīs* began to indirectly accuse Kṛṣṇa by citing so many similes.

Uddhava understood that the *gopīs* of Vṛndāvana were all simply absorbed in the thought of Kṛṣṇa and His childhood activities. While talking about Kṛṣṇa with Uddhava, they forgot all about their household business. They even forgot about themselves as their interest in Kṛṣṇa increased more and more.

One of the *gopīs*, namely Śrīmatī Rādhārāṇī, was so much absorbed in thoughts of Kṛṣṇa by dint of Her personal touch with Him that She actually began to talk with a bumblebee which was flying there and trying to touch Her lotus feet. While another *gopī* was talking with Kṛṣṇa's messenger Uddhava, Śrīmatī Rādhārāṇī took that bumblebee to be a messenger from Kṛṣṇa and began to talk with it as follows. "Bumblebee, you are accustomed to drinking honey from the flowers, and therefore you have preferred to be a messenger of Kṛṣṇa, who is of the same nature as you. I have seen on your moustaches the red powder of *kuṅkuma,* which was smeared on the flower garland of Kṛṣṇa while He was pressing the breast of some other girl who is My competitor. You are feeling very proud by touching that flower, and your moustaches have become reddish. You have come here carrying a message for Me. You are anxious to touch My feet. But my dear bumblebee, let me warn you–don't touch Me! I don't want any messages from your unreliable master. You are the unreliable servant of an unreliable master." It may be that Śrīmatī Rādhārāṇī purposely addressed that bumblebee sarcastically in order to criticize the messenger Uddhava. Indirectly, Śrīmatī Rādhārāṇī saw Uddhava as not only resembling Kṛṣṇa's bodily features but as being equal to Kṛṣṇa. In this way She indicated that Uddhava was as unreliable as Kṛṣṇa Himself. Śrīmatī Rādhārāṇī wanted to give specific reasons why She was dissatisfied with Kṛṣṇa and His messengers.

She addressed the bumblebee, "Your master Kṛṣṇa is exactly of your quality. You sit down on a flower, and after taking a little honey you immediately fly away and sit in another flower and taste. You're just like your master Kṛṣṇa. He gave us the chance of tasting the touch of His lips and then left altogether. I know also that the goddess of fortune, Lakṣmī, who is always in the midst of the lotus flower, is constantly engaged in Kṛṣṇa's service. But I do not know why she has become so captivated by Kṛṣṇa. She is attached to Him, although she knows His actual character. As far as we are concerned, we are more intelligent than that goddess of fortune. We are not going to be cheated anymore by Kṛṣṇa or His messengers."

According to expert opinion, Lakṣmī, the goddess of fortune is a subordinate expansion of Śrīmatī Rādhārāṇī. As Kṛṣṇa has numerous expansions of Viṣṇu-*mūrtis,* so His pleasure potency, Rādhārāṇī, also has innumerable expansions of goddesses of fortune. Therefore the goddess of fortune, Lakṣmījī, is always anxious to be elevated to the position of the *gopīs*.

Śrīmatī Rādhārāṇī continued: "You foolish bumblebee, you are trying to satisfy Me and get a reward by singing the glories of Kṛṣṇa, but it is a useless attempt. We are bereft of all our possessions. We are away from our homes and families. We know very well about Kṛṣṇa. We know even more than you. So whatever you make up about Him will be old stories to us. Kṛṣṇa is now in the city and is better known as the friend of Arjuna. He now has many new girl friends, and they are no doubt very happy in association with Him. Because the lusty burning sensation of their breasts has been satisfied by Kṛṣṇa, they are now happy. If you go there and glorify Kṛṣṇa, they may be pleased to reward you. You are just trying to pacify Me by your behavior as a flatterer, and therefore you have put your head under My feet. But I know the trick which you are trying to play. I know that you are a messenger coming from a great trickster, Kṛṣṇa. Therefore please leave me.

"I can understand that you are very expert in reuniting two opposing parties, but at the same time you must know that I cannot place My reliance upon you, nor upon your master Kṛṣṇa. We left our families, husbands, children and relatives only for Kṛṣṇa, and yet He did not feel any obligation in exchange. He has left us for lost. Do you think we can place our faith in Him again? We know that Kṛṣṇa cannot be long without the association of young women. That is His nature. He is finding difficulty in Mathurā because He is no longer in the village among innocent cowherd girls. He is in the aristocratic society and must be feeling difficulty in making friendships with the young girls. Perhaps you have come here to canvass again or to take us there. But why should Kṛṣṇa expect us to go there? He is greatly qualified to entice all other girls, not only in Vṛndāvana or Mathurā, but all over the universe. His wonderfully enchanting smile is so attractive and the movement of His eyebrows so beautiful that He can call for any woman from the heavenly, middle or plutonic planets. Mahā-Lakṣmī, the greatest of all goddesses of fortune, also hankers to render Him some service. In comparison to all these women of the universe, what are we? We are very insignificant.

"Kṛṣṇa advertises Himself as very magnanimous, and He is praised by great saints. His qualifications could be perfectly utilized if He would only show us mercy because we are downtrodden and neglected by Him. You poor messenger, you are only a less intelligent servant. You do not know much about Kṛṣṇa, how ungrateful and hardhearted He has been, not only in this life, but in His previous lives also. We have all heard this from our grandmother, Paurṇamāsī. She has informed us that Kṛṣṇa was born in a *kṣatriya* family previous to this birth and was known as Rāmacandra. In that birth, instead of killing Vāli, an enemy of His friend, in the manner of a *kṣatriya,* He killed him just like a hunter. A hunter takes a secure hiding place and then kills an animal without facing it. So Lord Rāmacandra, as a *kṣatriya,* should have fought with Vāli face to face, but instigated by His friend, He killed him from behind a tree. Thus He deviated from the religious principles of a *kṣatriya.* Also, He was so attracted by the beauty of Sītā that He converted Śūrpaṇakhā, the sister of Rāvaṇa, into an ugly woman by cutting off her nose and ears. Śūrpaṇakhā proposed an intimate relationship with Him, and as a *kṣatriya,*

He should have satisfied her. But He was so selfish that He could not forget Sītādevī and converted Śūrpaṇakhā into an ugly woman. Before that birth as a *kṣatriya*, He took His birth as a *brāhmaṇa* boy known as Vāmanadeva and asked charity from Bali Mahārāja. Bali Mahārāja was so magnanimous that he gave Him whatever he had, yet Kṛṣṇa as Vāmanadeva ungratefully arrested him just like a crow and pushed him down to the Pātāla kingdom. We know all about Kṛṣṇa and how ungrateful He is. But here is the difficulty: in spite of His being so cruel and hardhearted, it is very difficult for us to give up talking about Him. Not only are we unable to give up this talk, but great sages and saintly persons are also engaged in talking about Him. We *gopīs* of Vṛndāvana do not want to make anymore friendships with this blackish boy, but we do not know how we shall be able to give up remembering and talking about His activities."

Since Kṛṣṇa is absolute, His so-called unkind activities are as relishable as His kind activities. Saintly persons and great devotees like the *gopīs* cannot give up Kṛṣṇa in any circumstances. Lord Caitanya therefore prayed, "Kṛṣṇa, You are free and independent in all respects. You can either embrace me or crush me under Your feet—whatever You like. You may make me brokenhearted by not letting me see You throughout my whole life, but You are my only object of love."

"In my opinion," Śrīmatī Rādhārāṇī continued, "one should not hear about Kṛṣṇa, because as soon as a drop of the nectar of His transcendental activities is poured into the ear, one immediately rises above the platform of duality, attraction and rejection. Being completely freed from the attraction of material attachment, one gives up the attachment for this material world, family, home, wife, children and everything which is materially dear to every person. Being dispossessed of all material acquisition, one makes his relatives and himself unhappy. Then he wanders in search of Kṛṣṇa, either as a human being or in other species of life, even as a bird. It is very difficult to actually understand Kṛṣṇa, His name, His quality, His form, His pastimes, His paraphernalia and His entourage."

Śrīmatī Rādhārāṇī continued to speak to the black messenger of Kṛṣṇa. "Please do not talk anymore about Kṛṣṇa. It is better to talk about something else. We are already doomed, like the black-spotted she-deer in the forest who are enchanted by the sweet musical vibration of the hunter. In the same way, we have been enchanted by the sweet words of Kṛṣṇa, and again and again we are thinking of the rays of the nails of His toes. We are becoming more and more lustful for His association; therefore, I request you not to talk of Kṛṣṇa anymore."

This talk of Rādhārāṇī with the bumblebee messenger and Her accusing

Kṛṣṇa, and, at the same time, Her inability to give up talking about Him, are symptoms of the topmost transcendental ecstasy, called *mahābhāva.* The ecstatic *mahābhāva* manifestation is possible only in the persons of Rādhārāṇī and Her associates. Great *ācāryas* like Śrīla Rūpa Gosvāmī and Viśvanātha Cakravartī Ṭhākur have analyzed these *mahābhāva* speeches of Śrīmatī Rādhārāṇī, and they have described the different sentiments such as *udghūrṇā,* bewilderment, and *jalpapratijalpa,* talking in different ways. In Rādhārāṇī is found the science of *ujjala,* or the brightest jewel or love of God. While Rādhārāṇī was talking with the bee and the bee was flying hither and thither, it all of a sudden disappeared from Her sight. She was in full mourning due to separation from Kṛṣṇa and was feeling ecstasy by talking with the bee. But as soon as the bee disappeared, She became almost mad, thinking that the messenger-bee might have returned to Kṛṣṇa to inform Him all about Her talking against Him. "Kṛṣṇa must have been very sorry to hear it," She thought. In this way She was very much overwhelmed with another type of ecstasy.

In the meantime, the bee, flying hither and thither, appeared before Her again. She thought, "Kṛṣṇa is still kind to Me. In spite of the messenger carrying disruptive messages, He is so kind that He has again sent the bee to take Me to Him." Śrīmatī Rādhārāṇī was very careful this time not to say anything against Kṛṣṇa. "My dear friend, I welcome you," she said. "Kṛṣṇa is so kind that He has again sent you. Kṛṣṇa is so kind and affectionate to Me that He has sent you back, fortunately, in spite of your carrying My message against Him. My dear friend, you can ask from Me whatever you want. I shall give you anything because you are so kind upon Me. You have come to take Me to Kṛṣṇa because He is not able to come here. He is surrounded by new girl friends in Mathurā. But you are a tiny creature. How can you take Me there? How will you be able to help Me in meeting Kṛṣṇa while He is taking rest there along with the goddess of fortune and embracing her to His chest? Never mind. Let us forget all these things about My going there or sending you. Please let Me know how Kṛṣṇa is faring in Mathurā. Tell Me if He still remembers His foster father, Nanda Mahārāja, His affectionate mother, Yaśodā, His cowherd friends and His poor friends like us, the *gopīs.* I am sure that He must sometimes sing about us. We served Him just like maidservants, without any payment. Is there any possibility that Kṛṣṇa will again come back and place His arms around us? His limbs are always fragrant with the *aguru* scent. Please put all these inquiries to Kṛṣṇa."

Uddhava was standing near, and he heard Rādhārāṇī talking in this way, as if She had become almost mad after Kṛṣṇa. He was exceedingly surprised at how the *gopīs* were accustomed to think of Kṛṣṇa constantly in that topmost ecstasy of *mahābhāva* love. He had brought a message in writing from Kṛṣṇa, and now he wanted to present it before the *gopīs*, just to pacify them. He said, "My dear *gopīs*, your mission of human life is now successful. You are all wonderful devotees of the Supreme Personality of Godhead; therefore you are eligible to be worshiped by all kinds of people. You are worshipable throughout the three worlds because your minds are wonderfully absorbed in the thought of Vāsudeva, Kṛṣṇa. He is the goal of all kinds of pious activities and ritualistic performances, such as giving in charity, rigidly following the austerity of vows, undergoing severe penances and igniting the fire of sacrifice. He is the purpose behind the chanting of different *mantras*, the reading of the *Vedas*, controlling the senses and concentrating the mind in meditation. These are some of the many different processes for self-realization and attainment of perfection of life. But actually they are only meant for realizing Kṛṣṇa and dovetailing oneself in the transcendental loving service of the Supreme Personality of Godhead. This is the last instruction of *Bhagavad-gītā* also; although there are descriptions of different kinds of processes of self-realization, at the end Kṛṣṇa recommended one should give up everything and simply surrender unto Him. All other processes are meant for teaching one how to surrender ultimately unto the lotus feet of Kṛṣṇa. The *Bhagavad-gītā* also says that this surrendering process is completed by a sincere person executing the processes of self-realization in wisdom and austerity after many births."

Since the perfection of such austerity was completely manifested in the life of the *gopīs*, Uddhava was fully satisfied upon seeing their transcendental position. He continued to say: "My dear *gopīs*, the mentality which you have developed in relationship with Kṛṣṇa is very, very difficult to attain, even for great sages and saintly persons. You have attained the highest perfectional stage of life. It is a great boon for you that you have fixed your mind upon Kṛṣṇa and have decided to have Kṛṣṇa only, giving up your family, home, relatives, husbands and children for the sake of the Supreme Personality. Because your mind is now fully absorbed in Kṛṣṇa, the Supreme Soul, universal love has automatically developed in you. I think myself very fortunate that I have been favored, by your grace, to see you in this situation."

When Uddhava said that he had a message from Kṛṣṇa, the *gopīs* were more interested in hearing the message than in hearing about their exalted position. They did not very much like being praised for their high position. They showed their anxiety to hear the message which Uddhava had brought from Kṛṣṇa. Uddhava said, "My dear *gopīs,* I am especially deputed to carry this message to you, who are such great and gentle devotees. Kṛṣṇa has specifically sent me to you because I am His most confidential servitor."

The written message which Uddhava brought from Kṛṣṇa was not delivered to the *gopīs* by Uddhava, but he personally read it before them. The message was very gravely written, so that not only the *gopīs,* but all empiric philosophers might understand how pure love of God is intrinsically integrated with all the different energies of the Supreme Lord. From Vedic information it is understood that the Supreme Lord has multi-energies, *parāsya śaktir vividhaiva śrūyate.* Also, the *gopīs* were such intimate personal friends of Kṛṣṇa that while He was writing the message for them, He was much moved and could not write distinctly. Uddhava, as the student of Bṛhaspati, had very sharp intelligence, so instead of handing over the written message, he thought it wise to read it personally and explain it to them.

Uddhava continued: "These are the words from the Personality of Godhead. 'My dear *gopīs,* My dear friends, please know that separation between ourselves is impossible at any time, at any place or under any circumstances, because I am all-pervading.'"

This all-pervasiveness of Kṛṣṇa is explained in the *Bhagavad-gītā,* both in the Ninth and Seventh Chapters. Kṛṣṇa is all-pervasive in His impersonal feature; everything is resting in Him, but He is not personally present everywhere. In the Seventh Chapter also, it is stated that the five gross elements, earth, water, fire, air and sky, and the three subtle elements, mind, intelligence, and ego, are all His inferior energies. But there is another, superior energy, which is called the living entity. The living entities are also directly part and parcel of Kṛṣṇa. Therefore Kṛṣṇa is the source of both the material and spiritual energies. He is always intermingled with everything as cause and effect. Not only the *gopīs,* but all living entities are always inseparably connected with Kṛṣṇa in all circumstances. The *gopīs,* however, are perfectly and thoroughly in cooperation in their relationship with Kṛṣṇa, whereas the living entities under the spell of *māyā* are forgetful of Kṛṣṇa. They think themselves as separate identities having no connection with Kṛṣṇa.

Love of Kṛṣṇa, or Kṛṣṇa consciousness, is therefore the perfectional stage of real knowledge in understanding things as they are. Our minds can never be vacant. The mind is constantly occupied with some kind of thought, and the subject matter of such thought cannot be outside the eight elements of Kṛṣṇa's energy. One who knows this philosophical aspect of all thoughts is actually a wise man, and he surrenders unto Kṛṣṇa. The *gopīs* are the typical example of this perfectional stage of knowledge. They are not simple mental speculators. Their minds are always in Kṛṣṇa. The mind is nothing but the energy of Kṛṣṇa. Actually, any person who can think, feel, act and will cannot be separated from Kṛṣṇa. But the stage in which he can understand his eternal realtionship is called Kṛṣṇa consciousness. The diseased condition in which he cannot understand his eternal relationship with Kṛṣṇa is the contaminated stage, or *māyā.* Since the *gopīs* are on the platform of pure transcendental knowledge, their minds are always filled with Kṛṣṇa consciousness. For example, as there is no separation between fire and air, so there is no separation between Kṛṣṇa and the living entities. When the living entities forget Kṛṣṇa, they are not in their normal condition. As for the *gopīs,* because they are always thinking of Kṛṣṇa they are on the absolute stage of perfection in knowledge. The so-called empiric philosophers sometimes think that the path of *bhakti* is meant for the less intelligent, but unless the so-called man of knowledge comes to the platform of *bhakti,* his knowledge is certainly impure and imperfect. Actually, the stage of perfecting one's eternal relationship with Kṛṣṇa is love in separation. But that is also illusory because there is no separation. The *gopīs* were never separated from Kṛṣṇa. Even from the philosophical point of view, there was no separation.

The cosmic manifestation is also not separate from Kṛṣṇa. "Nothing is separate from Me; the whole cosmic manifestation is resting on Me and is not separate from Me. Before the creation, I was existing." This is confirmed in the Vedic literature: before creation, there was only Nārāyaṇa. There were no Brahmā and no Śiva as assistants. The whole cosmic manifestation is manipulated by the three modes of material nature. Brahmā is the incarnation of the quality of passion. It is said that Brahmā created this universe, but Brahmā is the secondary creator; the original creator is Narāyaṇa. This is also confirmed by Śaṅkarācārya: *nārāyaṇaḥ paro'vyaktāt.* Nārāyaṇa is transcendental, beyond this cosmic creation.

Kṛṣṇa creates, maintains, and annihilates the whole cosmic manifestation by expanding Himself in different incarnations. Everything is Kṛṣṇa, and everything is depending on Kṛṣṇa, but He is not perceived in the material energy. Material energy is called *māyā,* or illusion. In the spiritual energy, however, Kṛṣṇa is perceived at every step, in all circumstances. This perfectional stage of understanding is present in the *gopīs.* As Kṛṣṇa is always aloof from the cosmic manifestation, although it is completely dependent on Him, so a living entity is also completely aloof from his material conditional life. The material body has developed on the basis of spiritual existence. In the *Bhagavad-gītā* the whole cosmic manifestation is accepted as the mother of the living entities, and Kṛṣṇa is the father. As the father impregnates the mother by injecting the living entity within the womb, so all the living entities are injected by Kṛṣṇa in the womb of the material nature. They come out in different bodies according to their different fruitive activities. In all circumstances, the living entity is aloof from this material conditional life.

If we simply study our own bodies, we can understand how a living entity is always aloof from this bodily encagement. Every action of the body is taking place by the interaction of the three modes of material nature. We can see at every moment many changes taking place in bodies, but the spirit soul is aloof from all changes. One can neither create nor annihilate nor interfere with the actions of material nature. The living entity is therefore entrapped by the material body and is conditioned in three stages, namely while awake, asleep and unconscious. The mind is acting through all the three conditions of life; the living entity in his sleeping or dreaming condition sees something as real, and in his awake condition he sees the same thing as unreal. It is concluded, therefore, that under certain circumstances he accepts something as real, and under other circumstances he accepts the very same thing as unreal. These matters are the subject matter of study for the empiric philosopher or the *sāṅkhya-yogī.* In order to come to the right conclusion, *sāṅkhya-yogīs* undergo severe austerities and penances. They practice control of the senses and renunciation.

All these different ways of determining the ultimate goal of life are compared to rivers. Kṛṣṇa is the ocean. As the rivers flow down toward the ocean, all attempts for knowledge flow toward Kṛṣṇa. After many, many births of endeavor, when one actually comes to Kṛṣṇa, he attains the perfectional stage. Kṛṣṇa says in the *Bhagavad-gītā:* All are pursuing the path of realizing Me, but those who have adopted courses without any *bhakti* find their endeavor very troublesome." *Kleśo'dhikataras teṣām:* Kṛṣṇa cannot be understood unless one comes to the point of *bhakti.*

Three paths are enunciated in the *Gītā: karma-yoga, jñāna-yoga* and *bhakti-yoga.* Those who are too addicted to fruitive activities are advised to perform actions which will bring them to *bhakti.* Those who are addicted to the frustration of empiric philosophy are also advised to realize *bhakti. Karma-yoga* is different from ordinary *karma,* and *jñāna-yoga* is different from *jñāna.* Ultimately, as stated by the Lord in the *Bhagavad-gītā, bhaktyā māṁ abhijānāti:* only through execution of devotional service can one understand Kṛṣṇa. The perfectional stage of devotional service was achieved by the *gopīs* because they did not care to know anything but Kṛṣṇa. It is confirmed in the *Vedas, yasmin eva vijñāte sarvam eva vijñātam bhavanti.* This means that simply by knowing Kṛṣṇa all other knowledge is automatically acquired.

Kṛṣṇa continued: "Transcendental knowledge of the Absolute is no longer necessary for you. You were accustomed to love Me from the very beginning of your lives." Knowledge of the Absolute Truth is specifically required for persons who want liberation from material existence. But one who has attained love for Kṛṣṇa is already on the platform of liberation. As stated in the *Bhagavad-gītā,* anyone engaged in unalloyed devotional service is to be considered situated on the transcendental platform of liberation. The *gopīs* were not actually feeling any pangs of material existence, but they were feeling the separation of Kṛṣṇa. Kṛṣṇa therefore said, "My dear *gopīs,* in order to increase your superexcellent love for Me, I have purposely separated Myself from you. I have done this so that you may be in constant meditation on Me."

The *gopīs* are in the perfectional stage of meditation. The *yogīs* are generally more fond of meditation than the execution of devotional service to the Lord, but they do not know that the perfectional stage of devotion is the attainment of the perfection of the *yoga* system. This constant meditation on Kṛṣṇa by the *gopīs* is confirmed in the *Bhagavad-gītā* to be the topmost *yoga.* Kṛṣṇa knew very well the psychology of women. When a woman's beloved is away, she thinks of him meditatively, and he is present before her. Kṛṣṇa wanted to teach through the behavior of the *gopīs.* One who is constantly in trance like the *gopīs* surely attains the lotus feet of Kṛṣṇa.

Lord Caitanya taught people in general the method of *vipralambha,* which is the method of rendering service unto the Supreme Personality of Godhead in the feeling of separation. The six Gosvāmīs also taught worship of Kṛṣṇa in the feeling of the *gopīs* in separation. The prayers of Śrīnivāsa Ācārya about the Gosvāmīs explain these matters very clearly. Śrīnivāsa Ācārya said that the Gosvāmīs were always absorbed in the ocean of transcendental feelings in the mood of the *gopīs.* When they lived in Vṛndāvana they were searching for Kṛṣṇa, crying, "Where is Kṛṣṇa? Where are the *gopīs?* Where are You, Śrīmatī Rādhārāṇī?" They never said, "We have now seen Rādhā and Kṛṣṇa, and therefore our mission is fulfilled." Their mission remained always unfulfilled; they never met Rādhā and Kṛṣṇa. At the time of the *rāsa* dance, those *gopīs* who could not join the *rāsa-līlā* with Kṛṣṇa gave up their bodies simply by thinking of Him. Absorption in Kṛṣṇa consciousness by feeling separation is thus the quickest method for attainment of the lotus feet of Kṛṣṇa. By the personal statement of Kṛṣṇa, the *gopīs* were convinced about the strength of feelings of separation. They were actually experiencing the supernatural method of Kṛṣṇa worship and were much relieved and happy to understand it.

They began to speak as follows: "We have heard that King Kaṁsa, who was always a source of trouble for the Yadu dynasty, has now been killed. This is good news for us. We hope, therefore, that the members of the Yadu dynasty are very happy in the association of Kṛṣṇa, who can fulfill all the desires of His devotees. My dear Uddhava, kindly let us know whether Kṛṣṇa sometimes thinks of us while in the midst of highly enlightened society girls in Mathurā. We know that the women and girls in Mathurā are not village women. They are enlightened and beautiful. Their bashful smiling glances and other feminine features must be very pleasing to Kṛṣṇa. We know very well that Kṛṣṇa is always fond of the behavior of beautiful women. It seems, therefore, that He has been entrapped by the women of Mathurā. My dear Uddhava, will you kindly let us know if Kṛṣṇa sometimes remembers us while He is in the midst of other women?"

Another *gopī* inquired: "Does He remember that night in the midst of *kumadini* flowers and moonlight, when Vṛndāvana became exceedingly beautiful? Kṛṣṇa was dancing with us, and the atmosphere was surcharged with the sound of foot bells. We exchanged pleasing conversation then. Does He remember that particular night? We remember that night, and we feel separation. Separation from Kṛṣṇa makes us agitated, as if there were fire in our bodies. He proposed to come back to Vṛndāvana to extinguish the fire, just as a cloud appears in the sky to extinguish the forest fire by its downpour."

Another *gopī* said, "Kṛṣṇa has killed His enemy, and He has victoriously achieved the kingdom of Kaṁsa. Maybe He is married with a king's daughter by this time and living very happily among His kinsmen and friends. Therefore, why should He come to this village of Vṛndāvana?"

Another *gopī* said, "Kṛṣṇa is the Supreme Personality of Godhead, the husband of the goddess of fortune, and He is self-sufficient. He has no business either with us, the girls in the Vṛndāvana forest, or with the city girls in Mathurā. He is the great Supersoul; He has nothing to do with any of us, either here or there."

Another *gopī* said, "It is an unreasonable hope for us to expect Kṛṣṇa to come back to Vṛndāvana. We should try instead to be happy in disappointment. Even Piṅgalā, the great prostitute, said that disappointment is the greatest pleasure. We all know these things, but it is very difficult for us to give up the expectation of Kṛṣṇa's coming back again. Who can forget a solitary conversation with Kṛṣṇa, on whose breast the goddess of fortune always remains, in spite of Kṛṣṇa's not desiring her? My dear Uddhava, Vṛndāvana is the land of rivers, forests and cows. Here the vibration of the flute is heard, and Kṛṣṇa, along with His elder brother, Śrī Balarāma, enjoyed the atmosphere in our company. Thus the environment of Vṛndāvana is constantly reminding us of Kṛṣṇa and Balarāma. The impression of His footprints is on the land of Vṛndāvana, which is the residential place of the goddess of fortune, but such signs cannot help us to get Kṛṣṇa."

The *gopīs* further expressed that Vṛndāvana was still full of all opulence and good fortune; there was no scarcity or want in Vṛndāvana as far as material necessities were concerned, but in spite of such opulence they could not forget Kṛṣṇa and Balarāma.

"We are constantly remembering various attractive features of beautiful Kṛṣṇa, His walking, His smiling and His joking words. We have all become lost by the dealings of Kṛṣṇa, and it is impossible for us to forget Him. We are always praying for Him, exclaiming, 'Dear Lord, dear husband of the goddess of fortune, dear Lord of Vṛndāvana and deliverer of the distressed devotees! We are now fallen and merged into an ocean of distress. Please, therefore, come back again to Vṛndāvana and deliver us from this pitiable condition."

Uddhava minutely studied the transcendental abnormal condition of the *gopīs* in their separation from Kṛṣṇa, and he thought it wise to repeat all the pastimes of Śrī Kṛṣṇa over and over again. Materialistic persons are always in a burning condition on account of the blazing fire of material miseries. The *gopīs* also were burning in a transcendental blazing fire due to separation from Kṛṣṇa. The blazing fire which was exasperating the *gopīs*, however, is different from the fire of the material world. The *gopīs* constantly want the association of Kṛṣṇa, whereas the materialistic person wants the advantage of material comforts.

It is stated by Viśvanātha Cakravartī Ṭhākur that Kṛṣṇa saved the cowherd boys from the blazing forest fire within a second, while their eyes were closed. Similarly, Uddhava advised the *gopīs* that they could be saved from the fire of separation by closing their eyes and meditating on the activities of Kṛṣṇa from the very beginning of their association with Him. From the outside, the *gopīs* could visualize all the pastimes of Kṛṣṇa by hearing the descriptions of Uddhava, and from inside they could remember those pastimes. From the instruction of Uddhava, the *gopīs* could understand that Kṛṣṇa was not separate from them. As they were constantly thinking of Kṛṣṇa, Kṛṣṇa was also thinking of them constantly while at Mathurā.

Uddhava's messages and instructions saved the *gopīs* from immediate death, and the *gopīs* acknowledged the benediction from Uddhava. Uddhava practically acted as the preceptor spiritual master of the *gopīs*, and they in return worshiped him as they would worship Kṛṣṇa. It is recommended in authoritative scriptures that the spiritual master should be worshiped on the level of the Supreme Personality of Godhead, because of his being His very confidential servitor, and it is accepted by great authorities that the spiritual master is the external manifestation of Kṛṣṇa. The *gopīs* were relieved from their transcendental burning condition by realizing that Kṛṣṇa was with them. Internally, they remembered His association within their hearts, and externally Uddhava helped them to appreciate Kṛṣṇa by conclusive instructions.

The Supreme Personality of Godhead is described in the scriptures as *adhokṣaja,* which indicates that He is beyond the perception of all material senses. Although He is beyond the perception of material senses, He is present in everyone's heart. At the same time, He is present everywhere by His all-pervasive feature of Brahman. All three transcendental features of the Absolute Truth (*Bhagavān* the Personality of Godhead, *Paramātmā* the localized Supersoul, and the all-pervasive *Brahman*) can be realized simply by studying the condition of the *gopīs* in their meeting with Uddhava, as described by the *Śrīmad-Bhāgavatam.*

It is said by Śrīnivāsa Ācārya that the six Gosvāmīs were always merged in thoughts of the activities of the *gopīs.* Caitanya Mahāprabhu has also recommended the *gopīs'* method of worship of the Supreme Personality of Godhead as superexcellent. Śrīla Śukadeva Gosvāmī has also recommended that anyone who hears from the right source about the dealings of the *gopīs* with Kṛṣṇa and who follows the instructions will be elevated to the topmost position of devotional service and will be able to give up the lust of material enjoyment.

All the *gopīs* were solaced by the instruction of Uddhava, and they requested him to stay in Vṛndāvana for a few days more. Uddhava agreed to their proposal and stayed with them not only for a few days, but for a few months. He always kept them engaged in thinking of the transcendental message of Kṛṣṇa and His pastimes, and the *gopīs* were feeling as if they were experiencing direct association with Kṛṣṇa. While Uddhava remained in Vṛndāvana, the inhabitants enjoyed his association. As they discussed the activities of Kṛṣṇa, the days passed just like moments. Vṛndāvana's natural atmosphere, with the presence of the River Yamunā, its nice orchards of trees decorated with various fruits, Govardhana Hill, caves, blooming flowers—all combined to inspire Uddhava to narrate Kṛṣṇa's pastimes. The inhabitants enjoyed Uddhava's association in the same way as they enjoyed the association of Kṛṣṇa.

Uddhava was attracted by the attitude of the *gopīs* because they were completely attached to Kṛṣṇa, and Uddhava was inspired by the *gopīs'* anxiety for Kṛṣṇa. He began to offer them his respectful obeisances and composed songs in praise of their transcendental qualities as follows: "Among all the living entities who have accepted the human form of life, the *gopīs* are superexcellently successful in their mission. Their thought is thoroughly absorbed in the lotus feet of Kṛṣṇa. Great sages and saintly persons are also trying to be absorbed in meditation upon the lotus feet of Kṛṣṇa, who is Mukunda Himself, the giver of liberation, but the *gopīs,* having lovingly accepted the Lord, are automatically accustomed to this habit. They do not depend on any yogic practice. The conclusion is that one who has attained the *gopīs'* condition of life does not have to take birth as Lord Brahmā or be born in a *brāhmaṇa* family or be initiated as a *brāhmaṇa.*"

Śrī Uddhava confirmed the statement of *Bhagavad-gītā* spoken by Lord Kṛṣṇa; one who takes shelter of Him for the right purpose, be he a *śūdra* or lower, will attain the highest goal of life. The *gopīs* have set the standard of devotion for the whole world. By following in the footsteps of the *gopīs* by constantly thinking of Kṛṣṇa, one can attain the highest perfectional stage of spiritual life. The *gopīs* were not born of any highly cultured family; they were born of cowherd men, and yet they developed the highest love of Kṛṣṇa. For self-realization or God realization there is no need to take birth in a high family. The only thing needed is ecstatic development of love of God. In achieving perfection in Kṛṣṇa consciousness, no other qualification is required than to be constantly engaged in the loving service of Kṛṣṇa. Kṛṣṇa is the supreme nectar, the reservoir of all pleasure. The effect of taking up Kṛṣṇa consciousness is just like that of drinking nectar; with or without one's knowledge, it will act. The active principle of Kṛṣṇa consciousness will manifest itself everywhere; it does not matter how and where one has taken his birth. Kṛṣṇa will bestow His benediction upon anyone who takes to Kṛṣṇa consciousness, without any doubt. The supreme benediction attained by the *gopīs* in spite of their being born in the family of cowherd men was never attained even by the goddess of fortune herself, and certainly not by the denizens of heaven, though their bodily forms are like lotuses. The *gopīs* are so fortunate that during *rāsa-līlā* Kṛṣṇa personally embraced them with His arms. Kṛṣṇa kissed them face to face. Certainly it is not possible for any women in the three worlds to achieve this except the *gopīs.*

Uddhava appreciated the exalted position of the *gopīs* and wished to fall down and take the dust of their feet on his head. Yet he did not dare to ask the *gopīs* to offer the dust from their feet; perhaps they would not be agreeable. He therefore desired to have his head smeared with the dust of the *gopīs'* feet without their knowledge. He desired to become only an insignificant clump of grass or herbs in the land of Vṛndāvana.

The *gopīs* were so much attracted to Kṛṣṇa that when they heard the vibration of His flute, they instantly left their families, children, honor and feminine bashfulness and ran towards the place where Kṛṣṇa was standing. They did not consider whether they were passing over the road or through the jungles. Imperceptibly, the dust of their feet was bestowed on small grasses and herbs of Vṛndāvana. Not daring to place the dust of the *gopīs'* feet on his own head, Uddhava aspired to have a future birth in the position of a clump of grass and herbs. He would then be able to have the dust of the *gopīs'* feet.

Uddhava appreciated the extraordinary fortune of the *gopīs,* who relieved themselves of all kinds of material contamination by placing on their high, beautiful breasts the lotus feet of Kṛṣṇa, which are not only worshiped by the goddess of fortune, but by such exalted demigods as Brahmā and Lord Śiva, and which are meditated upon by great *yogīs* within their hearts. Thus Uddhava desired to be able to constantly pray to be honored by the dust of the *gopīs'* lotus feet. The *gopīs'* chanting of the transcendental pastimes of Lord Kṛṣṇa has become celebrated all over the three worlds.

After living in Vṛndāvana for some days, Uddhava desired to go back to Kṛṣṇa, and he begged permission to leave from Nanda Mahārāja and Yaśodā. He had a farewell meeting with the *gopīs,* and taking permission of them also, he mounted his chariot to start for Mathurā.

When Uddhava was about to leave, all the inhabitants of Vṛndāvana, headed by Mahārāja Nanda and Yaśodā, came to bid him good-bye and presented him with various kinds of valuable goods secured in Vṛndāvana. They expressed their feelings with tears in their eyes due to intense attachment for Kṛṣṇa. All of them desired benediction from Uddhava. They desired always to remember the glorious activities of Kṛṣṇa and wanted their minds to be always fixed upon His lotus feet, their words always engaged in glorifying Kṛṣṇa, and their bodies always engaged in bowing down and constantly remembering Him. This prayer of the inhabitants of Vṛndāvana is the superexcellent type of self-realization. The method is very simple: to fix the mind always on the lotus feet of Kṛṣṇa, to talk always of Kṛṣṇa without passing on to any other subject matter, and to engage the body in Kṛṣṇa's service constantly. Specifically in this human form of life, one should engage his life, his resources, words and intelligence for the service of the Lord. Such kinds of activities only can elevate a human being to the highest level of perfection. This is the verdict of all authorities.

The inhabitants of Vṛndāvana said: "By the will of the supreme authority and according to the results of our own work, we may take our birth anywhere. It doesn't matter where we are born, but our only prayer is that we may simply be engaged in Kṛṣṇa consciousness." A pure devotee of Lord Kṛṣṇa never desires to be promoted to the heavenly planets, or even to Vaikuṇṭha or Goloka Vṛndāvana, because he has no desire for his own personal satisfaction. A pure devotee regards both heaven and hell to be on an equal level. Without Kṛṣṇa, heaven is hell; and with Kṛṣṇa, hell is heaven. When Uddhava had sufficiently honored the worship of the pure devotees of Vṛndāvana, he returned to Mathurā and to his master, Kṛṣṇa. After offering respects by bowing down before Lord Kṛṣṇa and Balarāma, he began to describe the wonderful devotional life of the inhabitants of Vṛndāvana. He presented all of the gifts given by the inhabitants of Vṛndāvana to Vasudeva, the father of Kṛṣṇa, and Ugrasena, the grandfather of Kṛṣṇa.

Thus ends the Bhaktivedanta purport of the Second Volume, Twelfth Chapter of* Kṛṣṇa, *"Delivery of the Message of Kṛṣṇa to the Gopīs."

13 / Kṛṣṇa Pleases His Devotees

For days together, Kṛṣṇa heard from Uddhava all the details of his visit to Vṛndāvana, of the condition of His father and mother, and of the *gopīs* and the cowherd boys. Lord Kṛṣṇa was fully satisfied that Uddhava was able to solace them by his instruction and by the message delivered to them.

Lord Kṛṣṇa then decided to go to the house of Kubjā, the hunchback woman who had pleased Him by offering Him sandalwood when He was entering the city of Mathurā. As stated in the *Bhagavad-gītā,* Kṛṣṇa always tries to please His devotees, and the devotees try to please Kṛṣṇa. As the devotees always think of Kṛṣṇa within their hearts, so Kṛṣṇa also thinks of His devotees within Himself. When Kubjā was converted into a beautiful society girl, she wanted Kṛṣṇa to come to her place so that she could try to receive and worship Him in her own way. Society girls generally try to satisfy their clients by offering their bodies to the men to enjoy. But this society girl, Kubjā, was actually captivated by a lust to satisfy her senses with Kṛṣṇa. When Kṛṣṇa desired to go to the house of Kubjā, He certainly had no desire for sense gratification. By supplying the sandalwood pulp to Kṛṣṇa, Kubjā had already satisfied His senses. On the plea of her sense gratification, He decided to go to her house, not actually for sense gratification, but to turn her into a pure devotee. Kṛṣṇa is always served by many thousands of goddesses of fortune; therefore He has no need to satisfy His senses by going to a society girl. But as He is kind to everyone, He decided to go there. It is said that the moon does not withhold its shining from the courtyard of a crooked person. Similarly, Kṛṣṇa's transcendental mercy is never denied to anyone, whether one has rendered service unto Him through lust, anger, fear or pure love. In the *Caitanya-caritāmṛta* it is stated that if one wants to serve Kṛṣṇa and at the same time wants to satisfy his own lusty desires, Kṛṣṇa will handle it so that the devotee forgets his lusty desire and becomes fully purified and constantly engaged in the service of the Lord.

In order to fulfill His past promise, Kṛṣṇa, along with Uddhava, went to the house of Kubjā. When Kṛṣṇa reached her house, He saw that it was completely decorated in a way to excite the lusty desires of a man. This suggests that there were many nude pictures, on top of which were canopies and flags embroidered with pearl necklaces, along with comfortable beds and cushioned chairs. The rooms were provided with flower garlands and were nicely scented with incense and sprinkled with scented water. And the rooms were illuminated by nice lamps.

When Kubjā saw that Lord Kṛṣṇa had come to her house in order to fulfill His promised visit, she immediately got up from the chair to receive Him. Accompanied by her many girl friends, she began to talk with Him with great respect and honor. After offering Him a nice place to sit, she worshiped Lord Kṛṣṇa in a manner just suitable to her position. Uddhava was similarly received by Kubjā and her girl friends, but he was not on an equal level with Kṛṣṇa, and he simply sat down on the floor.

Without wasting time, as one does in such situations, Kṛṣṇa entered the bedroom of Kubjā. In the meantime, Kubjā took her bath and smeared her body with sandalwood pulp. She dressed herself with nice garments, valuable jewelry, ornaments and flower garlands. Chewing betel nut and other intoxicating eatables and spraying herself with scents, she appeared before Kṛṣṇa. Her smiling glance and moving eyes were full of feminine bashfulness as she stood gracefully before Lord Kṛṣṇa, who is known as Mādhava, the husband of the goddess of fortune. When Kṛṣṇa saw that Kubjā was hesitating to come before Him, He immediately caught hold of her hand, which was decorated with bangles. With great affection, He dragged her beside Him and made her sit by His side. Simply by having previously supplied pulp of sandalwood to the Supreme Lord, Kṛṣṇa, Kubjā became free from all sinful reactions and eligible to enjoy with Him. She then took Kṛṣṇa's lotus feet and placed them on her breasts, which were burning with the blazing fire of lust. By smelling the fragrance of Kṛṣṇa's lotus feet, she immediately became relieved of all lusty desires. She was thus allowed to embrace Kṛṣṇa with her two arms and thus mitigate her long-cherised desire to have Kṛṣṇa as a visitor in her house.

It is stated in the *Bhagavad-gītā* that without being freed of all material sinful reactions, one cannot be engaged in the transcendental loving service of the Lord. Simply by supplying sandalwood pulp to Kṛṣṇa, Kubjā was thus rewarded. She was not trained to worship Kṛṣṇa in any other way; therefore she wanted to satisfy Him by her profession. It is confirmed in the *Bhagavad-gītā* that the Lord can be worshiped even by one's profession, if it is sincerely offered for the pleasure of the Lord. Kubjā then told

Kṛṣṇa, "My dear friend, kindly remain with me at least for a few days. Enjoy with me, You and Your lotus-eyed friend. I cannot leave You immediately. Please grant my request."

As stated in the Vedic versions, the Supreme Personality of Godhead has multi-potencies. According to expert opinion, Kubjā represents the *puruṣa-śakti* potency of Kṛṣṇa, just as Śrīmatī Rādhārāṇī represents His *cit-śakti* potency. Although she requested Kṛṣṇa to remain with her for some days, Kṛṣṇa politely impressed upon her that it was not possible for Him to stay. Kṛṣṇa visits this material world occasionally, whereas His connection with the spiritual world is eternal. Kṛṣṇa is always present either in the Vaikuṇṭha planets or in the Goloka Vṛndāvana planet. The technical term for His presence in the spiritual world is *prakaṭa-līlā.*

After satisfying Kubjā with sweet words, Kṛṣṇa returned to His place along with Uddhava. There is a warning in the *Śrīmad-Bhāgavatam* that Kṛṣṇa is not very easily worshiped because He is the Supreme Personality of Godhead, the chief among the *Viṣṇu-tattvas.* To worship Kṛṣṇa or have association with Him is not a very easy job. Specifically, there is a warning for devotees who are attracted to Kṛṣṇa through conjugal love; it is not good for them to desire to have sense gratification by direct association with Kṛṣṇa. Actually, the activities of sense gratification are material. In the spiritual world there are symptoms like kissing and embracing, but there is no sense-gratificatory process as it exists in the material world. This warning is specifically for those known as *sahajiyā,* who take it for granted that Kṛṣṇa is an ordinary human being. They desire to enjoy sex life with Him in a perverted way. In a spiritual relationship, sense gratification is most insignificant. Anyone who desires a relationship of perverted sense gratification with Kṛṣṇa must be considered to be less intelligent. His mentality requires to be reformed.

After a while, Kṛṣṇa fulfilled His promise to visit Akrūra at his house. Akrūra was in relationship with Kṛṣṇa as His servitor, and Kṛṣṇa wanted to get some service from him. He went there accompanied by both Lord Balarāma and Uddhava. When Kṛṣṇa, Balarāma and Uddhava were approaching the house of Akrūra, Akrūra came forward, embraced Uddhava and offered respectful obeisances, bowing down before Lord Kṛṣṇa and Balarāma. Kṛṣṇa, Balarāma and Uddhava offered him obeisances in turn and were offered appropriate sitting places by Akrūra. When all were comfortably seated, Akrūra washed their feet and sprinkled the water on his head. Then he offered nice flowers and sandalwood pulp in regular worship. All three of them became very satisfied by the behavior of Akrūra. Akrūra then bowed down before Kṛṣṇa, putting his head on the ground.

Then, keeping Kṛṣṇa's lotus feet on his lap, Akrūra began to gently massage them. When Akrūra was fully satisfied in the presence of Kṛṣṇa and Balarāma, his eyes became filled with tears of love for Kṛṣṇa, and he began to offer his prayers as follows.

"My dear Lord Kṛṣṇa, it is very kind of You to have killed Kaṁsa and his associates. You have delivered the whole family of the Yadu dynasty from the greatest calamity. Your saving of the great Yadu dynasty will always be remembered by them. My dear Lord Kṛṣṇa and Balarāma, You are the original personality from whom everything has emanated. You are the original cause of all causes. You have inconceivable energy, and You are all-pervasive. But for Yourself, there is no other cause and effect, gross or subtle. You are the Supreme Brahman realized by the study of the *Vedas.* By Your inconceivable energy, You are actually visible before us. You create this cosmic manifestation by Your own potencies, and You enter into it Yourself. As the five material elements, earth, water, fire, air, and sky, are distributed in everything manifested by different kinds of bodies, so You alone enter into different varieties of bodies, created by Your own energy. You enter the body as the individual soul as well as independently as the Supersoul. The material body is created by Your inferior energy. The living entities, individual souls, are part and parcel of You, and the Supersoul is Your localized representation. This material body, the living entity and the Supersoul constitute an individual living being, but originally they are all different energies of the one Supreme Lord.

"In the material world, You are creating, maintaining and dissolving the whole manifestation by interaction of three qualities, namely goodness, passion and ignorance. You are not implicated by the activities of those material qualities because Your supreme knowledge is never overcome, as is the case with the individual living entity."

As the Supreme Lord enters into this material creation and thus the creation, maintenance and destruction are going on in their due course, so the part and parcel living entity enters the material elements and has his material body created for him. The difference between the living entity and the Lord is that the living entity is part and parcel of the Supreme Lord and has the tendency to be overcome by the interaction of material qualities. Kṛṣṇa, the *Parambrahman* or the Supreme Brahman, being always situated in full knowledge, is never overcome by such activities. Therefore Kṛṣṇa's name is *Acyuta,* meaning He who never falls down. Kṛṣṇa's knowledge of spiritual identity is never overcome by material action, whereas the identity of the minute part and parcel living entities is prone to be overcome by material action. The individual living entities are eternally part and parcel of God. As minute sparks of the original fire, Kṛṣṇa, they have the tendency to become extinguished.

Akrūra continued: "The less intelligent class of men misunderstand Your transcendental form to be also made of material energy. That concept is not at all applicable to You. Actually, You are all spiritual, and there is no difference between You and Your body. Because of this, there is no question of Your being conditioned or liberated. You are ever-liberated in any condition of life. As stated in the *Bhagavad-gītā,* 'Only the fools and rascals consider You to be an ordinary man.' To consider Your Lordship to be one of us, conditioned by the material nature, is a mistake due to our imperfect knowledge. When people deviate from the original knowledge of the *Vedas,* they try to identify the ordinary living entities with Your Lordship. Your Lordship has appeared on this earth in Your original form in order to reestablish the real knowledge that the living entities are neither one with nor equal to the Supreme God. My dear Lord, You are always situated in uncontaminated goodness *(śuddha-sattva).* Your appearance is necessary to reestablish actual Vedic knowledge, as opposed to the atheistic philosophy which tries to establish that God and living entities are one and the same. My dear Lord Kṛṣṇa, this time You have appeared in the home of Vasudeva as His son, along with Your plenary expansion, Śrī Balarāma. Your mission is to kill all the atheistic royal families, along with their huge military strength. You have advented Yourself to minimize the overburden of the world, and in order to fulfill this mission, You have glorified the dynasty of Yadu, appearing in the family as one of its members.

"My dear Lord, today my home has become purified by Your presence. I have become the most fortunate person in the world. The Supreme Personality of Godhead, who is worshipable by all different kinds of demigods, Pitṛs, living entities, kings and emperors, and who is the Supersoul of everything, has come into my home. The water of His lotus feet is purifying the three worlds, and now He has kindly come to my place. Who is there in the three worlds among factually learned men who will not take shelter of Your lotus feet and surrender unto You? Who, knowing well that no one can be as affectionate as You are to Your devotees, is so foolish that he will decline to become Your devotee? Throughout the Vedic literature it is declared that You are the dearmost friend of every living entity. This is confirmed in the *Bhagavad-gītā: suhṛdaṁ sarva-bhūtānām.* You are the Supreme Personality of Godhead, completely capable of fulfilling the desires of Your devotees. You are the real friend of everyone. In spite of giving Yourself to Your devotees, You are never depleted of Your original potency. Your potency neither decreases nor increases in volume.

"My dear Lord, it is very difficult for even the great mystic *yogīs* and demigods to ascertain Your movement. You cannot be approached by them, and yet out of Your causeless mercy You have kindly consented to come to my home. This is the most auspicious moment in the journey of my material existence. By Your grace only, I can just understand that my home, my wife, my children and my worldly possessions are all different bonds to material existence. Please cut the knot and save me from this entanglement of false society, friendship and love."

Lord Śrī Kṛṣṇa was very pleased by Akrūra's offering of prayers. His smile was captivating Akrūra more and more. The Lord replied him as follows: "My dear Akrūra, in spite of your submissiveness, I consider you to be My superior, on the level with My father and teacher and most well-wishing friend. You are, therefore, worshipable by Me, and since You are My uncle, I am always to be protected by you. I desire to be maintained by you because I am one of your own children. Apart from this filial relationship, you are always to be worshiped. Anyone who desires good fortune must offer his respectful obeisances unto personalities like you. You are more than the demigods. People go to worship the demigods when they are in need of some sense gratification; the demigods offer benediction to their devotees after being worshiped by them. But a devotee like Akrūra is always ready to offer the greatest benediction to the people. A saintly person or devotee is free to offer benediction to everyone, whereas the demigods can offer benediction only after being worshiped. One can take advantage of the place of pilgrimage only after going there. By worshiping the particular demigod, it takes a long time for fulfillment of the desire; but saintly persons like you, My dear Akrūra, can immediately fulfill all the desires of the devotees. My dear Akrūra, you are always our friend and well-wisher. You are always ready to act for our welfare. Kindly, therefore, go to Hastināpura and see what arrangement has been made for the Pāṇḍavas."

Kṛṣṇa was very anxious to know about the sons of Pāṇḍu, because at a very young age, they had lost their father. Being very friendly to His devotees, Kṛṣṇa was anxious to know about them, and therefore He deputed Akrūra to go to Hastināpura and get information of the real situation. Kṛṣṇa continued to say, "I have heard that after the death of King Pāṇḍu, his young sons, Yudhiṣṭhira, Bhīma, Arjuna, Nakula and Sahadeva, along with their widowed mother, have come under the charge of Dhṛtarāṣṭra, who is to look after them as their guardian. But I have also heard that Dhṛtarāṣṭra is not only blind from birth, but also blind in his affection for his cruel son, Duryodhana. The five Pāṇḍavas are the sons of King Pāṇḍu, but Dhṛtarāṣṭra, due to his plans and designs, is not favorably disposed towards the Pāṇḍavas. Kindly go there and study how Dhṛtarāṣṭra is dealing with the Pāṇḍavas. On receipt of your report, I shall consider how to favor the Pāṇḍavas." In this way the Supreme Personality of Godhead, Kṛṣṇa, ordered Akrūra to go to Hastināpura, and then He returned home, accompanied by Balarāma and Uddhava.

Thus ends the Bhaktivedanta purport of the Second Volume, Thirteenth Chapter of* Kṛṣṇa, *"Kṛṣṇa Pleases His Devotees."

14 / Ill-motivated Dhṛtarāṣṭra

Thus being ordered by the Supreme Personality of Godhead, Śrī Kṛṣṇa, Akrūra visited Hastināpura. Hastināpura is said to be the site of what is now New Delhi. The part of New Delhi, which is still known as Indraprastha, is accepted by people in general as the old capital of the Pāṇḍavas. The very name Hastināpura suggests that there were many *hastīs,* or elephants. Because the Pāṇḍavas kept many elephants in the capital, it was called Hastināpura. Keeping elephants is a very expensive job; to keep many elephants, therefore, the kingdom must be very rich, and Hastināpura was full of elephants, horses, chariots and other opulences. When Akrūra reached Hastināpura, he saw that the capital was full of all kinds of opulences. The kings of Hastināpura were taken to be the ruling kings of the whole world. Their fame was widely spread throughout the entire kingdom, and their administration was conducted under the good counsel of learned *brāhmaṇas.*

After seeing the very opulent capital city, Akrūra met King Dhṛtarāṣṭra. He also saw grandfather Bhīṣma sitting with him. After meeting them, he went to see Vidura and then Vidura's sister, Kuntī. One after another, he saw the son of Somadatta, and the King of Bāhlīka, Droṇācārya, Kṛpācārya, Karṇa and Suyodhana. (Suyodhana is another name of Duryodhana.) He saw the five Pāṇḍava brothers and other friends and relatives living in the city. Akrūra was known as the son of Gāndī, so whomever he met was very pleased to receive him. He was offered a good seat at his receptions, and he inquired all about his relatives' welfare and other activities.

Since he was deputed by Lord Kṛṣṇa to visit Hastināpura, it is understood that he was very intelligent in studying a diplomatic situation. Dhṛtarāṣṭra was unlawfully occupying the throne after the death of the King Pāṇḍu, despite the presence of Pāṇḍu's sons. Akrūra wanted to study the whole situation by remaining there. He could understand very well that ill-motivated Dhṛtarāṣṭra was much inclined in favor of his own sons. In fact, Dhṛtarāṣṭra had already usurped the kingdom and was now instigating and planning to dispose of the five Pāṇḍava brothers. Akrūra knew also that all the sons of Dhṛtarāṣṭra, headed by Duryodhana, were very crooked politicians. Dhṛtarāṣṭra did not act in accordance with the good instruction given by Bhīṣma and Vidura, but he was being conducted by the ill instruction of such persons as Karṇa, Śakuni and others. Akrūra decided to stay in Hastināpura for a few months to study the whole political situation.

Gradually Akrūra learned from Kuntī and Vidura that Dhṛtarāṣṭra was very intolerant and envious of the five Pāṇḍava brothers because of their extraordinary learning in military science and their greatly developed bodily strength. They acted as true chivalrous heroes, exhibited all the good qualities of *kṣatriyas,* and were very responsible princes, always thinking of the welfare of the citizens. Akrūra also learned that the envious Dhṛtarāṣṭra, in consultation with his ill-advised son, had tried to kill the Pāṇḍavas by poisoning them.

Akrūra happened to be one of the cousins of Kuntī; therefore, after meeting him, she began to inquire about her paternal relatives. Thinking of her birthplace, she began to cry. She asked Akrūra whether her father, mother, brothers, sisters and other friends at home were still remembering her. She especially inquired about Kṛṣṇa and Balarāma, her glorious nephews. She asked: "Does Kṛṣṇa, who is the Supreme Personality of Godhead, who is very affectionate to His devotees, remember my sons? Does Balarāma remember us?" Inside herself, Kuntī felt like a she-deer in the midst of tigers, and actually her position was like that. After the death of her husband, King Pāṇḍu, she was supposed to take care of the five Pāṇḍava children, but Dhṛtarāṣṭra was always planning to kill them. She was certainly living as a poor innocent animal in the midst of several tigers. Being a devotee of Lord Kṛṣṇa, she was always thinking of Him and expecting that one day Kṛṣṇa would come and save them from their dangerous position. She inquired from Akrūra whether Kṛṣṇa proposed to come to advise the fatherless Pāṇḍavas how to get free of the intriguing policy of Dhṛtarāṣṭra and his sons. By talking with Akrūra about all these affairs, she felt herself helpless and began to exclaim: "My dear Kṛṣṇa, my dear Kṛṣṇa, You are the supreme mystic, the Supersoul of the universe. You are the real well-wisher of the whole universe. My dear Govinda, at this time You are far away from me, yet I pray to surrender unto Your lotus feet. At the present moment I am very much griefstricken with my five fatherless sons. I can fully understand that but for Your lotus feet there is no shelter or protection. Your lotus feet can deliver all aggrieved souls because You are the Supreme Personality of Godhead. One can be safe from the clutches of repeated birth and death by Your mercy only. My dear Kṛṣṇa, You are the supreme pure one, the Supersoul and the master of all *yogīs.* What can I say? I can simply offer my respectful obeisances unto You. Accept me as Your fully surrendered devotee."

Although Kṛṣṇa was not present before her, Kuntī offered her prayers to Him as if she were in His presence face to face. This is possible for anyone following in the footsteps of Kuntī. Kṛṣṇa does not have to be physically present everywhere. He is actually present everywhere by spiritual potency, and one simply has to surrender unto Him sincerely. When Kuntī was offering her prayers very feelingly to Kṛṣṇa, she could not check herself and began to cry loudly before Akrūra. Vidura was also present, and both Akrūra and Vidura became very sympathetic to the mother of the Pāṇḍavas. They began to solace her by glorifying her sons, Yudhiṣṭhira, Arjuna and Bhīma. They pacified her, saying that her sons were extraordinarily powerful; she should not be perturbed about them, since they were born of great demigods, Yamarāja, Indra and Vāyu.

Akrūra decided to return and report on the extreme circumstances in which he found Kuntī and her five sons. He first wanted to give good advice to Dhṛtarāṣṭra, who was so favorably inclined toward his own son and unfavorably inclined toward the Pāṇḍavas. When Kuntī and Dhṛtarāṣṭra were sitting among friends and relatives, Akrūra began to address him, calling him "Vārcitravīrya." *Vārcitravīrya* means the son of Vicitravīrya. Vicitravīrya was the name of the father of Dhṛtarāṣṭra, but Dhṛtarāṣṭra was not actually the begotten son of Vicitravīrya. He was the begotten son of Vyāsadeva. Formerly it was the system that if a man were unable to beget a child, his brother could beget a child in the womb of his wife. That system is now forbidden in this age of Kali. Akrūra called Dhṛtarāṣṭra "Vārcitravīrya" sarcastically because he was not actually begotten by his father. He was the son of Vyāsadeva. When a child was begotten in the wife by the husband's brother, the child was claimed by the husband, but of course the child was not begotten by the husband. This sarcastic remark pointed out that Dhṛtarāṣṭra was falsely claiming the throne on heriditary grounds. Actually the son of Pāṇḍu was the rightful king, and in the presence of Pāṇḍu's sons, the Pāṇḍavas, Dhṛtarāṣṭra should not have occupied the throne.

Akrūra then said, "My dear son of Vicitravīrya, you have unlawfully usurped the throne of the Pāṇḍavas. Anyway, somehow or other you are now on the throne. Therefore I beg to advise you to please rule the kingdom on moral and ethical principles. If you do so and try to teach your subjects in that way, then your name and fame will be perpetual." Akrūra hinted that although Dhṛtarāṣṭra was ill-treating his nephews, the Pāṇḍavas, they happened to be his subjects. "Even if you treat them not as the owners of the throne, but as your subjects, you should impartially think of their welfare as though they were your own sons. But if you do not follow this principle and act in just the opposite way, then you will be unpopular among your subjects, and in the next life you will have to live in a hellish condition. I therefore hope you will treat your sons and the sons of Pāṇḍu equally. Akrūra hinted that if Dhṛtarāṣṭra did not treat the Pāṇḍavas and his sons as equals, then surely there would be a fight between the two camps of cousins. Since the Pāṇḍavas' cause was just, they would come out victorious, and the sons of Dhṛtarāṣṭra would be killed. This was a prophecy told by Akrūra to Dhṛtarāṣṭra.

Akrūra further advised Dhṛtarāṣṭra, "In this material world, no one can remain as an eternal companion to another. By chance only we assemble together in the family, in the society, in the community or in the nation, but at the end, because every one of us has to give up the body, we must be separated. One should not, therefore, be unnecessarily affectionate toward family members." Dhṛtarāṣṭra's affection was also unlawful and did not show much intelligence. In plain words, Akrūra hinted to Dhṛtarāṣṭra that his staunch family affection was due to his gross ignorance of fact. Although we appear to be combined together in family, society or nation, each one of us has an individual destiny. Everyone takes birth according to individual past work; therefore everyone has to individually enjoy or suffer the result of his own *karma.* There is no possibility of improving one's destiny by cooperate living. Sometimes it happens that one's father accumulates wealth by illegal ways, and the son takes away the money, although it is hard-earned by the father. It is just like a small fish in the ocean who eats the material body of the large, old fish. One ultimately cannot accumulate wealth illegally for the gratification of his family, society, community or nation. That many great empires which developed in the past are no longer existing because their wealth was squandered away by later descendants is an illustration of this principle. One who does not know this subtle law of fruitive activities and thus gives up the principles of moral and ethical principles only carries with him the reactions of his sinful activities. His ill-gotten wealth and possessions are taken by someone else, and he goes to the darkest region of hellish life. One should not, therefore, accumulate more wealth than is allotted to him by destiny; otherwise he will be factually blind to his own interest. Instead of fulfilling his self-interest, he will act in just the opposite way for his own downfall.

Akrūra continued: "My dear Dhṛtarāṣṭra, I beg to advise you not to be blind about the fact of this material existence. Material conditional life, either in distress or in happiness, is to be accepted as a dream. One should try to bring his mind and senses under control and live very peacefully for spiritual advancement in Kṛṣṇa consciousness." In the *Caitanya-caritāmṛta* it is said that except for persons who are in Kṛṣṇa consciousness, everyone is always in a disturbed condition of mind and is full of anxiety. Even those who are trying for liberation, or merging into the Brahman effulgence, or the *yogīs* who are trying to achieve perfection in mystic power, cannot have peace of mind. Pure devotees of Kṛṣṇa have no demands to make of Kṛṣṇa. They are simply satisfied with service to Him. Actual peace and mental tranquility can be attained only in perfect Kṛṣṇa consciousness.

After hearing moral instructions from Akrūra, Dhṛtarāṣṭra replied: "My dear Akrūra, you are very charitable in giving me good instructions, but unfortunately I cannot accept it. A person who is destined to die does not utilize the effect of nectar, although it may be administered to him. I can understand that your instructions are very valuable. Unfortunately, they do not stay in my flickering mind, just as the glittering lightning in the sky does not stay in a fixed cloud. I can understand only that no one can stop the onward progress of the supreme will. I understand that the Supreme Personality of Godhead, Kṛṣṇa, has appeared in the family of the Yadus in order to decrease the overburdened load of this earth."

Dhṛtarāṣṭra gave hints to Akrūra that he had complete faith in Kṛṣṇa, the Supreme Personality of Godhead. At the same time, he was very much partial to his family members. In the very near future, Kṛṣṇa would vanquish all the members of his family, and in a helpless condition, Dhṛtarāṣṭra would take shelter of Kṛṣṇa's feet. In order to show His special favor to a devotee, Kṛṣṇa usually takes away all the objects of his material affection. He thus forces the devotee to be materially helpless, with no alternative than to accept the lotus feet of Kṛṣṇa. This actually happened to Dhṛtarāṣṭra after the end of the Battle of Kurukṣetra.

Dhṛtarāṣṭra could realize two opposing factors acting before him. He could understand that Kṛṣṇa was there to remove all the unnecessary burdens of the world. His sons were an unnecessary burden, and so he expected that they would be killed. At the same time, he could not rid himself of his unlawful affection for his sons. Understanding these two contradictory factors, he began to offer his respectful obeisances to the Supreme Personality of Godhead. "The contradictory ways of material existence are very difficult to understand; they can only be taken as the inconceivable execution of the plan of the Supreme, who by His inconceivable energy creates this material world and enters into it and sets into action the three modes of nature. When everything is created, He enters into each and every living entity and into the smallest atom. No one can understand the incalculable plans of the Supreme Lord."

After hearing this statement, Akrūra could clearly understand that Dhṛtarāṣṭra was not going to change his policy of discriminating against the Pāṇḍavas in favor of his sons. He at once took leave of his friends in Hastināpura and returned to his home in the kingdom of the Yadus. After returning home, he vividly informed Lord Kṛṣṇa and Balarāma of the actual situation in Hastināpura and the intentions of Dhṛtarāṣṭra. Akrūra was sent to Hastināpura by Kṛṣṇa to study. By the grace of the Lord, he was successful and informed Kṛṣṇa about the actual situation.

Thus ends the Bhaktivedanta purport of the Second Volume, Fourteenth Chapter of* Kṛṣṇa, *"Ill-motivated Dhṛtarāṣṭra."

15 / Kṛṣṇa Erects the Dvārakā Fort

After his death, Kaṁsa's two wives became widows. According to Vedic civilization, a woman is never independent. She has three stages of life: In childhood a woman should live under the protection of her father, a youthful woman should live under the protection of her young husband, and in the event of the death of her husband she should live either under the protection of her grown-up children, or if she has no grown-up children, she must go back to her father and live as a widow under his protection. It appears that Kaṁsa had no grown-up sons. After becoming widows, his wives returned to the shelter of their father. Kaṁsa had two queens. One was Asti, and the other Prāpti, and both happened to be the daughters of King Jarāsandha, the lord of the Behar Province (known in those days as Magadharāja). After reaching home, both queens explained their awkward position following Kaṁsa's death. The King of Magadha, Jarāsandha, was mortified on hearing their pitiable condition due to the slaughter. When informed of the death of Kaṁsa, Jarāsandha decided on the spot that he would rid the world of all the members of the Yadu dynasty. He decided that since Kṛṣṇa had killed Kaṁsa, the whole dynasty of the Yadus should be killed.

He began to make extensive arrangements to attack the kingdom of Mathurā with his innumerable military phalanxes, consisting of many thousands of chariots, horses, elephants and infantry soldiers. Jarāsandha prepared thirteen such military phalanxes in order to retaliate the death of Kaṁsa. Taking with him all his military strength, he attacked the capital of the Yadu kings, Mathurā, surrounding it from all directions. Śrī Kṛṣṇa, who appeared as an ordinary human being, saw the immense strength of Jarāsandha, which appeared as an ocean about to cover a beach at any moment. He also perceived that the inhabitants of Mathurā were overwhelmed with fear. He began to think within Himself about the situation of His mission as an incarnation and how to tackle the present situation before Him. His mission was to diminish the overburdened population of the whole world; therefore He took the opportunity of facing so many men, chariots, elephants, and horses. The military strength of Jarāsandha had appeared before Him, and He decided to kill the entire force of Jarāsandha so that they would not be able to go back and again reorganize their military strength.

While Lord Kṛṣṇa was thinking in that way, two military chariots, fully equipped with drivers, weapons, flags and other implements, arrived for Him from outer space. Kṛṣṇa saw the two chariots present before Him, and immediately addressed His attendant brother, Balarāma, who is also known as Saṅkarṣaṇa: "My dear elder brother, You are the best among the Āryans, You are the Lord of the universe, and specifically, You are the protector of the Yadu dynasty. The members of the Yadu dynasty sense great danger before the soldiers of Jarāsandha, and they are very much aggrieved. Just to give them protection, Your chariot is also here, filled with military weapons. I request You to sit down on Your chariot and kill all these soldiers, the entire military strength of the enemy. Naturally, both of Us have descended on this earth just to annihilate such unnecessary bellicose forces and to give protection to the pious devotees. So we have the opportunity to fulfill Our mission. Please let Us execute it." Thus Kṛṣṇa and Balarāma, the descendants of the Gadaha King, Daśārha, decided to annihilate the thirteen military companies of Jarāsandha.

Kṛṣṇa went upon the chariot on which Dāruka was the driver and with a small army, and to the blowing of conchshells, He came out of the city of Mathurā. Curiously enough, although the other party was equipped with greater military strength, just after hearing the vibration of Kṛṣṇa's conchshell, their hearts were shaken. When Jarāsandha saw both Balarāma and Kṛṣṇa, he was a little bit compassionate, because both Kṛṣṇa and Balarāma happened to be related to him as grandsons. He specifically addressed Kṛṣṇa as Puruṣādhama, meaning the lowest among men. Actually Kṛṣṇa is known in all Vedic literatures as Puruṣottama, the highest among men. Jarāsandha had no intention of addressing Kṛṣṇa as Puruṣottama, but great scholars have determined the true meaning of the word *puruṣādhama* to be "one who makes all other personalities go downward." Actually no one can be equal to or greater than the Supreme Personality of Godhead.

Jarāsandha said, "It will be a great dishonor for me to fight with boys like Kṛṣṇa and Balarāma." Because Kṛṣṇa had killed Kaṁsa, Jarāsandha specifically addressed Him as the killer of His own relatives. Kaṁsa had killed so many of his own nephews, yet Jarāsandha did not take notice of it; but because Kṛṣṇa had killed His maternal uncle, Kaṁsa, Jarāsandha tried to criticize Him. That is the way of demoniac dealing. Demons do not try to find their own faults, but try to find the faults of their friends. Jarāsandha also criticized Kṛṣṇa for not even being a *kṣatriya.* Because He was raised by Mahārāja Nanda, Kṛṣṇa was not a *kṣatriya,* but a *vaiśya. Vaiśyas* are generally called *guptas,* and the word *gupta* can also be used to mean "hidden." So Kṛṣṇa was both hidden and raised by Nanda Mahārāja. Jarāsandha accused Kṛṣṇa of three faults: that He killed His own maternal uncle, that He was hidden in His childhood, and that He was not even a *kṣatriya.* And therefore Jarāsandha felt ashamed to fight with Him.

Next he turned toward Balarāma and addressed Him: "You, Balarāma! If You like You can fight along with Him, and if You have patience, then You can wait to be killed by my arrows. Thus You can be promoted to heaven." It is stated in the *Bhagavad-gītā* that a *kṣatriya* can become benefited in two ways while fighting. If a *kṣatriya* gains victory in the fight, he enjoys the results of victory, but even if he is killed in the fight, he is promoted to the heavenly kingdom.

After hearing Jarāsandha speak in that way, Kṛṣṇa answered: "My dear King Jarāsandha, those who are heroes do not talk much. Rather, they show their prowess. Because you are talking much, it appears that you are assured of your death in this battle. We do not care to hear you anymore, because it is useless to hear the words of a person who is going to die or one who is very distressed." In order to fight with Kṛṣṇa, Jarāsandha surrounded Him from all sides with great military strength, and the sun appeared covered by the cloudy air and dust. Similarly, Kṛṣṇa, the supreme sun, was covered by the military strength of Jarāsandha. Kṛṣṇa's and Balarāma's chariots were marked with pictures of Garuḍa and palm trees. The women of Mathurā were all standing on the tops of the houses and palaces and gates to see the wonderful fight, but when Kṛṣṇa's chariot was surrounded by Jarāsandha's military force, they became so frightened that some of them fainted. Kṛṣṇa saw Himself overwhelmed by the military strength of Jarāsandha. His small number of soldiers were being harassed by them, so He immediately took up His bow, named Śārṅga.

He began to take His arrows from their case, and one after another He set them on the bowstring and shot them toward the enemy. They were so accurate that the elephants, horses and infantry soldiers of Jarāsandha were quickly killed. The incessant arrows thrown by Kṛṣṇa appeared as a whirlwind of blazing fire killing all the military strength of Jarāsandha. As Kṛṣṇa released His arrows, gradually all the elephants began to fall down, their heads severed by the arrows. Similarly, all the horses fell, and the chariots also, along with their flags. The chariot fighters and the chariot drivers fell as well. Almost all the infantry soldiers fell on the field of battle, their heads, hands and legs cut off. In this way, many thousands of elephants and horses were killed, and their blood began to flow just like the waves of a river. In that river, the severed arms of the men appeared to be snakes, their heads appeared to be tortoises, and the dead bodies of the elephants appeared to be small islands. The dead horses appeared to be sharks. By the arrangement of the supreme will, there was a great river of blood filled with paraphernalia. The hands and legs of the infantry soldiers were floating like seaweed, and the floating bows of the soldiers appeared to be waves of the river. And all the jewelry from the bodies of the soldiers and commanders appeared to be so many pebbles flowing down the river of blood.

Lord Balarāma, who is also known as Saṅkarṣaṇa, began to fight with His club in such a heroic way that the river of blood created by Kṛṣṇa overflooded. Those who were cowards became very much afraid upon seeing the ghastly and horrible scene, and those who were heroes began to talk delightedly among themselves about the heroism of the two brothers. Although Jarāsandha was equipped with a vast ocean of military strength, the fighting of Lord Kṛṣṇa and Balarāma converted the whole situation into a ghastly scene which was far beyond ordinary fighting. Persons of ordinary mind cannot estimate how it could be possible, but when such activities are accepted as pastimes of the Supreme Personality of Godhead, under whose will everything is possible, then this can be understood. The Supreme Personality of Godhead is creating, maintaining and dissolving the cosmic manifestation by His will only. For Him to create such a vast scene of devastation while fighting with an enemy is not so wonderful. And yet, because Kṛṣṇa and Balarāma were fighting with Jarāsandha just like ordinary human beings, the affair appeared to be wonderful.

All the soldiers of Jarāsandha were killed, and he was the only one left alive. Certainly he became very depressed at this point. Śrī Balarāma immediately arrested him, just as, with great strength, one lion captures another lion. But while Lord Balarāma was binding Jarāsandha with the rope of Varuṇa and ordinary ropes also, Lord Kṛṣṇa, with a greater plan in mind for the future, asked Him not to arrest him. Jarāsandha was then released by Kṛṣṇa. As a great fighting hero, Jarāsandha became very much ashamed, and he decided that he would no longer live as a king, but would resign from his position in the royal order and go to the forest to practice meditation under severe austerities and penances.

As he was returning home with other royal friends, however, they advised him not to retire, but to regain strength to fight again with Kṛṣṇa in the near future. The princely friends of Jarāsandha began to instruct him that ordinarily it would not have been possible for him to have been defeated by the strength of the Yadu kings, but the defeat which he had experienced was simply due to his ill luck. The princely order encouraged King Jarāsandha. His fighting, they said, was certainly heroic; therefore, he should not take his defeat very seriously, as it was due only to his past mistakes. After all, there was no fault in his fighting.

In this way, Jarāsandha, the King of Magadha Province, having lost all his strength and having been insulted by his arrest and subsequent release, could do nothing but return to his kingdom. Thus Lord Kṛṣṇa conquered the soldiers of Jarāsandha. Although Kṛṣṇa's army was tiny in comparison to Jarāsandha's, not a pinch of His strength was lost, whereas all of Jarāsandha's men were killed.

At that time the denizens of heaven became very pleased and began to offer their respects by chanting in glorification of the Lord and by showering Him with flowers. They accepted the victory with great appreciation. Jarāsandha returned to his kingdom, and Mathurā City was made safe from the danger of an imminent attack. The citizens of Mathurā organized the combined services of a circus of professional singers, like *sūtas, māgadhas,* and poets who could compose nice songs, and they began to chant the victory glorification of Lord Kṛṣṇa. When Lord Kṛṣṇa entered the city after the victory, many bugles, conches and kettledrums were sounded, and the vibrations of various musical instruments, like *bherya, tūrya, vīṇā,* flute and *mṛdaṅga*—all joined together to make a beautiful reception. While Kṛṣṇa was entering, the whole city was very much cleansed, all the different streets and roads were sprinkled with water, and the inhabitants, being joyous, decorated their respective houses, roads and shops with flags and festoons. The *brāhmaṇas* chanted Vedic *mantras* at numerous places. The people constructed road crossings, entrances, lanes and streets. When Lord Kṛṣṇa was entering the nicely decorated city of Mathurā in a festive attitude, the ladies and girls of Mathurā prepared different kinds of flower garlands to make the ceremony more auspicious. In accordance with the Vedic custom, they took yogurt mixed with freshly grown green grass and began to strew it here and there to make the victory jubilation even more auspicious. As Kṛṣṇa passed through the street, all the ladies and women began to regard Him with great affection. Kṛṣṇa and Balarāma carried various kinds of booty, ornaments and jewels carefully collected from the battlefield and presented them to King Ugrasena. Kṛṣṇa thus offered His respect to His grandfather because he was at that time the crowned king of the Yadu dynasty.

Jarāsandha, the King of Magadha, not only besieged the city of Mathurā once, but he attacked it seventeen times in the same way, equipped with the same number of military phalanxes. Each and every time, he was defeated, and all his soldiers were killed by Kṛṣṇa, and each time he had to return disappointed in the same way. Each time, the princely order of the Yadu dynasty arrested Jarāsandha in the same way and again released him in an insulting manner, and each time Jarāsandha shamelessly returned home.

While Jarāsandha was attempting one such attack, a Yavana king somewhere to the south of Mathurā became attracted by the opulence of the Yadu dynasty and also attacked the city. It is said that the king of the Yavanas, known as Kālayavana, was induced to attack by Nārada. This story is narrated in the *Viṣṇu Purāṇa.* Once, Gargamuni, the priest of the Yadu dynasty, was taunted by his brother-in-law. When the kings of the Yadu dynasty heard the taunt they laughed at him, and Gargamuni became angry at the Yadu kings. He decided that he would produce someone who would be very fearful to the Yadu dynasty, so he pleased Lord Śiva and received from him the benediction of a son. He begot this son, Kālayavana, in the wife of a Yavana king. This Kālayavana inquired from Nārada, "Who are the most powerful kings in the world?" Nārada informed him that the Yadus were the most powerful. Being thus informed by Nārada, Kālayavana attacked the city of Mathurā at the same time that Jarāsandha attempted to attack it for the eighteenth time. Kālayavana was very anxious to declare war on a king of the world who would be a suitable combatant for him, but he had not found any. However, being informed about Mathurā by Nārada, he thought it wise to attack this city. When he attacked Mathurā he brought with him thirty million Yavana soldiers. When Mathurā was thus besieged, Lord Śrī Kṛṣṇa began to consider how much the Yadu dynasty was in distress, being threatened by the attacks of two formidable enemies, Jarāsandha and Kālayavana. Time was growing very short. Kālayavana was already besieging Mathurā from all sides, and it was expected that the next day Jarāsandha would also come, equipped with the same number of divisions of soldiers as in his previous seventeen attempts. Kṛṣṇa was certain that Jarāsandha would take advantage of the opportunity to capture Mathurā when it was also being besieged by Kālayavana. He therefore thought it wise to take precautionary measures to defend the strategic points of Mathurā. If both Kṛṣṇa and Balarāma were engaged in fighting with Kālayavana at one place, Jarāsandha might come at another place to attack the whole Yadu family and take his revenge. Jarāsandha was very powerful, and having been defeated seventeen times, he might vengefully kill the members of the Yadu family or arrest them and take them to his kingdom. Kṛṣṇa therefore decided to construct a formidable fort in a place where no two-legged animal, either man or demon, could enter. He decided to keep His relatives there so that He would then be free to fight with the enemy. It appears that formerly Dvārakā was also part of the kingdom of Mathurā, because in the *Śrīmad-Bhāgavatam* it is stated that Kṛṣṇa constructed a fort in the midst of the sea. Remnants of the fort which Kṛṣṇa constructed are still existing on the Bay of Dvārakā.

He first of all constructed a very strong wall covering ninety-six square miles, and the wall itself was within the sea. It was certainly wonderful and was planned and constructed by Viśvakarmā. No ordinary architect could construct such a fort within the sea, but an architect like Viśvakarmā, who is considered to be the engineer among the demigods, can execute such wonderful craftmanship anywhere in any part of the universe. If huge planets can be floated in weightlessness in the outer space by the arrangement of the Supreme Personality of Godhead, surely the architectural construction of a fort within the sea covering a space of ninety-six square miles was not a very wonderful act.

It is stated in the *Śrīmad-Bhāgavatam* that this new, well-constructed city, developed within the sea, had regular planned roads, streets and lanes. Not only were there well-planned roads, streets and lanes, but there were well-planned paths and gardens filled with plants known as *kalpavṛkṣas,* or desire trees. These desire trees are not like the ordinary trees of the material world; the desire trees are found in the spiritual world. By Kṛṣṇa's supreme will, everything is possible, so such desire trees were planted in this city of Dvārakā constructed by Kṛṣṇa. The city was also filled with many palaces and *gopuras,* or big gates. These *gopuras* are still found in some of the larger temples. They are very high and constructed with extreme artistic skill. Such palaces and gates held golden waterpots *(kalaśa).* These water pots on the gates or in the palaces are considered to be auspicious signs.

Almost all the palaces were skyscrapers. In each and every house there were big pots of gold and silver and grains stocked in underground rooms. And there were many golden waterpots within the rooms. The bedrooms were all bedecked with jewels, and the floors were mosiac pavements of *marakata* jewels. The Viṣṇu Deity, worshiped by the descendants of Yadu, was installed in each house in the city. The residential quarters were so arranged that the different castes, *brāhmaṇas, kṣatriyas, vaiśyas* and *śūdras,* had their respective quarters. It appears from this that the caste system was existing even at that time. In the center of the city there was another residential quarter made specifically for King Ugrasena. This place was the most dazzling of all the houses.

When the demigods saw that Kṛṣṇa was constructing a particular city of His own choice, they sent the celebrated *pārijāta* flower of the heavenly planet to be planted in the new city, and they also sent a parliamentary house, Sudharmā. The specific quality of this assembly house was that anyone participating in a meeting within it would overcome the influence of invalidity due to old age. The demigod Varuṇa also presented a horse, which was all white except for black ears and which could run at the speed of the mind. Kuvera, the treasurer of the demigods, presented the art of attaining the eight perfectional stages of material opulences. In this way, all the demigods began to present their respective gifts according to their different capacities. There are thirty-three million demigods, and each of them is entrusted with a particular department of universal management. All the demigods took the opportunity of the Supreme Personality of Godhead's constructing a city of His own choice to present their respective gifts, making the city of Mathurā unique within the universe. This proves that there are undoubtedly innumerable demigods, but none of them are independent of Kṛṣṇa. As stated in the *Caitanya-caritāmṛta,* Kṛṣṇa is the supreme master, and all others are servants. So all the servants took the opportunity of rendering service to Kṛṣṇa when He was personally present within this universe. This example should be followed by all, especially those who are Kṛṣṇa conscious, for they should serve Kṛṣṇa by their respective abilities.

When the new city was fully constructed according to plan, Kṛṣṇa transferred all the inhabitants of Mathurā and entrusted Śrī Balarāma as the city father. After this He consulted with Balarāma, and being garlanded with lotus flowers, He came out of the city to meet Kālayavana, who had already seized Mathurā without taking up any weapons.

When Kṛṣṇa came out of the city, Kālayavana, who had never seen Kṛṣṇa before, saw Him to be extraordinarily beautiful, dressed in yellow garments. Passing through His assembly of soldiers, Kṛṣṇa appeared like the moon in the sky passing through the assembled clouds. Kālayavana was fortunate enough to see the lines of *Śrīvatsa,* a particular impression on the chest of Śrī Kṛṣṇa, and the *Kaustubha* jewel which He was wearing.

Kālayavana saw Him, however, in His Viṣṇu form, with a well-built body, with four hands, and eyes like newly blooming lotus petals. Kṛṣṇa appeared blissful, with a handsome forehead and beautiful face, with smiling restless eyes and moving earrings. Before seeing Kṛṣṇa, Kālayvana had heard about Him from Nārada, and now the descriptions of Nārada were confirmed. He noticed Kṛṣṇa's specific marks and the jewels on His chest, His beautiful garland of lotus flowers, His lotus-like eyes and similarly beautiful bodily features. He concluded that this beautiful personality must be Vāsudeva, because every description of Nārada's which he had heard previously was substantiated by the presence of Kṛṣṇa. Kālayavana was very much astonished to see that He was passing through without any weapon in His hands and without any chariot. He was simply walking on foot. Kālayavana had come to fight with Kṛṣṇa, and yet he had sufficient principles not to take up any kind of weapon. He decided to fight with Him hand to hand. Thus he prepared to capture Kṛṣṇa and fight.

Kṛṣṇa, however, went ahead without looking at Kālayavana, and Kālayavana began to follow Him with a desire to capture Him. But in spite of all his swift running, he could not capture Kṛṣṇa. Kṛṣṇa cannot be captured even by the mental speed attained by great *yogīs*. He can be captured only by devotional service, and Kālayavana was not practiced in devotional service. He wanted to capture Kṛṣṇa, and as he could not do so he was following him from behind.

Kālayavana began running very fast, and he was thinking, "Now I am nearer; I will capture Him," but he could not. Kṛṣṇa led him far away, and He entered the cave of a hill. Kālayavana thought that Kṛṣṇa was trying to avoid fighting with him and was therefore taking shelter of the cave. He began to chastise Him with the following words: "Oh You, Kṛṣṇa! I heard that You are a great hero born in the dynasty of Yadu, but I see that You are verily running away from fighting, like a coward. It is not worthy of Your good name and family tradition." Kālayavana was following, running very fast, but still he could not catch Kṛṣṇa because he was not freed from all contaminations of sinful life.

According to Vedic culture, anyone who does not live following the regulative principles of life observed by the higher castes like the *brāhmaṇas, kṣatriyas, vaiśyas* and even the laborer class is called *mleccha.* The Vedic social situation is so planned that persons who are accepted as *śūdras* can gradually be elevated to the position of *brāhmaṇas* by the cultural advancement known as *saṁskāra,* or the purificatory process. The version of the Vedic scriptures is that no one becomes a *brāhmaṇa* or a *mleccha* simply by birth; by birth everyone is accepted as *śūdra.* One has to elevate himself by the purificatory process to the stage of brahminical life. If he doesn't, if he degrades himself further, then he is called *mleccha.* Kālayavana belonged to the class of *mleccha* and *yavanas.* He was contaminated by sinful activities and could not approach Kṛṣṇa. The principles from which higher class men are restricted, namely illicit sex indulgence, meat eating, gambling and intoxication, are part and parcel of the lives of the *mlecchas* and *yavanas.* Being bound by such sinful activities one cannot make any advancement in God realization. The *Bhagavad-gītā* confirms that only one who is completely freed from all sinful reactions can be engaged in devotional service or Kṛṣṇa consciousness.

When Kṛṣṇa entered the cave of the hill, Kālayavana followed, chastising Him with various harsh words. Kṛṣṇa suddenly disappeared from the demon's sight, but Kālayavana followed and also entered the cave. The first thing he saw was a man lying down asleep within the cave. Kālayavana was very anxious to fight with Kṛṣṇa, and when he could not see Kṛṣṇa, but saw instead only a man lying down, he thought that Kṛṣṇa was sleeping within this cave. Kālayavana was very puffed up and proud of his strength, and he thought Kṛṣṇa was avoiding the fight. Therefore, he very strongly kicked the sleeping man, thinking him to be Kṛṣṇa. The sleeping man had been lying down for a very long time. When he was awakened by the kicking of Kālayavana, he immediately opened his eyes and began to look around in all directions. At last he began to see Kālayavana, who was standing nearby. This man was untimely awakened and therefore very angry, and when he looked upon Kālayavana in his angry mood, rays of fire emanated from his eyes, and Kālayavana burned into ashes within a moment.

Thus ends the Bhaktivedanta purport of the Second Volume, Fifteenth Chapter of* Kṛṣṇa, *"Kṛṣṇa Erects the Dvārakā Fort."

16 / Deliverance of Mucukunda

When Mahārāja Parīkṣit heard this incident of Kālayavana's being burned to ashes, he inquired about the sleeping man from Śukadeva Gosvāmī: "Who was he? Why was he sleeping there? How had he achieved so much power that instantly, by his glance, Kālayavana was burned to ashes? How did he happen to be lying down in the cave of the hill?" Many questions were put before Śukadeva Gosvāmī, and Śukadeva also answered, as follows.

"My dear King, this person was born in the very great family of King Ikṣvāku, in which Lord Rāmacandra was also born, and he happened to be the son of a great king known as Māndhātā. He himself was also a great soul and was known popularly as Mucukunda. King Mucukunda was a very strict follower of the Vedic principles of brahminical culture, and he was truthful to his promise. He was so powerful that even demigods like Indra and others used to ask him to please help in fighting with the demons, and as such, he often fought against the demons to protect the demigods."

The commander-in-chief of the demigods, known as Kārttikeya, was satisfied with the fighting of King Mucukunda, but once he asked that the King, having taken too much trouble in fighting with the demons, retire from fighting and take rest. The commander-in-chief, Kārttikeya, addressed King Mucukunda, "My dear King, you have sacrificed everything for the sake of the demigods. You had a very nice kingdom undisturbed by any kind of enemy. You left that kingdom, you neglected your opulence and possessions, and you never cared for fulfillment of your personal ambition. Due to your long absence from your kingdom while fighting with the demons on behalf of the demigods, your family, your children, your relatives and your ministers have all passed away in due course of time. Time and tide wait for no living man. Now even if you retire to your home, you will find that no one is living there. The influence of time is very strong; all your relatives have passed away in due course of time. Time is so strong and powerful because it is a representation of the Supreme Personality of Godhead; time is therefore stronger than the strongest. By the influence of time, changes in subtle things can be effected without any difficulty. No one can check the process of time. As an animal tamer tames the animals according to his own will, so time also enters things according to its own will. None can supersede the arrangement made by the supreme time."

Thus addressing Mucukunda, the demigods requested him to ask for any kind of benediction he might be pleased with, excepting the benediction of liberation. Liberation cannot be awarded by any living entity except the Supreme Personality of Godhead, Viṣṇu. Therefore another name of Lord Viṣṇu or Kṛṣṇa is Mukunda, He who can award liberation.

King Mucukunda had not slept for many, many years. He was engaged in the duty of fighting, and therefore he was very tired. So when the demigod offered benediction, Mucukunda simply thought of sleeping. He replied as follows: "My dear Kārttikeya, the best of the demigods, I want to sleep now, and I want from you the following benediction. Grant me the power to burn, by my mere glance, anyone to ashes who tries to disturb my sleeping and awakens me untimely. Please give me this benediction." The demigod agreed and also gave him the benediction that he would be able to take complete rest. Then King Mucukunda entered the cave of the mountain.

On the strength of the benediction of Kārttikeya, Kālayavana was burnt into ashes simply by Mucukunda's glancing at him. When the incident was over, Kṛṣṇa came before King Mucukunda. Kṛṣṇa had actually entered the cave to deliver King Mucukunda from his austerity, but He did not first appear before him. He arranged that first Kālayavana should come before him. That is the way of the activities of the Supreme Personality of Godhead; He does one thing in such a way that many other purposes are served. He wanted to deliver King Mucukunda, who was sleeping in the cave, and at the same time He wanted to kill Kālayavana, who had attacked Mathurā city. By this action He served all purposes.

When Lord Kṛṣṇa appeared before Mucukunda, the King saw Him dressed in a yellow garment, His chest marked with the symbol of *Śrīvatsa*, and the *Kaustubha-maṇi* hanging around His neck. Kṛṣṇa appeared before him with four hands, as Viṣṇu-mūrti, with a garland called *vaijayantī* hanging from His neck down to His knees. He was looking very lustrous, His face was very beautifully smiling, and He had nice jeweled earrings in both His ears. Kṛṣṇa appeared more beautiful than a human can conceive.

Not only did He appear in this feature, but He glanced over Mucukunda with great splendor, attracting the King's mind. Although He was the Supreme Personality of Godhead, the oldest of all, He looked like a fresh young boy, and His movement was just like that of a free deer. He appeared extremely powerful; His excellence in power is so great that every human being should be afraid of Him.

When King Mucukunda saw Kṛṣṇa's magnificent features, he wondered about His identity, and with great humility he began to inquire from the Lord: "My dear Lord, may I inquire how it is that You happened to be in the cave of this mountain? Who are You? I can see that Your feet are just like soft lotus flowers. How could You walk in this forest full of thorns and hedges? I am simply surprised to see this! Are You not, therefore, the Supreme Personality of Godhead, who is the most powerful amongst the powerful? Are You not the original source of all illumination and fire? Can I consider You one of the great demigods, like the sun, the moon, or Indra, King of heaven? Or are You the predominating deity of any other planet?"

Mucukunda knew well that every higher planetary system has a predominating deity. He was not ignorant like modern men who consider that this earthly planet is full of living entities and all others are vacant. The inquiry from Mucukunda about Kṛṣṇa's being the predominating deity of a planet unknown to him is quite appropriate. Because he was a pure devotee of the Lord, King Mucukunda could immediately understand that Lord Kṛṣṇa, who had appeared before him in such an opulent feature, could not be one of the predominating deities in the material planets. He must be the Supreme Personality of Godhead, Kṛṣṇa, who has His many Viṣṇu forms. He therefore took Him to be Puruṣottama, Lord Viṣṇu. He could see also that the dense darkness within the mountain cave had already been dissipated due to the Lord's presence; therefore He could not be other than the Supreme Personality of Godhead. He knew very well that wherever the Lord is personally present by His transcendental name, quality, form, etc., there cannot be any darkness of ignorance. He is like a lamp placed in the darkness; He immediately illuminates a dark place.

King Mucukunda became very much anxious to know about the identity of Lord Kṛṣṇa, and therefore he said, "O best of human beings, if You think that I am fit to know about Your identity, then kindly tell me who You are. What is Your parentage? What is Your occupational duty, and what is Your family tradition?" King Mucukunda thought it wise, however, to identify himself to the Lord; otherwise he had no right to ask the Lord's identity. Etiquette is such that a person of less importance cannot ask the identity of a person of higher importance without first disclosing his own identity. King Mucukunda therefore informed Lord Kṛṣṇa, "My dear Lord, I must inform You of my identification. I belong to the most celebrated dynasty of King Ikṣvāku, but personally I am not as great as my forefather. My name is Mucukunda. My father's name was Māndhātā, and my grandfather's name was Yuvanāśva, the great king. I was very much fatigued due to not resting for many thousands of years, and because of this all my bodily limbs were flattened and almost incapable of acting. In order to revive my energy, I was taking rest in this solitary cave, but I have been awakened by some unknown man who has forced me to wake up although I was not willing to do so. For such an offensive act, this person has been burnt into ashes simply by my glancing over him. Fortunately, now I can see You in Your grand and beautiful features. I think, therefore, that You are the cause of killing my enemy. My dear Lord, I must admit that due to the effulgence of Your body, unbearable to my eyes, I cannot see You properly. I can fully realize that by the influence of Your effulgence my powerful potency has been diminished. I can understand that You are quite fit for being worshiped by all living entities."

Seeing King Mucukunda so anxious to know about His identity, Lord Kṛṣṇa began to answer smilingly, as follows: "My dear King, it is practically impossible to tell about My birth, appearance, disappearance and activities. Perhaps you know that My incarnation Anantadeva has unlimited mouths, and for an unlimited time he has been trying to narrate fully about My name, fame, qualities, activities, appearance, disappearance and incarnation, but still he has not been able to finish. Therefore, it is not possible to know exactly how many names and forms I possess. It may be possible for a material scientist to estimate the number of atomic particles which make up this earthly planet, but the scientist cannot enumerate My unlimited names, forms and activities. There are many great sages and saintly persons who are trying to make a list of My different forms and activities, yet they have failed to make a complete list. But since you are so anxious to know about Me, I may inform you that presently I have appeared on this planet just to annihilate the demoniac principles of the people in general and to reestablish the religious principles enjoined in the *Vedas*. I have been invited for this purpose by Brahmā, the superintending deity of this universe, and thus I have now appeared in the dynasty of the Yadus as one of their family members. I have specifically taken My birth as the son of Vasudeva in the Yadu Dynasty, and people therefore know Me as Vāsudeva, the son of Vasudeva. You may also know that I have killed Kaṁsa, who was in a previous life known as Kālanemi, as well as Pralambāsura and many other demons. They have acted as My enemies and have been killed by Me. The demon who was present before you also acted as My enemy, and you have very kindly burned him into ashes by glancing over him. My dear King Mucukunda, you are My great devotee, and just to show you My causeless mercy, I have appeared in this form. I am very affectionately inclined toward My devotees, and in your previous life, before your present condition, you acted as My great devotee and prayed for My causeless mercy. I have, therefore, come to see you to fulfill your desire. Now you can see Me to your heart's content. My dear King, now you can ask from Me any benediction that you wish, and I am prepared to fulfill your desire. It is my eternal principle that anyone who comes under My shelter must have all his desires fulfilled by My grace."

When Lord Kṛṣṇa ordered King Mucukunda to ask a benediction from Him, the King became very joyful, and he immediately remembered the prediction of Gargamuni, who had foretold long before that in the twenty-eighth millennium of Vaivasvata Manu, Lord Kṛṣṇa would appear on this planet. As soon as he remembered this prediction, he began to understand that the Supreme Person, Nārāyaṇa, was present before Him as Lord Kṛṣṇa. He immediately fell down at His lotus feet and began to pray as follows.

"My dear Lord, O Supreme Personality of Godhead, I can understand that all living entities on this planet are illusioned by Your external energy and are enamored of the illusory satisfaction of sense gratification. Being fully engaged in illusory activities, they are reluctant to worship Your lotus feet, and because they are unaware of the benefits of surrendering unto Your lotus feet they are subjected to various miserable conditions of material existence. They are foolishly attached to so-called society, friendship and love, which simply produce different kinds of miserable conditions. Illusioned by Your external energy, everyone, both man and woman, is attached to this material existence, and all are engaged in cheating one another in a great society of the cheaters and the cheated. These foolish persons do not know how fortunate they are to have obtained this human form of life, and they are reluctant to worship Your lotus feet. By the influence of Your external energy, they are simply attached to the glare of material activities. They are attached to so-called society, friendship and love like dumb animals that have fallen into a dark well." The example of a dark well is given because in the fields there are many wells, unused for years and covered over by grass, and the poor animals, without knowing of them, fall into them, and unless they are rescued, they die. Being captivated by a few blades of grass, the animals fall into a dark well and meet death. Similarly, foolish persons, without knowing the importance of the human form of life, spoil it simply for sense gratification and die unnecessarily, without any useful purpose.

"My dear Lord, I am not an exception to this universal law of material nature. I am also one of those foolish persons who has wasted his time for nothing. And my position is especially difficult. On account of my being situated in the royal order, I was more puffed up than ordinary persons. An ordinary man thinks of becoming the proprietor of his body or of his family, but I began to think in that way on a larger scale. I wanted to be the master of the whole world, and as I became puffed up with ideas of sense gratification, my bodily concept of life became stronger and stronger. My attachment for home, wife and children, for money and for supremacy over the world, became more and more acute; in fact, it was limitless. So I remained always attached to thoughts of my material living conditions.

Therefore, my dear Lord, I wasted so much of my valuable lifetime without any benefit. My misconception of life having been intensified, I began to think of this material body, which is just a bag of flesh and bones, as the all in all, and in my vanity I was like a dog who believes that he has become the king of human society. In this misconception of bodily life, I began to travel all over the world, accompanied by my military strength—soldiers, charioteers, elephants and horses. Assisted by many commanders and puffed up by power, I could not trace out Your Lordship, who is always sitting within my heart as the most intimate friend. I did not care for You, and this was the fault of my so-called exalted material condition. I think that, like me, all living creatures are careless about spiritual realization and are always full of anxieties, thinking, 'What is to be done?' 'What is next?' But because we are strongly bound by material desires, we continue to remain in craziness.

"Yet in spite of our being so absorbed in material thought, inevitable time, which is only a form of Yourself, is always careful about its duty, and as soon as the allotted time is over, Your Lordship immediately ends all the activities of our material dreams. As the time factor, You end all our activities, as the hungry blacksnake swiftly swallows up a small rat without any leniency. Due to the action of cruel time, the royal body which was always decorated with gold ornaments during life and which moved on a chariot drawn by beautiful horses or on the back of an elephant nicely decorated with golden ornaments, and which was advertised as the king of human society—that same royal body decomposes under the influence of inevitable time and becomes fit for being eaten by worms and insects or being turned into ashes or the stool of an animal.

This beautiful body may be nice while in the living condition, but after death even the body of a king is eaten by an animal and therefore turns into stool or is cremated in the crematorium and turned into ashes or is put into an earthly grave where different kinds of worms and insects are produced out of it.

"My dear Lord, not only do we become under the full control of this inevitable time after death, but also while living, in a different way. For example, I may be a powerful king, and yet when I come home after conquering over the world I become subjected to many material conditions. It may be that when I come back after being victorious all subordinate kings come and offer their respects, but as soon as I enter into the inner section of my palace, I myself become an instrument in the hands of the queens, and for sense gratification I have to fall down at the feet of women. The material way of life is so complicated that before taking the enjoyment of material life one has to work so hard that there is scarcely an opportunity for enjoying. And to attain the youthful condition with all material facilities one has to undergo severe austerities and penances and become elevated to the heavenly planets. If one gets the opportunity of taking birth in a very rich or royal family, even then in that condition he is always anxious to maintain the status quo and prepare for the next life by performing various kinds of sacrifices and by distributing charity. Even in the royal condition of life one is not only full of anxieties because of political administration, but he is also in anxiety over being elevated to heavenly planets.

"It is therefore very difficult to get out of the material entanglement, but somehow or other if one is favored by You, by Your mercy only he is given the opportunity to associate with a pure devotee. That is the beginning point of liberation from the entanglement of material conditional life. My dear Lord, only by the association of pure devotees is one entrapped by Your Lordship, who is the controller of both the material and spiritual existences. You are the supreme goal of all pure devotees, and by association with pure devotees one can develop his dormant love for You. Therefore, development of Kṛṣṇa consciousness in the association of pure devotees is the cause of liberation from this material entanglement.

"My dear Lord, You are so merciful that in spite of my being reluctant to associate with Your great devotees You have shown Your extreme mercy upon me as a result of my slight contact with a pure devotee like Gargamuni. By Your causeless mercy only have I lost all my material opulences, my kingdom and my family. I do not think that I could have gotten rid of all these entanglements without Your causeless mercy. Kings and emperors accept the life of austerity to forget the royal condition of life, but by Your special causeless mercy I have already been bereft of the royal condition. Other kings exert themselves to get out of the attachment of kingdom and family by acceptance of the hardships of renunciation, but by Your mercy I do not need to become a mendicant or to practice renunciation.

"My dear Lord, I therefore pray that I may simply be engaged in rendering transcendental loving service unto Your lotus feet, which is the ambition of the pure devotees who are freed from all kinds of material contamination. You are the Supreme Personality of Godhead, and You can offer me anything I want, including liberation. But who is such a foolish person that after pleasing You he would ask from You something which might be the cause of entanglement in this material world? I do not think any sane man would ask such a benediction from You. I therefore surrender unto You because You are the Supreme Personality of Godhead, You are the Supersoul living in everyone's heart, and You are the impersonal Brahman effulgence. Moreover, You are also this material world, because this material world is only the manifestation of Your external energy. Therefore, from any angle of vision, You are the supreme shelter for everyone. Everyone, either in the material plane or in the spiritual plane, must take shelter under Your lotus feet. I therefore submit unto You, my Lord. For many, many births I have been suffering from the threefold miseries of this material existence, and I am now tired of it. I have simply been impelled by my senses, and I was never satisfied. I therefore take shelter of Your lotus feet, which are the source of all peaceful conditions of life and which can eradicate all kinds of lamentation caused by material contamination. My dear Lord, You are the Supersoul of everyone, and You can understand everything. Now I am free from all contamination of material desire. I do not wish to enjoy this material world, nor do I wish to take advantage of merging into Your spiritual effulgence, nor do I wish to meditate upon Your localized aspect of Paramātmā, for I know that simply by taking shelter of You, I shall become completely peaceful and undisturbed."

On hearing this statement of King Mucukunda, Lord Kṛṣṇa replied, "My dear King, I am very much pleased with your statement. You have been the King of all the lands on this planet, but I am surprised to find that your mind is now freed from all material contamination. You are now fit to execute devotional service. I am most pleased to see that although I offered you the opportunity of asking from Me any kind of benediction, you did not take advantage of asking for material benefit. I can understand that your mind is now fixed in Me, and it is not disturbed by any material fault.

"The material qualities are three, namely goodness, passion and ignorance. When one is placed in the mixed material qualities of passion and ignorance, he is impelled by various kinds of dirtiness and lusty desires to try to find comfort in this material world. When he is situated in the material quality of goodness, he tries to purify himself by performing various kinds of penances and austerities. When one reaches the platform of a real *brāhmaṇa,* he aspires to merge into the existence of the Lord, but when one desires simply to render service unto the lotus feet of the Lord, that is transcendental to all these three qualities. The pure Kṛṣṇa conscious person is therefore always free from all material qualities. My dear King, I offered to give you any kind of benediction, just to test how much you have advanced in devotional service. Now I can see that you are on the platform of the pure devotees because your mind is not disturbed by any kind of greedy or lusty desires of this material world. The *yogīs* who are trying to elevate themselves by controlling the senses and who meditate upon Me by practicing the breathing exercise of *prāṇāyāma* are not so thoroughly freed from material desires. It has been seen in several cases that as soon as there is allurement, such *yogīs* again come down to the material platform."

The vivid example verifying this statement is Viśvāmitra Muni. Viśvāmitra Muni was a great *yogī* who practiced *prāṇāyāma,* a breathing exercise, but still when he was visited by Menakā, a society woman of the heavenly planet, he lost all control and begot in her a daughter named Śakuntalā. But the pure devotee Haridāsa Ṭhākur was never disturbed, even when all such allurements were offered by the prostitutes.

"My dear King," Lord Kṛṣṇa continued, "I therefore give you the special benediction that you will always think of Me. Thus you will be able to traverse this material world freely, without being contaminated by the qualities." This statement of the Lord confirms that a person in true Kṛṣṇa consciousness, engaged in the transcendental loving service of the Lord under the direction of the spiritual master, is never subjected to the contamination of material qualities.

"My dear King," the Lord said, "because you are a *kṣatriya,* you have committed the offense of slaughtering animals, both in hunting and in political engagements. To become purified, just engage yourself in *bhakti-yoga* practice and always keep your mind absorbed in Me. Very soon you will be freed from all reactions to such sordid activities." In this statement it appears that although the *kṣatriyas* are allowed to kill animals in the hunting process, they are not freed from the contamination of other sinful reactions. Therefore it does not matter whether one is *kṣatriya, vaiśya,* or *brāhmaṇa;* everyone is recommended to take *sannyāsa* at the end of life, to engage himself completely in the service of the Lord and thus become freed from all sinful reactions of his past life.

The Lord then assured King Mucukunda, "In your next life you will take your birth as a first-class Vaiṣṇava, the best of *brāhmaṇas,* and in that life your only business will be to engage yourself in My transcendental service." The Vaiṣṇava is the first-class *brāhmaṇa,* because one who has not acquired the qualification of a bona fide *brāhmaṇa* cannot come to the platform of a Vaiṣṇava. When one comes to the platform of a Vaiṣṇava, he is completely engaged in welfare activities for all living entities. The highest welfare activity for living entities is the preaching of Kṛṣṇa consciousness. It is stated herein that those who are specifically favored by the Lord can become absolutely Kṛṣṇa conscious and be engaged in the preaching work of the Vaiṣṇava philosophy.

Thus ends the Bhaktivedanta purport of the Second Volume, Sixteenth Chapter of Kṛṣṇa, *"Deliverance of Mucukunda."*

17 / Kṛṣṇa, the Ranchor

When Mucukunda, the celebrated descendant of the Ikṣvāku dynasty, was favored by Lord Kṛṣṇa, he circumambulated the Lord within the cave and then came out. On coming out of the cave, Mucukunda saw that the stature of the human species had surprisingly been reduced to pigmy size. Similarly, the trees had also far reduced in size, and Mucukunda could immediately understand that the current age was Kali-yuga. Therefore, without diverting his attention, he began to travel north. Eventually he reached the mountain known as Gandhamādana. It appeared there were many trees on this mountain, such as sandalwood and other flower trees, the flavor of which made anyone joyful who reached them. He decided to remain in that Gandhamādana Mountain region in order to execute austerities and penances for the rest of his life. It appears that this place is situated in the northernmost part of the Himalayan Mountains, where the abode of Nara-Nārāyaṇa is situated. This place is still existing and is called Badarikāśrama. In Badarikāśrama he engaged himself in the worship of Lord Kṛṣṇa, forgetting all pain and pleasure and the other dualities of this material world. Lord Kṛṣṇa also returned to the vicinity of the city of Mathurā and began to fight with the soldiers of Kālayavana and kill them one after another. After this, He collected all the booty from the dead bodies, and under His direction, it was loaded on bullock carts by big men and brought back to Dvārakā.

Meanwhile, Jarāsandha again attacked Mathurā, this time with bigger divisions of soldiers, numbering twenty-three *akṣauhiṇīs.*

Lord Śrī Kṛṣṇa wanted to save Mathurā from the eighteenth attack of the great military divisions of King Jarāsandha. In order to prevent further killing of soldiers and to attend to other important business, Lord Kṛṣṇa left the battlefield without fighting. Actually He was not at all afraid, but He pretended to be an ordinary human being frightened by the immense quantity of soldiers and resources of Jarāsandha. Without any weapons He left the battlefield. Although His lotus feet were as soft as the petals of the lotus flower, He proceeded for a very long distance on foot.

This time, Jarāsandha thought that Kṛṣṇa and Balarāma were very much afraid of His military strength and were fleeing from the battlefield. He began to follow Them with all his chariots, horses and infantry. He thought Kṛṣṇa and Balarāma to be ordinary human beings, and he was trying to measure the activities of the Lord. Kṛṣṇa is known as Ranchor, which means "one who has left the battlefield." In India, especially in Gujarat, there are many temples of Kṛṣṇa which are known as temples of Ranchorjī. Ordinarily, if a king leaves the battlefield without fighting he is called a coward, but when Kṛṣṇa enacts this pastime, leaving the battlefield without fighting, He is worshiped by the devotee. A demon always tries to measure the opulence of Kṛṣṇa, whereas the devotee never tries to measure His strength and opulence, but always surrenders unto Him and worships Him. By following the footsteps of pure devotees we can know that Kṛṣṇa, the Ranchorjī, did not leave the battlefield because He was afraid, but because He had some other purpose. The purpose, as it will be revealed, was to attend to a confidential letter sent by Rukmiṇī, His future first wife. The act of Kṛṣṇa's leaving the battlefield is a display of one of His six opulences. Kṛṣṇa is the supreme powerful, the supreme wealthy, the supreme famous, the supreme wise, the supreme beautiful; similarly He is the supreme renouncer. *Śrīmad-Bhāgavatam* clearly states that He left the battlefield in spite of having ample military strength. Even without His militia, however, He alone would have been sufficient to defeat the army of Jarāsandha, as He had done seventeen times before. Therefore, His leaving the battlefield is an example of His supermost opulence of renunciation.

After traversing a very long distance, the brothers pretended to become very tired. To mitigate Their weariness They climbed up a very high mountain several miles above sea level. This mountain was called Pravarṣaṇa due to constant rain. The peak was always covered with clouds sent by Indra. Jarāsandha took it for granted that the two brothers were afraid of his military power and had hidden Themselves at the top of the mountain. First he tried to find Them, searching for a long time, but when he failed he decided to trap and kill Them by setting fires around the peak. He therefore surrounded the peak with oil and set it on fire. As the blaze spread more and more, Kṛṣṇa and Balarāma jumped from the top of the mountain down to the ground—a distance of eighty-eight miles. Thus, while the peak was burning up, Kṛṣṇa and Balarāma escaped without being seen by Jarāsandha. Jarāsandha concluded that the two brothers had been burned to ashes and that there was no need of further fighting. Thinking himself successful in his efforts, he left the city of Mathurā and returned to his home in the kingdom of Magadha. Gradually Kṛṣṇa and Balarāma reached the city of Dvārakā, which was surrounded on all sides by the sea.

Following this, Śrī Balarāma married Revatī, daughter of King Raivata, ruler of the Ānarta province. This is explained in the Ninth Canto of *Śrīmad-Bhāgavatam.* After the marriage of Baladeva, Kṛṣṇa married Rukmiṇī. Rukmiṇī was the daughter of King Bhīṣmaka, ruler of the province known as Vidarbha. Just as Kṛṣṇa is the Supreme Personality of Godhead, Vāsudeva, Rukmiṇī is the supreme goddess of fortune, Mahā-Lakṣmī According to the authority of *Caitanya-caritāmṛta,* the expansion of Kṛṣṇa and Śrī Rādhārāṇī is simultaneous; Kṛṣṇa expands Himself into various *Viṣṇu-tattva* forms, and Śrīmatī Rādhārāṇī expands Herself into various *śakti-tattva* forms by Her internal potency, as multi-forms of the goddess of fortune.

According to Vedic convention, there are eight kinds of marriages. In the first-class marriage system, the parents of the bride and bridegroom arrange the marriage date. Then, in royal style, the bridegroom goes to the house of the bride, and in the presence of *brāhmaṇas,* priests and relatives, the bride is given in charity to the bridegroom. Besides this, there are other systems, such as the *gandharva* and *rākṣasa* marriages. Rukmiṇī was married to Kṛṣṇa in the *rākṣasa* style because she was kidnapped by Him in the presence of His many rivals, like Śiśupāla, Jarāsandha, Śālva and others. While Rukmiṇī was being given in charity to Śiśupāla, she was snatched from the marriage arena by Kṛṣṇa, exactly as Garuḍa snatched the pot of nectar from the demons. Rukmiṇī, the only daughter of King Bhīṣmaka, was exquisitely beautiful. She was known as Rucirānanā, which means "one who has a beautiful face, expanding like a lotus flower."

Devotees of Kṛṣṇa are always anxious to hear about the transcendental activities of the Lord. His activities of fighting, kidnapping and running away from the battlefield are all transcendental, being on the absolute platform, and devotees take a transcendental interest in hearing of them. The pure devotee does not make the distinction that some activities of the Lord should be heard and others should be avoided. There is, however, a class of so-called devotees known as *prākṛta sahajiyā* who are very interested in hearing about Kṛṣṇa's *rāsa-līlā* with the *gopīs,* but not about His fighting activities with His enemies. They do not know that His bellicose activities and His friendly activities with the *gopīs* are equally transcendental, being on the absolute platform. The transcendental pastimes of

Kṛṣṇa described in the *Śrīmad-Bhāgavatam* are relished by pure devotees through submissive aural reception. They do not reject even a drop.

The story of Kṛṣṇa's marriage with Rukmiṇī is described as follows. The King of Vidarbha, Mahārāja Bhīṣmaka, was a very qualified and devoted prince. He had five sons and only one daughter. The first son was known as Rukmī; the second, Rukmaratha; the third, Rukmabāhu; the fourth and youngest, Rukmakeśa; and the fifth, Rukmamālī. The brothers had one young sister, Rukmiṇī. She was beautiful and chaste and was meant to be married to Lord Kṛṣṇa. Many saintly persons and sages like Nārada Muni and others used to visit the palace of King Bhīṣmaka. Naturally Rukmiṇī had a chance to talk with them, and in this way she obtained information about Kṛṣṇa. She was informed about the six opulences of Kṛṣṇa, and simply by hearing about Him, she desired to surrender herself to His lotus feet and become His wife. Kṛṣṇa had also heard of Rukmiṇī. She was the reservoir of all transcendental qualities: intelligence, liberal-mindedness, exquisite beauty and righteous behavior. Kṛṣṇa therefore decided that she was fit to be His wife. All of the family members and relatives of King Bhīṣmaka decided that Rukmiṇī should be given in marriage to Kṛṣṇa. However her elder brother, Rukmī, despite the desire of the others, arranged for her marriage with Śiśupāla, a determined enemy of Kṛṣṇa. When the black-eyed, beautiful Rukmiṇī heard the settlement, she immediately became very morose. However, being a king's daughter, she understood political diplomacy and decided that there was no use in simply becoming morose. Some steps should be taken immediately. After some deliberation, she decided to send a message to Kṛṣṇa, and so that she might not be deceived, she selected a qualified *brāhmaṇa* as her messenger. Such a qualified *brāhmaṇa* is always truthful and is a devotee of Viṣṇu. Without delay, the *brāhmaṇa* was sent to Dvārakā.

Reaching the gate of Dvārakā, the *brāhmaṇa* informed the doorkeeper of his arrival, and the doorkeeper led him to the place where Kṛṣṇa was sitting on a golden throne. Since the *brāhmaṇa* had the opportunity of being Rukmiṇī's messenger, he was fortunate enough to see the Supreme Personality of Godhead, Kṛṣṇa, who is the original cause of all causes. A *brāhmaṇa* is the spiritual teacher of all the social divisions. Lord Śrī Kṛṣṇa, in order to teach everyone the Vedic etiquette of how to respect a *brāhmaṇa*, immediately got up and offered him His throne. When the *brāhmaṇa* was seated on the golden throne, Lord Śrī Kṛṣṇa began to worship him exactly in the manner in which the demigods worship Kṛṣṇa. In this way, He taught everyone that worshiping His devotee is more valuable than worshiping Himself.

In due time, the *brāhmaṇa* took his bath, accepted his meals and took to rest on a bedstead completely bedecked with soft silk. As he was resting, Lord Śrī Kṛṣṇa silently approached and, with great respect, put the *brāhmaṇa's* legs on His lap and began to massage them. In this way, Kṛṣṇa appeared before the *brāhmaṇa* and said, "My dear *brāhmaṇa*, I hope that you are executing the religious principles without any difficulty and that your mind is always in a peaceful condition." Different classes of people in the social system are engaged in various professions, and when one inquires as to the well-being of a particular person, it must be done on the basis of that person's occupation. Therefore, when one inquires as to the welfare of a *brāhmaṇa*, the questions should be worded according to his condition of life so as not to disturb him. A peaceful mind is the basis for becoming truthful, clean, equipoised, self-controlled and tolerant. Thus by attaining knowledge and knowing its practical application in life, one becomes convinced about the Absolute Truth. The *brāhmaṇa* knew Kṛṣṇa to be the Supreme Personality of Godhead, and still he accepted the respectful service of the Lord on the grounds of Vedic social convention. Lord Śrī Kṛṣṇa was playing just like a human being. Belonging to the *kṣatriya* division of the social system, and being a young boy, it was His duty to show respect to such a *brāhmaṇa*.

Lord Kṛṣṇa continued: "O best of all the *brāhmaṇas*, you should always remain satisfied because if a *brāhmaṇa* is always self-satisfied he will not deviate from his prescribed duties; and simply by sticking to one's prescribed duties, everyone, especially the *brāhmaṇas*, can attain the highest perfection of all desires. Even if a person is as opulent as the King of heaven, Indra, if he is not satisfied he inevitably has to transmigrate from one planet to another. Such a person can never be happy under any circumstances; but if a person's mind is satisfied, even if he is bereft of his high position, he can be happy living anywhere and everywhere."

This instruction of Kṛṣṇa to the *brāhmaṇa* is very significant. The purport is that a true *brāhmaṇa* should not be disturbed in any situation. In this modern age of Kali-yuga, the so-called *brāhmaṇas* have accepted the abominable position of the *śūdras* or less than *śūdras* and still want to pass as qualified *brāhmaṇas*. Actually, a qualified *brāhmaṇa* always sticks to his own duties and never accepts those of a *śūdra* or of one less than a *śūdra*. It is advised in the authorized scriptures that a *brāhmaṇa* may, under awkward circumstances, accept the profession of a *kṣatriya* or even a *vaiśya*, but never is he to accept the profession of a *śūdra*. Lord Kṛṣṇa declared that a *brāhmaṇa* should never be disturbed by any adverse conditions of life if he scrupulously sticks to his religious principles. In conclusion, Lord Śrī Kṛṣṇa said: "I offer My respectful obeisances to the *brāhmaṇas* and Vaiṣṇavas, because the *brāhmaṇas* are always self-satisfied, and the Vaiṣṇavas are always engaged in actual welfare activities for the human society. They are the best friends of the people in general; both are free from false egoism and are always in a peaceful condition of mind."

Lord Kṛṣṇa then desired to know about the rulers (*kṣatriyas*) in the *brāhmaṇa's* kingdom, so He inquired whether the citizens of the kingdom were all happy. A king's qualification is judged by the temperament of the people in the kingdom. If they are very happy in all respects, it is to be understood that the king is honest and executing his duties rightly. Kṛṣṇa said that the king in whose kingdom the citizens are happy is very dear to Him. Of course Kṛṣṇa could understand that the *brāhmaṇa* had come with a confidential message; therefore he said, "If you have no objection, I am giving you permission to speak about your mission." Thus, being very satisfied by these transcendental pastimes with the Lord, the *brāhmaṇa* narrated the whole story of his mission to come and see Kṛṣṇa. He got out the letter which Rukmiṇī had written to Kṛṣṇa and said, "These are the words of Princess Rukmiṇī: 'My dear Kṛṣṇa, O infallible and most beautiful one, any human being who happens to hear about Your transcendental form and pastimes immediately absorbs through his ears Your name, fame and qualities; thus all his material pangs subside, and he fixes Your form in his heart. Through such transcendental love for You, he sees You always within himself; and by this process all his desires become fulfilled. Similarly, I have heard of Your transcendental qualities. I may be shameless in expressing myself so directly, but You have captivated me and taken my heart. You may suspect that I am an unmarried girl, young in age, and may doubt my steadiness of character, but my dear Mukunda, You are the supreme lion among the human beings, the supreme person among persons. Any girl, although not yet out of her home, or any woman who may be of the highest chastity, would desire to marry You, being captivated by Your unprecedented character, knowledge, opulence and position. I know that You are the husband of the goddess of fortune and that You are very kind toward Your devotees; therefore I have decided to become Your eternal maidservant. My dear Lord, I dedicate my life and soul unto Your lotus feet. I have accepted Your Lordship as my selected husband, and I therefore request You to accept me as Your wife. You are the supreme powerful, O lotus-eyed one. Now I belong to You. If that which is enjoyable for the lion to eat is taken away by the jackal, it will be a ludicrous affair; therefore I request You to immediately take care of me before I am taken away by Śiśupāla and other princes like him.

My dear Lord, in my previous life I may have done public welfare work like digging wells and growing trees, or pious activities such as performing ritualistic ceremonies and sacrifices and serving the superior spiritual master, the *brāhmaṇas* and Vaiṣṇavas. By these activities, perhaps I have pleased the Supreme Personality of Godhead, Nārāyaṇa. If this is so, then I wish that You, Lord Kṛṣṇa, the brother of Lord Balarāma, would please come here and catch hold of my hand so that I may not be touched by Śiśupāla and his company.'"

Rukmiṇī's marriage with Śiśupāla was already settled; therefore she suggested that Kṛṣṇa kidnap her so that this might be changed. This sort of marriage, in which the girl is kidnapped by force, is known as *rākṣasa* and is practiced among the *kṣatriyas,* or the administrative, martial spirited type of men. Because her marriage was already arranged to take place the next day, Rukmiṇī suggested that Kṛṣṇa come there incognito to kidnap her and then fight with Śiśupāla and his allies like the King of Magadha. Knowing that no one could conquer Kṛṣṇa and that He would certainly emerge victorious, she addressed Him as Ajita—the unconquerable. Rukmiṇī told Kṛṣṇa not to be concerned that many of her family members, including other women, might be wounded or even killed if the fighting took place within the palace. As the king of a country thinks of diplomatic ways to achieve his object, similarly Rukmiṇī, being the daughter of a king, was diplomatic in suggesting how this unnecessary and undesirable killing could be avoided.

She explained that it was the custom of her family to visit the temple of the goddess Durgā, their family deity, before a marriage. (The *kṣatriya* kings were mostly staunch Vaiṣṇavas, worshiping Lord Viṣṇu in either the Rādhā-Kṛṣṇa or Lakṣmī-Nārāyaṇa form; still, for their material welfare, they used to worship the goddess Durgā. They never made the mistake, however, of accepting the demigods as the Supreme Lord on the level of *Viṣṇu-tattva,* as did some of the less intelligent men.) In order to avoid the unnecessary killing of her relatives, Rukmiṇī suggested that it would be easiest for Him to kidnap her while she was either going from the palace to the temple or else while she was returning home.

She also explained to Kṛṣṇa why she was so anxious to be married to Him, even though her marriage was to take place with Śiśupāla, who was also qualified, being the son of a great king. Rukmiṇī said that she did not think anyone was greater than Kṛṣṇa, not even Lord Śiva, who is known as Mahādeva, the greatest of all demigods. Lord Śiva also seeks the pleasure of Lord Kṛṣṇa in order to be delivered from his entanglement in the quality of ignorance within the material world. In spite of the fact that Lord

Śiva is the greatest of all great souls, *mahātmās,* he keeps on his head the purifying water of the Ganges, which emanates from a hole in this material universe made by the toe of Lord Viṣṇu. Lord Śiva is in charge of the material quality of ignorance, and in order to keep himself in a transcendental position, he always meditates on Lord Viṣṇu. Therefore Rukmiṇī knew very well that obtaining the favor of Kṛṣṇa was not an easy job. If even Lord Śiva must purify himself for this purpose, surely it would be difficult for Rukmiṇī, who was only the daughter of a *kṣatriya* king. Thus she desired to dedicate her life to observing severe austerities and penances, such as fasting and going without bodily comforts. If it were not possible in this lifetime to gain Kṛṣṇa's favor by these activities, she was prepared to do the same lifetime after lifetime. In the *Bhagavad-gītā* it is said that pure devotees of the Lord execute devotional service with great determination. Such determination, as exhibited by Rukmiṇīdevī, is the only price for purchasing Kṛṣṇa's favor and is the way to ultimate success in Kṛṣṇa consciousness.

After explaining Rukmiṇīdevī's statement to Kṛṣṇa, the *brāhmaṇa* said: "My dear Kṛṣṇa, chief of the Yadu dynasty, I have brought this confidential message for You from Rukmiṇī; now it is placed before You for Your consideration. After due deliberation You can act as You please, but if You want to do something, You must do it immediately. There is not much time left for action."

Thus ends the Bhaktivedanta purport of the Second Volume, Seventeenth Chapter of* Kṛṣṇa, *"Kṛṣṇa, the Ranchor."

18 / Kṛṣṇa Kidnaps Rukmiṇī

After hearing Rukmiṇī's statement, Lord Kṛṣṇa was very pleased. He immediately shook hands with the *brāhmaṇa* and said: "My dear *brāhmaṇa,* I am very glad to hear that Rukmiṇī is anxious to marry Me, since I am also anxious to get her hand. My mind is always absorbed in the thought of the daughter of Bhīṣmaka, and sometimes I cannot sleep at night because I am thinking of her. I can understand that the marriage of Rukmiṇī with Śiśupāla has been arranged by her elder brother in a spirit of animosity toward Me; so I am determined to give a good lesson to all of these princes. Just as fire is extracted and utilized after manipulating ordinary wood, similarly, after dealing with these demoniac princes, I shall bring forth Rukmiṇī, like fire, from their midst."

Kṛṣṇa, upon being informed of the specific date of Rukmiṇī's marriage, became anxious to leave immediately. He asked His driver, Dāruka, to harness the horses for His chariot and prepare to go to the kingdom of Vidarbha. The driver, just after hearing this order, brought Kṛṣṇa's four special horses. The names and descriptions of these horses are mentioned in the *Padma Purāṇa.* The first one, Śaivya, was greenish; the second, Sugrīva, was grayish like ice; the third, Meghapuṣpa, was the color of a new cloud; and the last, Balāhaka, was of ashen color. When the horses were yoked and the chariot ready to go, Kṛṣṇa helped the *brāhmaṇa* up and gave him a seat by His side. Immediately they started from Dvārakā and within one night arrived at the province of Vidarbha. The kingdom of Dvārakā is situated in the western part of India, and Vidarbha is situated in the northern part. They are separated by a distance of not less than 1,000 miles, but the horses were so fast that they reached their destination, a town called Kuṇḍina, within one night, or at most, twelve hours.

King Bhīṣmaka was not very enthusiastic about handing his daughter over to Śiśupāla, but he was obliged to accept the marriage settlement due to his affectionate attachment for his eldest son, who had negotiated it. As a matter of duty, he was decorating the city for the marriage ceremony and was acting in great earnestness to make it very successful. Water was sprinkled all over the streets, and the city was cleansed very nicely. Since India is situated in the tropical zone, the atmosphere is always dry. Due to this, dust always accumulates on the streets and roads; so they must be sprinkled with water at least once a day, and in big cities like Calcutta, twice a day. The roads of Kuṇḍina were arranged with colored flags and festoons, and gates were constructed at particular crossings. The whole city was decorated very nicely. The beauty of the city was enhanced by the inhabitants, both men and women, who were dressed in washed cloth, decorated with sandalwood pulp, pearl necklaces and flower garlands. Incense was burning everywhere, and fragrances like *aguru* scented the air. Priests and *brāhmaṇas* were sumptuously fed and, according to ritualistic ceremony, were given sufficient wealth and cows in charity. In this way, they were engaged in chanting Vedic hymns. The King's daughter, Rukmiṇī, was exquisitely beautiful. She was very clean and had beautiful teeth. The auspicious sacred girdle was tied on her wrist. She was given various types of jewelry to put on and long silken cloth to cover the upper and lower parts of her body. Learned priests gave her protection by chanting *mantras* from the *Sāma Veda, Ṛg Veda* and *Yajur Veda.* After this they chanted *mantras* from the *Atharva Veda* and offered oblations in the fire to pacify the ominous conjunctions of different stars.

King Bhīṣmaka was very experienced in dealing with the *brāhmaṇas* and priests when such ceremonies were held. He specifically distinguished the *brāhmaṇas* by giving them large quantities of gold and silver, grains mixed with molasses, and cows decorated with golden ornaments. Damaghoṣa, Śiśupāla's father, executed all kinds of ritualistic performances to invoke good fortune for his own family. Śiśupāla's father was known as Damaghoṣa due to his superior ability to cut down unregulated citizens. *Dama* means curbing down, and *ghoṣa* means famous; so he was famous for controlling the citizens. Damaghoṣa thought that if Kṛṣṇa came to disturb the marriage ceremony, he would certainly cut Him down with his military power. Therefore, after performing the various auspicious ceremonies, Damaghoṣa gathered his military divisions, known as Madasravi. He took many elephants, garlanded with golden necklaces, and many chariots and horses which were similarly decorated. It appeared that Damaghoṣa, along with his son and other companions, was going to Kuṇḍina, not completely forgetting the marriage, but mainly intent on fighting.

When King Bhīṣmaka learned that Damaghoṣa and his party were arriving, he left the city to receive them. Outside the city gate there were many gardens where the guests were welcomed to stay. In the Vedic system of marriage, the bride's father receives the large party of the bridegroom and accommodates them in a suitable place for two or three days until the marriage ceremony is performed. The party led by Damaghoṣa contained thousands of men, among whom the prominent kings and personalities were Jarāsandha, Dantavakra, Vidūratha and Pauṇḍraka. It was an open secret that Rukmiṇī was meant to be married to Kṛṣṇa but that her elder brother, Rukmī, had arranged her marriage to Śiśupāla. There was also some whispering going on about a rumor that Rukmiṇī had sent a messenger to Kṛṣṇa; therefore the soldiers suspected that Kṛṣṇa might cause a disturbance by attempting to kidnap Rukmiṇī. Even though they were not without fear, they were all prepared to give Kṛṣṇa a nice fight in order to prevent the girl from being taken away. Śrī Balarāma received the news that Kṛṣṇa had left for Kuṇḍina accompanied only by a *brāhmaṇa;* He also heard that Śiśupāla was there with a large number of soldiers. Suspecting that they would attack Kṛṣṇa, Balarāma took strong military divisions of chariots, infantry, horses and elephants and arrived at the precinct of Kuṇḍina.

Meanwhile, inside the palace, Rukmiṇī was expecting Kṛṣṇa to arrive, but when neither He nor the *brāhmaṇa* who took her message appeared, she became full of anxiety and began to think how unfortunate she was. "There is only one night between today and my marriage day, and still neither the *brāhmaṇa* nor Śyāmasundara has returned. I cannot ascertain any reason for this." Having little hope, she thought perhaps Kṛṣṇa had found reason to become dissatisfied and had rejected her fair proposal. As a result, the *brāhmaṇa* might have become disappointed and not come back. Although she was thinking of various causes for the delay, she expected them both at every moment.

Rukmiṇī further began to think that demigods such as Lord Brahmā, Lord Śiva and the goddess Durgā might have been displeased. It is generally said that the demigods become angry when they are not properly worshiped. For instance, when Indra found that the inhabitants of Vṛndāvana were not worshiping him (Kṛṣṇa having stopped the Indra-yajña), he became very angry and wanted to chastise them. Thus Rukmiṇī was thinking that since she did not worship Lord Śiva or Lord Brahmā very much, they might have become angry and tried to frustrate her plan. Similarly she thought that the goddess Durgā, the wife of Lord Śiva, might have taken the side of her husband. Lord Śiva is known as Rudra, and his wife is known as Rudrāṇī. Rudrāṇī and Rudra refer to those who are very accustomed to putting others in a distressed condition so they might cry forever. Rukmiṇī was thinking of the goddess Durgā as Girijā, the daughter of the Himalayan Mountains. The Himalayan Mountains are very cold and hard, and she thought of the goddess Durgā as hardhearted and cold. In her anxiety to see Kṛṣṇa, Rukmiṇī, who was after all still a child, thought this way about the different demigods. The *gopīs* worship goddess Kātyāyanī to get Kṛṣṇa as their husband; similarly Rukmiṇī was thinking of the various types of demigods, not for material benefit, but in respect to Kṛṣṇa. Praying to the demigods to achieve the favor of Kṛṣṇa is not irregular, and Rukmiṇī was fully absorbed in thoughts of Kṛṣṇa.

Even though she pacified herself by thinking that the time for Govinda to arrive had not yet expired, Rukmiṇī felt that she was hoping against hope. She began to shed tears, and when they became more forceful, she closed her eyes in helplessness. While Rukmiṇī was in such deep thought, auspicious symptoms appeared in different parts of her body. Trembling began to occur in her left eyelid and in her arms and thighs. When trembling occurs in these parts of the body, it is an auspicious sign indicating that something lucrative can be expected.

Just then, Rukmiṇī, full of anxiety, saw the *brāhmaṇa* messenger. Kṛṣṇa, being the Supersoul of all living beings, could understand Rukmiṇī's anxiety; therefore he sent the *brāhmaṇa* inside the palace to let her know that He had arrived. When Rukmiṇī saw the *brāhmaṇa,* she could understand the auspicious trembling of her body and immediately became elated. She smiled and inquired from him whether or not Kṛṣṇa had already come. The *brāhmaṇa* replied that the son of the Yadu dynasty, Śrī Kṛṣṇa, had arrived; he further encouraged her by saying that Kṛṣṇa had promised to carry her away without fail. Rukmiṇī was so elated by the *brāhmaṇa's* message that she wanted to give him in charity everything she possessed. However, finding nothing suitable for presentation, she simply offered him her respectful obeisances. The significance of offering respectful obeisances to a superior is that the one offering obeisances is obliged to the respected person. In other words, Rukmiṇī implied that she would remain ever grateful to the *brāhmaṇa.* Anyone who gets the favor of the goddess of fortune, as did this *brāhmaṇa,* is without a doubt always happy in material opulence.

When King Bhīṣmaka heard that Kṛṣṇa and Balarāma had come, he invited Them to see the marriage ceremony of his daughter. Immediately he arranged to receive Them, along with Their soldiers, in a suitable garden house. As was the Vedic custom, the King offered Kṛṣṇa and

Balarāma honey and fresh washed cloth. He was hospitable not only to Kṛṣṇa, Balarāma and kings such as Jarāsandha, but he also received many other kings and princes according to their respective personal strength, age and material possessions. Out of curiosity and eagerness, the people of Kuṇḍina assembled before Kṛṣṇa and Balarāma and began to drink the nectar of Their beauty. With tearful eyes, they offered Them their silent respects. They were very pleased, considering Lord Kṛṣṇa the suitable match for Rukmiṇī. They were so eager to unite Kṛṣṇa and Rukmiṇī that they began to pray to the Personality of Godhead: "My dear Lord, if we have performed any pious activities that You are satisfied with, kindly be merciful upon us and accept the hand of Rukmiṇī." It appears that Rukmiṇī was a very popular princess, and all the citizens, out of intense love for her, prayed for her best fortune. In the meantime, Rukmiṇī, being very nicely dressed and protected by bodyguards, came out of the palace to visit the temple of Ambikā, the goddess Durgā.

Deity worship in the temple has been in existence since the beginning of Vedic culture. There is a class of men described in the *Bhagavad-gītā* as the *veda-vāda-rata;* they only believe in the Vedic ritualistic ceremonies, but not in the temple worship. Such foolish people may here take note that although this marriage of Kṛṣṇa and Rukmiṇī took place more than 5,000 years ago, there were arrangements for temple worship. In the *Bhagavad-gītā* the Lord says, *yānti deva-vratā devān:* "The worshipers of the demigods attain the abodes of the demigods." There were many people who worshiped the demigods and many who directly worshiped the Supreme Personality of Godhead. The system of demigod worship was directed mainly to Lord Brahmā, Lord Siva, Lord Gaṇeśa, the sun-god and the goddess Durgā. Lord Śiva and the goddess Durgā were worshiped even by the royal families; other minor demigods were worshiped by silly inferior people. As far as the *brāhmaṇas* and Vaiṣṇavas are concerned, they simply worship Lord Viṣṇu, the Supreme Personality of Godhead. In the *Bhagavad-gītā* the worship of demigods is condemned, but not forbidden; there it is clearly stated that the less intelligent class of men worship the different kinds of demigods for material benefit. On the other hand, even though Rukmiṇī was the goddess of fortune, she went to the temple of the goddess Durgā because the family deity was worshiped there. In the *Śrīmad-Bhāgavatam* it is stated that as Rukmiṇī was proceeding towards the temple of the goddess Durgā, within her heart she was always thinking of the lotus feet of Kṛṣṇa. Therefore when Rukmiṇī went to the temple it was not with the intention of an ordinary person, who goes to beg for material benefits; her only target was Kṛṣṇa. When people go to the temple of a demigod, the objective is actually Kṛṣṇa, since it is He who empowers the demigods to provide material benefits.

As Rukmiṇī proceeded toward the temple, she was very silent and grave. Her mother and her girl friend were by her side, and the wife of a *brāhmaṇa* was in the center; surrounding her were royal bodyguards. (This custom of a would-be bride going to the temple of a demigod is still practiced in India.) As the procession continued, various musical sounds were heard. Drums, conchshells, and bugles of different sizes such as *paṇavas, turyas* and *bheris* combined to make a sound which was not only auspicious but very sweet to hear. There were thousands of wives of respectable *brāhmaṇas* present. These women were all dressed very nicely with suitable ornaments. They presented Rukmiṇī with flower garlands, sandalwood pulp and a variety of colorful garments to assist her in worshiping Lord Śiva and the goddess Durgā. Some of these ladies were very old and knew perfectly well how to chant prayers to the goddess Durgā and Lord Siva; so, followed by Rukmiṇī and others, they led these prayers before the deity.

Rukmiṇī offered her prayers to the deity by saying, "My dear goddess Durgā, I offer my respectful obeisances unto you as well as to your children." The goddess Durgā has four famous children: two daughters–the goddess of fortune, Lakṣmī, and the goddess of learning, Sarasvatī–and two famous sons, Lord Gaṇeśa and Lord Kārttikeya. They are all considered to be demigods and goddesses. Since the goddess Durgā is always worshiped along with her famous children, Rukmiṇī specifically offered her respectful obeisances to the deity in that way; however her prayers were different. Ordinary people pray to the goddess Durgā for material wealth, fame, profit, strength and so on; Rukmiṇī, however, desired to have Kṛṣṇa for her husband and therefore prayed to the deity to be pleased upon her and bless her. Since she desired only Kṛṣṇa, her worship of the demigods is not condemned. While Rukmiṇī was praying, a variety of items were presented before the deity, chief of which were water, different kinds of flames, incense, garments, garlands and various foodstuffs prepared with ghee, such as *puris* and *kacuris.* There were also fruits, sugar cane, betel nuts and spices offered. With great devotion, Rukmiṇī offered them to the deity according to the regulative principles directed by the old *brāhmaṇa* ladies. After this ritualistic ceremony, the ladies offered the remnants of the foodstuffs to Rukmiṇī as *prasādam,* which she accepted with great respect. Then Rukmiṇī offered her obeisances to the ladies and to the goddess Durgā. After the business of deity worship was finished, Rukmiṇī caught hold of the hand of one of her girl friends and left the temple, accompanied by the others.

All the princes and visitors who came to Kuṇḍina for the marriage were assembled outside the temple to see Rukmiṇī. The princes were especially very eager to see her because they all actually thought that they would have Rukmiṇī as their wife. Struck with wonder upon seeing Rukmiṇī, they thought that she was specially manufactured by the Creator to bewilder all the great chivalrous princes. Her body was well-constructed, the middle portion being thin. She had green eyes, pink lips, and a beautiful face which was enhanced by her scattered hair and by different kinds of earrings. Around her feet she wore jeweled lockets. The bodily luster and beauty of Rukmiṇī appeared as if painted by an artist perfectly presenting beauty following the description of great poets. The breast of Rukmiṇī is described as being a little bit high, indicating that she was just a youth not more than thirteen or fourteen years old. Her beauty was specifically intended to attract the attention of Krsna. Although the princes gazed upon her beautiful features, she was not at all proud. Her eyes moved restlessly, and when she smiled very simply, like an innocent girl, her teeth appeared just like lotus flowers. Expecting Kṛṣṇa to take her away at any moment, she proceeded very slowly towards her home. Her legs moved just like a full-grown swan, and her ankle bells tinkled very mildly.

As already explained, the great chivalrous princes who assembled there were so overwhelmed by Rukmiṇī's beauty that they almost became unconscious. Full of lust, they hopelessly desired Rukminī's hand, comparing their own beauty with hers. Śrīmatī Rukminī, however, was not interested in any of them; in her heart she was simply expecting Kṛṣṇa to come and carry her away. As she was adjusting the ornaments on her left-hand finger, she happened to look upon the princes and suddenly saw that Kṛṣṇa was present amongst them. Although Rukmiṇī had never before seen Kṛṣṇa, she was always thinking of Him; thus she had no difficulty in recognizing Him amongst the princely order. Kṛṣṇa, not being concerned with the other princes, immediately took the opportunity of placing Rukmiṇī on His chariot, marked by a flag bearing an image of Garuda. He then proceeded slowly, without fear, taking away Rukminī exactly as the lion takes the deer from the midst of the jackals. Meanwhile Balarāma appeared on the scene with the soldiers of the Yadu dynasty.

Jarāsandha, who had many times experienced defeat by Kṛṣṇa, began to roar: "How is this? Kṛṣṇa is taking Rukmiṇī away from us without any opposition! What is the use in our being chivalrous fighters with arrows? My dear princes, just look! We are losing our reputation by this action. It is just like the jackal taking away the booty from the lion."

Thus ends the Bhaktivedanta purport of the Second Volume, Eighteenth Chapter of* Kṛṣṇa, *"Kṛṣṇa Kidnaps Rukmiṇī."

19 / Kṛṣṇa Defeats All the Princes and Takes Rukmiṇī Home to Dvārakā

All the princes led by Jarāsandha became very angry at Kṛṣṇa's kidnapping Rukmiṇī. Struck by the beauty of Rukmiṇī, they had fallen from the backs of their horses and elephants, but now they began to stand up and properly arm themselves. Picking up their bows and arrows, they began to chase Kṛṣṇa on their chariots, horses and elephants. To check their progress, the soldiers of the Yadu dynasty turned and faced them. Thus terrible fighting between the two belligerant groups began. The princes opposing Kṛṣṇa were led by Jarāsandha, and they were all very expert in fighting. They began to shoot their arrows at the soldiers of Yadu just as a cloud splashes the face of a mountain with torrents of rain. Gathered on the face of a mountain, a cloud does not move very much, and therefore the force of rain is much more severe on a mountain than it is anywhere else.

The opposing princes were determined to defeat Kṛṣṇa and recapture Rukmiṇī from His custody, and they fought with Him as severely as possible. Rukmiṇī, seated by the side of Kṛṣṇa, saw arrows raining from the opposing party onto the faces of the soldiers of Yadu. In a fearful attitude, she began to look on the face of Kṛṣṇa, expressing her gratefulness that He had taken such a great risk for her sake only. Her eyes moving, she appeared to be very sorry, and Kṛṣṇa could immediately understand her mind. He encouraged her with these words: "My dear Rukmiṇī, don't worry. Please rest assured that the soldiers of the Yadu dynasty will kill all the opposing soldiers without delay."

As Kṛṣṇa was speaking with Rukmiṇī, the commanders of the Yadu dynasty's soldiers, headed by Lord Balarāma, who is also known as Saṅkarṣaṇa, as well as by Gadadhara, not tolerating the defiant attitude of the opposing soldiers, began to strike their horses, elephants, and chariots with arrows. As the fighting progressed, the princes and soldiers of the enemy camp began to fall from their horses, elephants and chariots. Within a very short time, it was seen that millions of severed heads, decorated with helmets and earrings, had fallen on the battlefield. The soldiers' hands were cut up along with their bows and arrows and clubs; one head was piled upon another, and one horse was piled upon another. All the infantry soldiers, as well as their camels, elephants and asses, fell down with severed heads.

When the enemy, headed by Jarāsandha, found that they were gradually being defeated by the soldiers of Kṛṣṇa, they thought it unwise to risk losing in the battle for the sake of Śiśupāla. Śiśupāla himself should have fought to rescue Rukmiṇī from the hands of Kṛṣṇa, but when the soldiers saw that Śiśupāla was not competent enough to fight with Kṛṣṇa, they decided not to lose their strength unnecessarily; therefore they ceased fighting and dispersed.

Some of the princes, as a matter of etiquette, appeared before Śiśupāla. They saw that Śiśupāla was very much discouraged, like one who has lost his wife. His face appeared to be dried up, he had lost all his energy, and all the luster of his body had disappeared. They began to address Śiśupāla thus: "My dear Śiśupāla, don't be discouraged in this way. You belong to the royal order and are the chief amongst the fighters. There is no question of distress or happiness for a person like you because neither of these conditions is everlasting. Take courage. Don't be disappointed by this temporary reverse. After all, we are not the final actor; as puppets dance in the hands of a magician, we are all dancing by the will of the Supreme, and according to His grace only we suffer distress or enjoy happiness, which therefore balance equally in all circumstances."

The whole catastrophe of the defeat was due to the envious nature of Rukmiṇī's elder brother, Rukmī. Having seen his sister forcibly taken away by Kṛṣṇa after he had planned to marry her with Śiśupāla, Rukmī was frustrated. So he and Śiśupāla, his friend and intended brother-in-law, returned to their respective homes. Rukmī, very much agitated, was determined to personally teach Kṛṣṇa a lesson. He called for his own soldiers—a military phalanx consisting of several thousand elephants, horses, chariots and infantry—and, equipped with this military strength, he began to follow Kṛṣṇa to Dvārakā. In order to show his prestige, Rukmī began to promise before all the returning kings, "You could not help Śiśupāla marry my sister Rukmiṇī, but I cannot allow Rukmiṇī to be taken away by Kṛṣṇa. I shall teach Him a lesson. Now I am going there." He presented himself as a big commander and vowed before all the princes present, "Unless I kill Krsna in the fight and bring back my sister from

His clutches, I shall no more return to my capital city, Kuṇḍina. I make this vow before you all, and you will see that I shall fulfill it." After thus vibrating all these boasting words, Rukmī immediately got on his chariot and told his chariot driver to pursue Kṛṣṇa. He said, "I want to fight with Him immediately. This cowherd boy has become very proud because of His tricky way of fighting with the *kṣatriyas,* but today I shall teach Him a good lesson. Because He has the impudency to kidnap my sister, I, with my sharpened arrows, shall teach Him very good lessons indeed." Thus this unintelligent man, Rukmī, ignorant of the extent of the strength and activities of the Supreme Personality of Godhead, began to voice impudent threats.

In great stupidity he soon stood before Kṛṣṇa, telling Him repeatedly, "Stop for a minute and fight with me!" After saying this he drew his bow and directly shot three forceful arrows against Kṛṣṇa's body. Then he condemned Kṛṣṇa as the most abominable descendant of the Yadu dynasty and asked Him to stand before him for a minute so that he could teach Him a good lesson. "You are carrying away my sister just like a crow stealing clarified butter meant for use in a sacrifice. You are simply proud of Your military strength, but You cannot fight according to regulative principles. You have stolen my sister; now I shall relieve You of Your false prestige. You can keep my sister under Your possession only as long as I do not pinion You to the ground for good with my arrows."

Lord Kṛṣṇa, after hearing all these crazy words from Rukmī, immediately shot an arrow and severed the string of Rukmī's bow, making him unable to use another arrow. Rukmī immediately took another bow and shot another five arrows at Kṛṣṇa. Being attacked for the second time by Rukmī, Kṛṣṇa again severed his bowstring. Rukmī took a third bow, and Kṛṣṇa again cut off its string. This time, in order to teach Rukmī a lesson, Kṛṣṇa personally shot six arrows at him, and then He shot another eight arrows. Thus four horses were killed by four arrows, the chariot driver was killed by another arrow, and the upper portion of Rukmī's chariot, including the flag, was chopped off with the remaining three arrows.

Having run out of arrows, Rukmī took the assistance of swords, shields, tridents, lances and similar other weapons used for fighting hand-to-hand, but Kṛṣṇa immediately severed them all in the same way. Being repeatedly baffled in his attempts, Rukmī simply took his sword and ran very swiftly toward Kṛṣṇa, just as a fly proceeds toward a fire. As soon as Rukmī reached Kṛṣṇa, Kṛṣṇa cut his weapon to pieces. This time Kṛṣṇa took out His sharp sword and was about to kill him immediately, but Rukmī's sister Rukmiṇī, understanding that this time Kṛṣṇa would not excuse her brother, fell down at the lotus feet of Kṛṣṇa and in a very grievous tone, trembling with great fear, began to plead with her husband.

Rukmiṇī first addressed Kṛṣṇa as "Yogeśvara." Yogeśvara means one who is possessed of inconceivable opulence and energy. Kṛṣṇa possesses inconceivable opulence and energy, whereas Rukmiṇī's brother had only limited military potency. Kṛṣṇa is immeasurable, whereas her brother was measured in every step of his life. Therefore, Rukmī was not even comparable to an insignificant insect before the unlimited power of Kṛṣṇa. She also addressed Kṛṣṇa as the God of the gods. There are many powerful demigods, such as Lord Brahmā, Lord Śiva, Indra, and Candra; Kṛṣṇa is the Lord of all these gods, whereas Rukmiṇī's brother was not only an ordinary human being, but was, in fact, the lowest of all because he had no understanding of Kṛṣṇa. In other words, a human being who has no conception of the actual position of Kṛṣṇa is the lowest in human society. Rukmiṇī also addressed Kṛṣṇa as "Jagatpati," the master of the whole cosmic manifestation. In comparison, her brother was only an ordinary prince.

In this way, Rukmiṇī compared the position of Rukmī to that of Kṛṣṇa and very feelingly pleaded with her husband not to kill her brother just before the auspicious time of her being united with Kṛṣṇa, but to excuse him. In other words, she displayed her real position as a woman. She was happy to get Kṛṣṇa as her husband just at the moment when her marriage to another was to be performed, but she did not want it to be at the loss of her elder brother, who, after all, loved his young sister and wanted to hand her over to one who was, according to his own calculations, a better man. While Rukmiṇī was praying to Kṛṣṇa for the life of her brother, her whole body trembled, and because of her anxiety, her face appeared to be dried up, her throat became choked, and, due to her trembling, the ornaments on her body loosened and fell scattered on the ground. Lord Kṛṣṇa immediately became compassionate and agreed not to kill the foolish Rukmī. But, at the same time, He wanted to give him some light punishment, so He tied him up with a piece of cloth and snipped at his moustache, beard and hair, keeping some spots here and there.

While Kṛṣṇa was dealing with Rukmī in this way, the soldiers of the Yadu dynasty, commanded by Balarāma Himself, broke the whole strength of Rukmī's army just as an elephant in a tank discards the feeble stem of a lotus flower. In other words, as an elephant breaks the whole construction of a lotus flower while bathing in the reservoir of water, so the military strength of the Yadus broke up Rukmī's forces. Yet when the commanders of the Yadu dynasty came back to see Kṛṣṇa, they were all surprised to see the condition of Rukmī. Lord Balarāma became especially compassionate for His sister-in-law, who was newly married to His brother. In order to please Rukmiṇī, Balarāma personally untied Rukmī, and in order to further please her, Balarāma, as the elder brother of Kṛṣṇa, spoke some words of chastisement. "Kṛṣṇa, Your action is not at all satisfactory," He said. "This is an abomination very much contrary to our family tradition! To cut someone's hair and shave his moustache and beard is almost comparable to killing him. Whatever Rukmī might have been, he is now our brother-in-law, a relative of our family, and You should not have put him in such a condition."

After this, in order to pacify her, Lord Balarāma said to Rukmiṇī, "You should not be sorry because your brother has been made very odd-looking. Everyone suffers or enjoys the results of his own actions." Lord Balarāma wanted to impress upon Rukmiṇī that she should not have been sorry for the consequences suffered by her brother due to his actions. There was no need of being too affectionate toward such a brother. Lord Balarāma again turned toward Kṛṣṇa and said, "My dear Kṛṣṇa, a relative, even though he commits such a blunder and deserves to be killed, should be excused. For when such a relative is conscious of his own fault, that consciousness itself is like death. Therefore, there is no need in killing him." He again turned toward Rukmiṇī and informed her that the current duty of the *kṣatriya* in the human society is so fixed that, according to the principles of fighting, one's own brother may become an enemy on the opposite side. A *kṣatriya* does not hesitate to kill his own brother. In other words, Lord Balarāma wanted to instruct Rukmiṇī that Rukmī and Kṛṣṇa were right in not showing mercy to each other in the fighting, despite the family consideration that they happened to be brothers-in-law. Śrī Balarāma continued to inform Rukmiṇī that *kṣatriyas* are typical emblems of the materialistic way of life; they become puffed-up whenever there is a question of material acquisition. Therefore, when there is a fight between two belligerent *kṣatriyas* on account of kingdom, land, wealth, women, prestige or power, they try to put one another into the most abominable condition. Balarāma instructed Rukmiṇī that her affection toward her brother Rukmī, who had created enmity with so many persons, was a perverse consideration befitting an ordinary materialistic person. Her brother's character was not at all adorable, considering his treatment toward other friends, and yet Rukmiṇī, as an ordinary woman, was so affectionate toward him. He was not fit to be her brother, and still Rukmiṇī was lenient toward him.

"Besides that," Balarāma continued, "the consideration that a person is neutral or is one's friend or enemy is generally made by persons who are in the bodily concept of life. Such foolish persons become bewildered by the illusory energy of the Supreme Lord. The spirit soul is of the same pure quality in any embodiment of matter, but those who are not sufficiently intelligent see only the bodily differentiations of animals and men, literates and illiterates, rich and poor, and so on, which cover the pure spirit soul. Such differentiation, observed purely on the basis of the body, is exactly like differentiation between fires in terms of the different types of fuel they consume. Whatever the size and shape of the fuel, there is no such variety of size and shape of the fire which comes out. Similarly, in the sky there are no differences in size or shape."

In this way Balarāma appeased them by His moral and ethical instruction. He stated further: "This body is part of the material manifestation. The living entity or spirit soul, being in contact with matter, is transmigrating, due to illusory enjoyment, from one body to another, and that is known as material existence. This contact of the living entity with the material manifestation has neither integration nor disintegration. My dear chaste sister-in-law, the spirit soul is, of course, the cause of this material body, as much as the sun is the cause of sunlight, eyesight and the forms of material manifestation. The example of the sunshine and the material manifestation is very appropriate in the matter of understanding the living entities' contact with this material world. In the morning, there is sunrise, and the heat and light expand gradually throughout the whole day. The sun is the cause of all material production and shapes and forms; it is due to the sun that integration and disintegration of material elements take place. But as soon as the sun is set, the whole manifestation is no longer connected to the sun, which has passed from one place to another. When the sun passes from the eastern to the western hemisphere, the result of interaction due to the sunshine in the eastern hemisphere remains, but the sunshine itself is visible again on the western hemisphere. Similarly, the living entity accepts or produces different bodies and different bodily relationships in a particular circumstance, but as soon as he gives up the present body and accepts another, he has nothing to do with the former body. Similarly, the living entity has nothing to do with the next body which he accepts. He is always free from the contact of this bodily contamination. Therefore, the conclusion is that the appearance and disappearance of the body have nothing to do with the living entity, as much as the waxing and waning of the moon have nothing to do with the moon. When there is waxing of the moon, we falsely think that the moon is developing, and when there is waning of the moon we think that the moon is decreasing. Factually the moon, as it is, is always the same; it has nothing to do with such visible waxing and waning activities.

"Consciousness of material existence can be compared to sleeping and dreaming. When a man sleeps, he dreams of many nonfactual happenings, and as a result of dreaming he becomes subjected to different kinds of distress and happiness. Similarly, when a person is in the dreaming condition of material consciousness, he suffers the effects of accepting a body and giving it up again in material existence. Opposite to this material consciousness is Kṛṣṇa consciousness. In other words, when a man is elevated to the platform of Kṛṣṇa consciousness he becomes free from this false conception of life."

In this way, Śrī Balarāma instructed them in spiritual knowledge. He addressed his sister-in-law thus: "Sweet, smiling Rukmiṇī, do not be aggrieved by false motives caused by ignorance. Due to false notions only one becomes unhappy, but this unhappiness is immediately removed by discussing the philosophy of actual life. Be happy on that platform only."

After hearing such enlightening instruction from Śrī Balarāma, Rukmiṇī immediately became pacified and happy and adjusted her mental condition, which was very much afflicted by seeing the degraded position of her brother, Rukmī. As far as Rukmī was concerned, neither was his promise fulfilled nor his mission successful. He had come from home with his soldiers and military phalanx to defeat Kṛṣṇa and release his sister, but on the contrary, he lost all his soldiers and military strength. He was personally much degraded, and in that condition he was very sorry; but by the grace of the Lord he could continue his life to the fixed destination. Because he was a *kṣatriya,* he could remember his promise that he would not return to his capital city, Kuṇḍina, without killing Kṛṣṇa and releasing his sister, which he had failed to do; therefore, he decided in anger not to return to his capital city, and he constructed a small cottage in the village known as Bhojakaṭa and began to reside there for the rest of his life.

After defeating all the opposing elements and forcibly carrying away Rukmiṇī, Kṛṣṇa brought her to His capital city, Dvārakā, and then married her according to the Vedic ritualistic principle. After this marriage, Kṛṣṇa became the King of the Yadus at Dvārakā. On the occasion of His marriage with Rukmiṇī, all the inhabitants were happy, and in every house there were great ceremonies. The inhabitants of Dvārakā City became so pleased that they dressed themselves with the nicest possible ornaments and garments, and they went to present gifts according to their means to the newly married couple, Kṛṣṇa and Rukmiṇī. All the houses of Yadupurī

(Dvārakā) were decorated with flags, festoons and flowers. Each and every house had an extra gate specifically prepared for this occasion, and on both sides of the gate there were big water jugs filled with water. The whole city was flavored by the burning of high quality incense, and at night there was illumination by thousands of lamps, decorating each and every building.

The entire city appeared jubilant on the occasion of Lord Kṛṣṇa's marriage with Rukmiṇī. Everywhere in the city there was profuse decoration of banana trees and betel nut trees. These two trees are considered very auspicious in happy ceremonies. At the same time there was an assembly of many elephants, who carried the respective kings of different friendly kingdoms. It is the habit of the elephant that whenever he sees some small plants and trees, out of his sportive frivolous nature, he uproots the trees and throws them hither and thither. The elephants assembled on this occasion also scattered the banana and betel nut trees, but in spite of such intoxicated action, the whole city, with the trees thrown here and there, looked very nice.

The friendly kings of the Kurus and the Pāṇḍavas were represented by Dhṛtarāṣṭra, the five Pāṇḍu brothers, King Drupada, King Santardana, as well as Rukmiṇī's father, Bhīṣmaka. Because of Kṛṣṇa's kidnapping Rukmiṇī, there was initially some misunderstanding between the two families, but Bhīṣmaka, King of Vidarbha, being approached by Śrī Balarāma and persuaded by many saintly persons, was induced to participate in the marriage ceremony of Kṛṣṇa and Rukmiṇī. Although the incidence of Kṛṣṇa's kidnapping was not a very happy occurrence in the kingdom of Vidarbha, kidnapping was not an unusual affair among the *kṣatriyas.* Kidnapping was, in fact, current in almost all marriages. Anyway, King Bhīṣmaka was from the very beginning inclined to hand over his beautiful daughter to Kṛṣṇa. In one way or another his purpose had been served, and so he was pleased to join the marriage ceremony, even though his eldest son was degraded in the fight. It is mentioned in the *Padma Purāṇa* that Mahārāja Nanda and the cowherd boys of Vṛndāvana joined the marriage ceremony. Kings from the kingdoms of Kuru, Sṛñjaya, Kekaya, Vidarbha and Kunti came to Dvārakā on this occasion with all their royal paraphernalia.

The story of Rukmiṇī's being kidnapped by Kṛṣṇa was poeticized, and the professional readers recited it everywhere. All the assembled kings and, especially, their daughters were struck with wonder and became very pleased upon hearing the chivalrous activities of Kṛṣṇa. In this way, all visitors as well as the inhabitants of Dvārakā City became joyful seeing Kṛṣṇa and Rukmiṇī together. In other words, the Supreme Lord, the maintainer of everyone, and the goddess of fortune were united, and all the people felt extremely jubilant.

Thus ends the Bhaktivedanta purport of the Second Volume, Nineteenth Chapter of* Kṛṣṇa, *"Kṛṣṇa Defeats All the Princes and Takes Rukmiṇī Home to Dvārakā."

20 / Pradyumna Born to Kṛṣṇa and Rukmiṇī

It is said that Cupid, who is directly part and parcel of Lord Vāsudeva and who was formerly burnt to ashes by the anger of Lord Śiva, took birth in the womb of Rukmiṇī begotten by Kṛṣṇa. This is Kāmadeva, a demigod of the heavenly planets especially capable of inducing lusty desires. The Supreme Personality of Godhead, Kṛṣṇa, has many grades of parts and parcels, but the quadruple expansions of Kṛṣṇa—Vāsudeva, Saṅkarṣaṇa, Pradyumna and Aniruddha—are directly in the Viṣṇu category. Kāma, or the Cupid demigod, who later on took his birth in the womb of Rukmiṇī, was also named Pradyumna, but he cannot be the Pradyumna of the Viṣṇu category. He belongs to the category of *jīva-tattva,* but for special power in the category of demigods, he was a part and parcel of the super prowess of Pradyumna. That is the verdict of the Gosvāmīs. Therefore, when Cupid was burnt into ashes by the anger of Lord Śiva he merged into the body of Vāsudeva, and in order to get his body again, he was begotten by Lord Kṛṣṇa Himself; he was directly released from his body in the womb of Rukmiṇī and was born as the son of Kṛṣṇa, celebrated by the name Pradyumna. Because he was begotten by Lord Kṛṣṇa directly, his qualities were most similar to those of Kṛṣṇa.

There was a demon of the name Śambara who was destined to be killed by this Pradyumna. The Śambara demon knew of his destiny, and as soon as he learned that Pradyumna was born, he took the shape of a woman and kidnapped the baby from the maternity home less than ten days after his birth. The demon took him and threw him directly into the sea. But, as it is said, "Whoever is protected by Kṛṣṇa, no one can kill; and whoever is destined to be killed by Kṛṣṇa, no one can protect." When Pradyumna was thrown in the sea, a big fish immediately swallowed him. Later on this fish was caught by the net of a fisherman, and the fish was later on sold to the Śambara demon. In the kitchen of the demon there was a maidservant whose name was Māyāvatī. This woman had formerly been the wife of Cupid, and had been called Rati. When the fish was presented to the demon Śambara, it was taken charge of by his cook, who was to make it into a palatable fish preparation. Demons and the *rākṣasas* are accustomed to eat meat, fish and similar non-vegetarian foods. Similarly, other demons, like Rāvaṇa, Kaṁsa and Hiraṇyakaśipu, although born of *brāhmaṇa* and *kṣatriya* fathers, used to take meat and flesh without discrimination. This practice is still prevalent in India, and those who are meat and fish eaters are generally called demons and *rākṣasas*.

When the cook was cutting the fish, he found a nice baby within the belly of the fish, and he immediately presented him to the charge of Māyāvatī, who was an assistant in the kitchen affairs. This woman was surprised to see how such a nice baby could remain within the belly of a fish, and the situation perplexed her. The great sage Nārada then appeared and explained to her about the birth of Pradyumna, how the baby had been taken away by Śambara and later on thrown into the sea, and so on. In this way the whole story was disclosed to Māyāvatī, who had formerly been Rati, the wife of Cupid. Māyāvatī knew that she had previously been the wife of Cupid; after her husband was burnt into ashes by the wrath of Lord Śiva, she was always expecting him to come back again in the material form. This woman was engaged for cooking rice and dahl in the kitchen, but when she got this nice baby and understood that he was Cupid, her own husband, she naturally took charge of him and with great affection began to bathe him. Miraculously, the baby very swiftly grew up, and within a very short period he became a very beautiful young man. His eyes were just like the petals of lotus flowers, his arms were very long, down to the knees, and any woman who happened to see him became captivated by his bodily beauty.

Māyāvatī could understand that her former husband, Cupid, born as Pradyumna, had grown into such a nice young man, and she also gradually became captivated and lusty. She was smiling before him with a feminine attractiveness, expressing her desire for sexual unity. He therefore inquired from her, "How is it possible that first of all you were affectionate like a mother, and now you are expressing the symptoms of a lusty woman? What is the reason for such a change?" On hearing this statement from Pradyumna, the woman, Rati, replied, "My dear sir, you are the son of Lord Kṛṣṇa. Before you were ten days old, you were stolen by the Śambara demon and later on thrown into the water and swallowed up by a fish. In this way you have come under my care, but actually, in your former life as Cupid, I was your wife; therefore, my manifestation of conjugal symptoms is not at all incompatible. Śambara wanted to kill you, and he is endowed with various kinds of mystic powers. Therefore, before he again attempts to kill you, please kill him as soon as possible with your divine power. Since you were stolen by Śambara, your mother, Rukmiṇīdevī, has been in a very grievous condition, like a cuckoo bird who has lost her babies. She is very affectionate toward you, and since you have been taken away from her, she has been living like a cow aggrieved over the loss of its calf."

Māyāvatī had mystic knowledge of supernatural power. Supernatural powers are generally known as *māyā,* and to supersede all such supernatural power there is another supernatural power, which is called *mahāmāyā.* Māyāvatī had the knowledge of the mystic power of *mahāmāyā,* and she delivered to Pradyumna this specific energetic power in order to defeat the mystic powers of the Śambara demon. Thus being empowered by his wife, Pradyumna immediately went before Śambara and challenged him to fight. Pradyumna began to address him in very strong language, so that his temper might be agitated and he would be moved to fight. At Pradyumna's words, the demon Śambara, being insulted, felt just like a snake feels after being struck by one's leg. A serpent cannot tolerate being kicked by another animal or by a man, and he immediately bites the opponent.

Śambara felt the words of Pradyumna as if they were a kick. He immediately took his club in his hand and appeared before Pradyumna to fight. In great anger, he began to beat Pradyumna with his club, just as a thunderbolt beats a mountain. The demon was also groaning and making a noise like a thundering cloud. Pradyumna protected himself with his own club, and eventually he struck the demon very severely. In this way, the fighting between Śambarāsura and Pradyumna began very seriously.

But Śambarāsura knew the art of mystic powers and could raise himself in the sky and fight from outer space. There is another demon of the name Maya, and Śambarāsura learned many mystic powers from him. He thus raised himself high in the sky and began to throw various types of nuclear weapons at the body of Pradyumna. In order to combat the mystic powers or Śambarāsura, Pradyumna remembered another mystic power, known as *mahāvidyā,* which was different from the black mystic power. The *mahāvidyā* mystic power is based on the quality of goodness. Understanding that his enemy was formidable, Śambara took assistance from various kinds of demonic mystic powers belonging to the *Guhyakas,* the *Gandharvas,* the *Piśācas,* the snakes and the *Rākṣasas.* But although the demon exhibited his mystic powers and took shelter of supernatural strength, Pradyumna was able to counteract his strength and powers by the superior power of *mahāvidyā.* When Śambarāsura was defeated in every respect, Pradyumna then took his sharpened sword and immediately cut off the demon's head, which was decorated with a helmet and with valuable jewels. When Pradyumna thus killed the demon, all the demigods in the higher planetary systems began to shower flowers on him.

Pradyumna's wife, Māyāvatī, could travel in outer space, and therefore they directly reached his father's capital, Dvārakā, by the airways. They passed above the palace of Lord Kṛṣṇa and began to come down as a cloud comes down with lightning. The inner section of a palace is known as *antaḥpura* (private apartments). Pradyumna and Māyāvatī could see that there were many women there, and they sat down among them. When the women saw Pradyumna, dressed in bluish garments, with very long arms, curling hair, beautiful eyes, a smiling reddish face, jewelry and ornaments, they first of all could not recognize him as Pradyumna, a personality different from Kṛṣṇa. They all felt themselves to be very much blessed by the sudden presence of Kṛṣṇa, and they wanted to hide in a different corner of the palace.

When the women saw, however, that all the characteristics of Kṛṣṇa were not present in the personality of Pradyumna, out of curiosity they came back again to see him and his wife, Māyāvatī. All of them were conjecturing as to who he was, for he was so beautiful. Among the women was Rukmiṇīdevī, who was equally beautiful, with her lotus-like eyes. Seeing Pradyumna, she naturally remembered her own son, and milk began to flow from her breast out of motherly affection. She then began to wonder, "Who is this beautiful young boy? He appears to be the most beautiful person. Who is the fortunate young woman able to give birth to this nice boy in her womb and become his mother? And who is that young woman who has accompanied him? How have they met? Remembering my own son, who was stolen even from the maternity home, I can only guess that if he is living somewhere, he might have grown by this time to be like this boy." Simply by intuition, Rukmiṇī could understand that Pradyumna was her own lost son. She could also observe that Pradyumna resembled Lord Kṛṣṇa in every respect. She was struck with wonder as to how he acquired all the symptoms of Kṛṣṇa. She therefore began to think more confidently that the boy must be her own grown-up son because she felt much affection for him, and, as an auspicious sign, her left arm was trembling.

At that very moment, Lord Kṛṣṇa, along with His father and mother, Devakī and Vasudeva, appeared on the scene. Kṛṣṇa, the Supreme Personality of Godhead, could understand everything, yet in that situation He remained silent. However, by the desire of Lord Śrī Kṛṣṇa, the great sage Nārada also appeared on the scene, and he began to disclose all the incidences–how Pradyumna had been stolen from the maternity home and how he had grown up and had come there with his wife Māyāvatī, who formerly had been Rati, the wife of Cupid. When everyone was informed of the mysterious disappearance of Pradyumna and how he had grown up, they all became struck with wonder because they had gotten back their dead son after they were almost hopeless of his return. When they understood that it was Pradyumna who was present, they began to receive him with great delight. One after another, all of the members of the family–Devakī, Vasudeva, Lord Śri Kṛṣṇa, Lord Balarāma, and Rukmiṇī and all the women of the family–began to embrace both Pradyumna and his wife Māyāvatī. When the news of Pradyumna's return was spread all over the city of Dvārakā, all the astonished citizens began to come with great anxiety to see the lost Pradyumna. They began to say, "The dead son has come back. What can be more pleasing than this?"

Śrīla Śukadeva Gosvāmī has explained that, in the beginning, all the residents of the palace, who were all mothers and stepmothers of Pradyumna, mistook him to be Kṛṣṇa and were all bashful, infected by the desire for conjugal love. The explanation is that Pradyumna's personal appearance is exactly like Kṛṣṇa's, and he was factually Cupid himself. There was no cause of astonishment, therefore, when the mothers of Pradyumna and other women mistook him in that way. It is clear from the statement that Pradyumna's bodily characteristics were so similar to Kṛṣṇa's that he was mistaken to be Kṛṣṇa even by his mother.

Thus ends the Bhaktivedanta purport of the Second Volume, Twentieth Chapter of Kṛṣṇa, *"Pradyumna Born to Kṛṣṇa and Rukmiṇī."*

21 / The Story of the Syamantaka Jewel

There was a king of the name Satrājit within the jurisdiction of Dvārakādhāma. He was a great devotee of the sun-god, who awarded him the benediction of a jewel known as Syamantaka. Because of this Syamantaka jewel, there was a misunderstanding between King Satrājit and the Yadu dynasty. Later on the matter was settled when Satrājit voluntarily offered Kṛṣṇa his daughter, Satyabhāmā, along with the jewel Syamantaka. Not only was Satyabhāmā married to Kṛṣṇa on account of the Syamantaka jewel, but Jāmbavatī, the daughter of Jāmbavān, was also married to Kṛṣṇa. These two marriages took place before the appearance of Pradyumna, as described in the last chapter. How King Satrājit offended the Yadu dynasty and how he later on came to his senses and offered his daughter and the Syamantaka jewel to Kṛṣṇa is described as follows.

Since he was a great devotee of the sun-god, King Satrājit gradually entered into a very friendly relationship with him. The sun-god was much pleased with him and delivered to him an exceptional jewel known as Syamantaka. When this jewel was worn by Satrājit in a locket around his neck, he appeared exactly like an imitation sun-god. Putting on this jewel, he would enter the city of Dvārakā, and people would think that the sun-god had come into the city to see Kṛṣṇa. They knew that Kṛṣṇa, being the Supreme Personality of Godhead, was sometimes visited by the demigods, so while Satrājit was visiting the city of Dvārakā all the inhabitants except Kṛṣṇa took him to be the sun-god himself. Although King Satrājit was known to everyone, he could not be recognized because of the dazzling effulgence of the Syamantaka jewel.

Once, mistaking him to be the sun-god, some of the important citizens of Dvārakā immediately went to Kṛṣṇa to inform Him that the sun-god had arrived to see Him. At that time, Kṛṣṇa was playing chess. One of the important residents of Dvārakā spoke thus: "My dear Lord Nārāyaṇa, You are the Supreme Personality of Godhead. In Your plenary portion of Nārāyaṇa or Viṣṇu, You have four hands with different symbols–the conchshell, disc, club and lotus flower. You are actually the owner of everything, but in spite of Your being the Supreme Personality of Godhead, Nārāyaṇa, You have descended in Vṛndāvana to act as the child of Yaśodāmātā, who sometimes used to tie You up with her ropes, and You are celebrated, therefore, by the name Dāmodara."

That Kṛṣṇa is the Supreme Personality of Godhead, Nārāyaṇa, as accepted by the citizens of Dvārakā, was later on confirmed by the great Māyāvādī philosophical leader, Śaṅkarācārya. By accepting the Lord as impersonal, he did not reject the Lord's personal form. He meant that everything which has form in this material world is subjected to creation, maintenance and annihilation, but the Supreme Personality of Godhead, Nārāyaṇa, does not have a material form subjected to these limitations. In order to convince the less intelligent class of men who take Kṛṣṇa to be an ordinary human being, Śaṅkarācārya therefore said that God is impersonal. This impersonality means that He is not a person of this material condition. He is a transcendental personality without a material body.

The citizens of Dvārakā addressed Lord Kṛṣṇa not only as Dāmodara, but also as Govinda, which indicates that Kṛṣṇa is very affectionate to the cows and calves; and just to refer to their intimate connection with Kṛṣṇa, they addressed Him as Yadunandana. He is the son of Vasudeva, born in the Yadu dynasty. In this way, the citizens of Dvārakā concluded that they were addressing Kṛṣṇa as the supreme master of the whole universe. They addressed Kṛṣṇa in many different ways, proud of being citizens of Dvārakā who could see Kṛṣṇa daily.

When Satrājit was visiting the city of Dvārakā, the citizens felt great pride to think that although Kṛṣṇa was living in Dvārakā like an ordinary human being, the demigods were coming to see Him. Thus they informed Lord Kṛṣṇa that the sun-god, with his appealing bodily effulgence, was coming to see Him. The citizens of Dvārakā confirmed that the sun-god's coming into Dvārakā was not very wonderful, because people all over the universe who were searching after the Supreme Personality of Godhead knew that He had appeared in the family of the Yadu dynasty and was living in Dvārakā as one of the members of that family. Thus the citizens expressed their joy on this occasion. On hearing the statement of His citizens, the all-pervasive Personality of Godhead, Kṛṣṇa, simply smiled. Being pleased with the citizens of Dvārakā, Kṛṣṇa informed them that the person whom they described as the sun-god was actually King Satrājit, who had come to visit Dvārakā City to show his opulence in the form of the valuable jewel obtained from the sun-god.

Satrājit, however, did not come to see Kṛṣṇa; he was instead overwhelmed by the jewel of Syamantaka. He installed the jewel in a temple to be worshiped by *brāhmaṇas* he engaged for this purpose. This is an instance of a less intelligent person worshiping a material thing. In the *Bhagavad-gītā* it is stated that less intelligent persons, in order to get immediate results from their fruitive activities, worship the demigods who are created within this universe. The word "materialist" means one concerned with gratification of the senses within this material world. Although Kṛṣṇa later asked for this Syamantaka jewel, King Satrājit did not deliver it to Him, but he installed the jewel for his purposes of worship. And who would not worship that jewel? The Syamantaka jewel was so powerful that it was daily producing a large quantity of gold. A quantity of gold is counted by a measurement called a *bhāra.* According to Vedic formulas, one *bhāra* is equal to sixteen pounds of gold; one *mound* equals eighty-two pounds. The jewel was producing about 170 pounds of gold every day. Besides that, it is learned from Vedic literature that in whatever part of the world this jewel is worshiped there is no possibility of famine; not only that, but wherever the jewel is present, there is no possibility of anything inauspicious, such as pestilence or disease.

Lord Kṛṣṇa wanted to teach the world that the best of everything should be offered to the ruling chief of the country. King Ugrasena was the overlord of many dynasties and happened to be the grandfather of Kṛṣṇa, and Kṛṣṇa asked Satrājit to present the Syamantaka jewel to King Ugrasena. Kṛṣṇa pleaded that the best should be offered to the king. But Satrājit, being a worshiper of the demigods, had become too materialistic and, instead of accepting the request of Kṛṣṇa, thought it wiser to worship the jewel in order to get the 170 pounds of gold every day. Materialistic persons who can achieve such huge quantities of gold every day are not interested in Kṛṣṇa consciousness. Sometimes, therefore, in order to show special favor, Kṛṣṇa takes away great accumulations of materialistic wealth from a person and thus makes him a great devotee. But Satrājit refused to abide by the order of Kṛṣṇa and did not deliver the jewel to him.

After this incident, Satrājit's younger brother, in order to display the opulence of the family, took the jewel, put it on his neck and rode on horseback into the forest making a show of his material opulence. While the brother of Satrājit, who was known as Prasena, was moving here and there in the forest, a big lion attacked him, killing both him and the horse on which he was riding, and took away the jewel to his cave. The news was received by the gorilla king, Jāmbavān, who then killed that lion in the cave and took away the jewel. Jāmbavān had been a great devotee of the Lord since the time of Lord Rāmacandra, so he did not take the valuable jewel as something he very much needed. He gave it to his young son to play with as a toy.

In the city, when Satrājit's younger brother Prasena did not return from the forest with the jewel, Satrājit became very upset. He did not know that his brother had been killed by a lion and that the lion had been killed by Jāmbavān. He was thinking instead that because Kṛṣṇa wanted that jewel and it had not been delivered to Him, Kṛṣṇa might have therefore taken the jewel away from Prasena by force and killed him. This idea grew into a rumor which was being spread by Satrājit in every part of Dvārakā.

The false rumor that Kṛṣṇa had killed Prasena and had taken away the jewel was spread everywhere like wildfire. Kṛṣṇa did not like to be defamed in that way, and therefore He decided that He would go to the forest and find the Syamantaka jewel, taking with Him some of the inhabitants of Dvārakā. Along with important men of Dvārakā, Kṛṣṇa went to search out Prasena, the brother of Satrājit, and He found him dead, killed by the lion. At the same time, Kṛṣṇa also found the lion which had been killed by Jāmbavān, who is generally called by the name Ṛkṣa. It was found that the lion had been killed by the hand of Ṛkṣa without the assistance of any weapon. Kṛṣṇa and the citizens of Dvārakā then found in the forest a great tunnel, said to be the path to Ṛkṣa's house. Kṛṣṇa knew that the inhabitants of Dvārakā would be afraid to enter the tunnel; therefore He asked them to remain outside, and He Himself entered the dark tunnel alone to find Ṛkṣa, Jāmbavān. After entering the tunnel, Kṛṣṇa saw that the very valuable jewel known as Syamantaka had been given to the son of Ṛkṣa as a toy, and in order to take the jewel from the child, He went there and stood before him. When the nurse who was taking care of Ṛkṣa's child saw Kṛṣṇa standing before her, she was afraid, thinking the valuable Syamantaka jewel might be taken away by Him. She began to cry loudly out of fear.

Hearing the nurse crying, Jāmbavān appeared on the scene in a very angry mood. Jāmbavān was actually a great devotee of Lord Kṛṣṇa, but because he was in an angry mood he could not recognize his master; he thought Him to be an ordinary man. This brings to mind the statement of the *Bhagavad-gītā* in which the Lord advises Arjuna to get free from anger, greed and lust in order to rise up to the spiritual platform. Lust, anger and greed run parallel in the heart and check one's progress on the spiritual path.

Not recognizing his master, Jāmbavān first challenged Him to fight. There was then a great fight between Kṛṣṇa and Jāmbavān in which they fought like two opposing vultures. Whenever there is an eatable corpse the vultures fight heartily over the prey. Kṛṣṇa and Jāmbavān first of all began fighting with weapons, then with stones, then with big trees, then hand to hand, until at last they were hitting one another with their fists, and the blows were like the striking of thunderbolts. Each was expecting victory over the other, but the fighting continued for days, both in daytime and at night, without stopping. In this way the fighting continued for twenty-eight days.

Although Jāmbavān was the strongest living entity of that time, practically all the joints of his bodily limbs became slackened and his strength reduced to practically nil after being constantly struck by the fists of Śrī Kṛṣṇa. Feeling very tired, with perspiration all over his body, Jāmbavān was astonished. Who was this opponent who was weakening him? Jāmbavān was quite aware of his own superhuman bodily strength, but when he felt tired from being struck by Kṛṣṇa, he could understand that Kṛṣṇa was no one else but his worshipable Lord, the Supreme Personality of Godhead. This incident has a special significance for the devotees. In the beginning, Jāmbavān could not understand Kṛṣṇa because his vision was obscured by material attachment. He was attached to his boy and to the greatly valuable Syamantaka jewel, which he did not want to spare for Kṛṣṇa. In fact, when Kṛṣṇa came there he became angry, thinking that He had come to take away the jewel. This is the material position; although one is very strong in body, that cannot help him understand Kṛṣṇa.

In a sporting attitude, Kṛṣṇa wanted to engage in a mock fight with His devotee. As we have experienced from the pages of the *Śrīmad-Bhāgavatam*, the Supreme Personality of Godhead has all the propensities and instincts of a human being. Sometimes, in a sportive spirit, He wishes to fight to make a show of bodily strength, and when He so desires, He selects one of His suitable devotees to give Him that pleasure. Kṛṣṇa desired this pleasure of mock fighting with Jāmbavān. Although Jāmbavān was a devotee by nature, he was without knowledge of Kṛṣṇa while giving service to the Lord by his bodily strength. But as soon as Kṛṣṇa was pleased by the fighting, Jāmbavān immediately understood that his opponent was none other than the Supreme Lord Himself. The conclusion is that he could understand Kṛṣṇa by his service. Kṛṣṇa is sometimes satisfied by fighting also.

Jāmbavān therefore said to the Lord, "My dear Lord, I can now understand who You are. You are the Supreme Personality of Godhead, Lord Viṣṇu, the source of everyone's strength, wealth, reputation, beauty, wisdom and renunciation." This statement of Jāmbavān's is confirmed by the *Vedānta-sūtra*, wherein the Supreme Lord is declared to be the source of everything. Jāmbavān identified Lord Kṛṣṇa as the Supreme Personality, Lord Viṣṇu: "My dear Lord, You are the creator of the creators of the universal affairs." This statement is very instructive to the ordinary man, who is amazed by the activities of a person with an exceptional brain. The ordinary man is surprised to see the inventions of a great scientist, but the statement of Jāmbavān confirms that although a scientist may be a creator of many wonderful things, Kṛṣṇa is the creator of the scientist. He is not only the creator of one scientist, but of millions and trillions, all over the universe. Jāmbavān said further, "You are not only creator of the creator, but You are also creator of the material elements which are manipulated by the so-called creators." Scientists utilize the physical elements or laws of material nature and do something wonderful, but actually such laws and elements are also the creation of Kṛṣṇa. This is actual scientific understanding. Less intelligent men do not try to understand who created the brain of the scientist; they are simply satisfied by seeing the wonderful creation or invention of the scientist.

Jāmbavān continued: "My dear Lord, the time factor which combines all the physical elements is also Your representative. You are the supreme time factor in which all creation takes place, is maintained, and is finally annihilated. And not only the physical elements and the time factors but also the persons who manipulate the ingredients and advantages of creation are part and parcel of You. The living entity is not, therefore, an independent creator. By studying all factors in the right perspective, one can see that You are the supreme controller and Lord of everything. My dear Lord, I can therefore understand that You are the same Supreme Personality of Godhead whom I worship as Lord Rāmacandra. My Lord Rāmacandra wanted to construct a bridge over the ocean, and I saw personally how the ocean became agitated simply by my Lord's glancing over it. And when the whole ocean became agitated, the living entities like the whales, alligators and *timiṅgila* fish, all became perturbed. [The *timiṅgila* fish in the ocean can swallow big aquatics like whales in one gulp.] In this way the ocean was forced to give way and allow Rāmacandra to cross to the island known as Laṅkā [now supposed to be Ceylon]. This construction of a bridge over the ocean from Cape Comorin to Ceylon is still well-known to everyone. After the construction of the bridge, a fire was set all over the kingdom of Rāvaṇa. During the fighting with Rāvaṇa, each and every part of Rāvaṇa's limbs was slashed and cut into pieces by Your sharp arrows, and his head fell to the face of the earth. Now I can understand that You are none other than my Lord Rāmacandra. No one else has such immeasurable strength; no one else could defeat me in this way."

Lord Kṛṣṇa became satisfied by the prayers and statements of Jāmbavān, and to mitigate the pains of his body, He began to smear the lotus palm of His hand all over the body of Jāmbavān. Jāmbavān at once felt relieved from the fatigue of the great fight. Lord Kṛṣṇa then addressed him as King Jāmbavān, because he and not the lion was actually the king of the forest; with his naked hand, without a weapon, Jāmbavān had killed the lion. Kṛṣṇa informed Jāmbavān that He had come to him to ask for the Syamantaka jewel because since the Syamantaka jewel had been stolen His name had been defamed by the less intelligent. Kṛṣṇa plainly informed him that he had come there to ask him for the jewel in order to be free from this defamation. Jāmbavān understood the whole situation, and to satisfy the Lord he not only immediately delivered the Syamantaka jewel, but he also brought his daughter Jāmbavatī, who was of marriageable age, and presented her to Lord Kṛṣṇa.

The episode of Jāmbavatī's marriage with Kṛṣṇa and the delivery of the jewel known as Syamantaka was finished within the mountain cave. Although the fighting between Kṛṣṇa and Jāmbavān went on for twenty-eight days, the inhabitants of Dvārakā waited outside the tunnel for twelve days, and after that they decided that something undesirable must have happened. They could not understand what had actually happened for certain, and being very sorry and tired, they had returned to the city of Dvārakā.

All the members of the family, namely the mother of Kṛṣṇa, Devakī, His father Vasudeva, and His chief wife Rukmiṇī, along with all other friends, relatives and residents of the palace, became very sorry when the citizens returned home without Kṛṣṇa. Because of their natural affection for Kṛṣṇa, they began to call Satrājit ill names, for he was the cause of Kṛṣṇa's disappearance. They went to worship the goddess Candrabhāgā, praying for the return of Kṛṣṇa. The goddess was satisfied by the prayers of the citizens of Dvārakā, and she immediately offered them her benediction. Simultaneously, Kṛṣṇa appeared on the scene accompanied by His new wife Jāmbavatī, and all the inhabitants of Dvārakā and relatives of Kṛṣṇa became joyful. The inhabitants of Dvārakā became as joyful as someone receiving a dear relative back from the dead. The inhabitants of Dvārakā had concluded that Kṛṣṇa had been put into great difficulties due to the fighting; therefore, they had become almost hopeless of His return. But when they saw that Kṛṣṇa had actually returned, not alone but with a new wife, Jāmbavatī, they immediately performed another celebration ceremony.

King Ugrasena then called for a meeting of all important kings and chiefs. He also invited Satrājit, and Kṛṣṇa explained before the whole assembly the incident of the recovery of the jewel from Jāmbavān. Kṛṣṇa wanted to return the valuable jewel to King Satrājit. Satrājit, however, became ashamed because he had unnecessarily defamed Kṛṣṇa. He accepted the jewel in his hand, but he remained silent, bending his head downwards, and without speaking anything in the assembly of the kings and chiefs, he returned home with the jewel. Then he thought about how he could clear himself from the abominable action he had performed by defaming Kṛṣṇa. He was conscious that he had offended Kṛṣṇa very grievously and that he had to find a remedial measure so that Kṛṣṇa would again be pleased with him.

King Satrājit was eager to get relief from the anxiety he had foolishly created due to being attracted by a material thing, specifically the Syamantaka jewel. Satrājit was truly afflicted by the offense he had committed toward Kṛṣṇa, and he sincerely wanted to rectify it. From within, Kṛṣṇa gave him good intelligence, and Satrājit decided to hand over to Kṛṣṇa both the jewel and his beautiful daughter, Satyabhāmā. There was no alternative for mitigating the situation, and therefore he arranged the marriage ceremony of Kṛṣṇa and his beautiful daughter. He gave in charity both the jewel and his daughter to the Supreme Personality of Godhead. Satyabhāmā was so beautiful and qualified that Satrājit, in spite of being asked for the hand of Satyabhama by many princes, was waiting to find a suitable son-in-law. By the grace of Kṛṣṇa he decided to hand his daughter over to Him.

Lord Kṛṣṇa, being pleased upon Satrājit, informed him that He did not have any need of the Syamantaka jewel. "It is better to let it remain in the temple as you have kept it," He said, "and every one of us will derive benefit from the jewel. Because of the jewel's presence in the city of Dvārakā, there will be no more famine or disturbances created by pestilence or excessive heat and cold."

Thus ends the Bhaktivedanta purport of the Second Volume, Twenty-first Chapter of **Kṛṣṇa, *"The Story of the Syamantaka Jewel."***

22 / The Killing of Satrājit and Śatadhanvā

After Akrūra visited Hastināpura and reported the condition of the Pāṇḍavas to Kṛṣṇa, there were further developments. The Pāṇḍavas were transferred to a house which was made of shellac and was later on set ablaze, and everyone understood that the Pāṇḍavas along with their mother, Kuntī, had been killed. This information was also sent to Lord Kṛṣṇa and Balarāma. After consulting together, They decided to go to Hastināpura to show sympathy to Their relatives. Kṛṣṇa and Balarāma certainly knew that the Pāṇḍavas could not have been killed in the devastating fire, but in spite of this knowledge They wanted to go to Hastināpura to take part in the bereavement. On arriving in Hastināpura, Kṛṣṇa and Balarāma first of all went to see Bhīṣmadeva, because he was the chief of the Kuru dynasty. They then saw Vidura, Gāndhārī and Droṇa. Other members of the Kuru dynasty were not sorry, because they wanted the Pāṇḍavas and their mother to be killed. But some family members, headed by Bhīṣma, were actually very sorry for the incident, and Kṛṣṇa and Balarāma expressed equal sorrow, without disclosing the actual situation.

When Kṛṣṇa and Balarāma were away from the city of Dvārakā, there was a conspiracy to take away the Syamantaka jewel from Satrājit. The chief conspirator was Śatadhanvā. Along with others, Śatadhanvā wanted to marry Satyabhāmā, the beautiful daughter of Satrājit. Satrājit had promised that he would give his beautiful daughter in charity to various candidates, but later on the decision was changed, and Satyabhāmā was given to Kṛṣṇa along with the Syamantaka jewel. Satrājit had no desire to give the jewel away along with his daughter, and Kṛṣṇa, knowing his mentality, accepted his daughter but returned the jewel. After getting back the jewel from Kṛṣṇa, he was satisfied and kept it with him always. But in the absence of Kṛṣṇa and Balarāma there was a conspiracy by many men, including even Akrūra and Kṛtavarmā, who were devotees of Lord Kṛṣṇa, to take the jewel from Satrājit. Akrūra and Kṛtavarmā joined the conspiracy because they wanted the jewel for Kṛṣṇa. They knew that Kṛṣṇa wanted the jewel and that Satrājit had not delivered it properly. Others joined the conspiracy because they were disappointed in not having the hand of Satyabhāmā. Some of them incited Śatadhanvā to kill Satrājit and take away the jewel.

The question is generally raised, Why did a great devotee like Akrūra join this conspiracy? And why did Kṛtavarmā, although a devotee of the Lord, join the conspiracy also? The answer is given by great authorities like Jīva Gosvāmī and others that although Akrūra was a great devotee, he was cursed by the inhabitants of Vṛndāvana because of his taking Kṛṣṇa away from their midst. Because of his wounding their feelings, Akrūra was forced to join the conspiracy declared by sinful men. Similarly, Kṛtavarmā was a devotee, but because of his intimate association with Kaṁsa, he was also contaminated by sinful reaction, and he also joined the conspiracy.

Being inspired by all the members of the conspiracy, Śatadhanvā one night entered the house of Satrājit and killed him while he was sleeping. Śatadhanvā was a sinful man of abominable character, and although due to his sinful activities he was not to live for many days, he decided to kill Satrājit while Satrājit was sleeping at home. When he entered the house to kill Satrājit, all the women there began to cry very loudly, but in spite of their great protests, Śatadhanvā mercilessly butchered Satrājit without hesitation, exactly as a butcher kills an animal in the slaughterhouse. Since Kṛṣṇa was absent from home, His wife Satyabhāmā was also present on the night Satrājit was murdered, and she began to cry, "My dear father! My dear father! How mercilessly you have been killed!" The dead body of Satrājit was not immediately removed for cremation because Satyabhāmā wanted to go to Kṛṣṇa in Hastināpura. Therefore the body was preserved in a tank of oil so that Kṛṣṇa could come back and see the dead body of Satrājit and take real action against Śatadhanvā. Satyabhāmā immediately started for Hastināpura to inform Kṛṣṇa about the ghastly death of her father.

When Kṛṣṇa was informed by Satyabhāmā of the murder of His father-in-law, He began to lament like an ordinary man. His great sorrow is, again, a strange thing. Lord Kṛṣṇa has nothing to do with action and reaction, but because He was playing the part of a human being He expressed His full sympathy for the bereavement of Satyabhāmā, and His eyes filled with tears upon hearing about the death of His father-in-law. He thus began to lament, "Oh, what unhappy incidents have taken place!" In this way both Kṛṣṇa and Balarāma, along with Satyabhāmā, the wife of Kṛṣṇa, immediately returned to Dvārakā and began to make plans to kill Śatadhanvā and take away the jewel. Although he was a great outlaw in the city, Śatadhanvā was still very much afraid of Kṛṣṇa's power, and thus he became most afraid on Kṛṣṇa's arrival.

Understanding Kṛṣṇa's plan to kill him, he immediately went to take shelter of Kṛtavarmā. But on being approached by him, Kṛtavarmā said, "I shall never be able to offend Lord Kṛṣṇa and Balarāma because They are not ordinary persons. They are the Supreme Personality of Godhead. Who can be saved from death if he has offended Balarāma and Kṛṣṇa? No one can be saved from Their wrath." Kṛtavarmā further said that Kaṁsa, although powerful and assisted by many demons, could not be saved from the wrath of Kṛṣṇa, and what to speak of Jarāsandha, who had been defeated by Kṛṣṇa eighteen times and each time had to return from the fighting in disappointment.

When Śatadhanvā was refused help by Kṛtavarmā he went to Akrūra and implored him to help. Akrūra also replied, "Both Balarāma and Kṛṣṇa are Themselves the Supreme Personality of Godhead, and anyone who knows Their unlimited strength would never dare to offend Them or fight with Them." He further informed Śatadhanvā, "Kṛṣṇa and Balarāma are so powerful that simply by willing They are creating the whole cosmic manifestation, maintaining it and dissolving it. Unfortunately, persons who are bewildered by the illusory energy cannot understand the strength of Kṛṣṇa, although the whole cosmic manifestation is fully under His control." He cited, as an example, that Kṛṣṇa, even at the age of seven years, had lifted Govardhana Hill and had continued to hold up the mountain for seven days, exactly as a child carries a small umbrella. Akrūra plainly informed Śatadhanvā that he would always offer his most respectful obeisances to Kṛṣṇa, the Supersoul of everything that is created and the original cause of all causes. When Akrūra also refused to give him shelter, Śatadhanvā decided to deliver to the hands of Akrūra the Syamantaka jewel. Then, riding on a horse which could run at great speed and up to four hundred miles at a stretch, he fled the city.

When Kṛṣṇa and Balarāma were informed of the flight of Śatadhanvā, They mounted Their chariot, its flag marked by the picture of Garuḍa, and followed immediately. Kṛṣṇa was particularly angry with Śatadhanvā and wanted to kill him because he had killed Satrājit, a superior personality. Satrājit happened to be the father-in-law of Kṛṣṇa, and it is the injunction of the *śāstras* that anyone who has rebelled against a superior person, or *gurudruha,* must be punished in proportion to the volume of offense. Because Śatadhanvā had killed His father-in-law, Kṛṣṇa was determined to kill him by any means.

Śatadhanvā's horse became exhausted and died near a garden house in Mithilā. Unable to take help of the horse, Śatadhanvā began to run with great speed. In order to be fair to Śatadhanvā, Kṛṣṇa and Balarāma also left Their chariot and began to follow Śatadhanvā on foot. While both Śatadhanvā and Kṛṣṇa were running on foot, Kṛṣṇa took His disk and cut off the head of Śatadhanvā. After Śatadhanvā was killed, Kṛṣṇa searched through his clothing for the Syamantaka jewel, but He could not find it. He then returned to Balarāma and said, "We have killed this person uselessly because the jewel is not to be found on his body." Śrī Balarāma suggested, "The jewel might have been kept in custody of another man in Dvārakā, so You'd better return and search it out." Śrī Balarāma expressed His desire to remain in Mithilā City for some days because He enjoyed an intimate friendship with the king. Therefore, Kṛṣṇa returned to Dvārakā, and Balarāma entered the city of Mithilā.

When the King of Mithilā saw the arrival of Śrī Balarāma in his city, he became most pleased and received the Lord with great honor and hospitality. He presented many valuable presents to Balarāmajī in order to seek His pleasure. At this time Śrī Balarāma lived in the city for several years as the honored guest of the King of Mithilā, Janaka Mahārāja. During this time, Duryodhana, the eldest son of Dhṛtarāṣṭra, took the opportunity of coming to Balarāma and learning from Him the art of fighting with a club.

After killing Śatadhanvā, Kṛṣṇa returned to Dvārakā, and in order to please His wife Satyabhāmā, He informed her of the death of Śatadhanvā, the killer of her father. But He also informed her that the jewel had not been found in his possession. Then, according to religious principles, Kṛṣṇa, along with Satyabhāmā, performed all kinds of ceremonies in honor of the death of His father-in-law. In that ceremony all the friends and relatives of the family joined together.

Akrūra and Kṛtavarmā, who were prominent members in the conspiracy to kill Satrājit, had incited Śatadhanvā to kill him, but when they heard of the death of Śatadhanvā at Kṛṣṇa's hand, and when they heard also that Kṛṣṇa had returned to Dvārakā, they both immediately left Dvārakā. The citizens of Dvārakā felt themselves threatened with pestilence and natural disturbances due to the absence of Akrūra from the city. This was a kind of superstition because while Lord Kṛṣṇa was present there could not be any pestilence, famine or natural disturbances. But in the absence of Akrūra there were some disturbances in Dvārakā. Once in the province of Kāśī within the barricade of Vārāṇasī there was severe drought and practically no rainfall. At that time the King of Kāśī arranged the marriage of his daughter, known as Gāndinī, with Śvaphalka, the father of Akrūra. This was done by the King of Kāśī on the advice of an astrologer, and actually it so happened that after the marriage of the King's daughter with Śvaphalka there was sufficient rainfall in the province. Due to this supernatural power of Śvaphalka, his son Akrūra was also considered equally powerful, and people were under the impression that wherever Akrūra or his father remained, there would be no natural disturbance, famine or drought. That kingdom is considered to be happy where there is no famine, pestilence, or excessive heat and cold and where people are happy mentally, spiritually and bodily. As soon as there is some disturbance, people consider the cause to be due to the absence of an auspicious personality in the city. Thus there was a rumor that because of the absence of Akrūra inauspicious things were happening. After the departure of Akrūra, some of the elderly members of the town began to perceive that there were also inauspicious signs due to the absence of the Syamantaka jewel. When Lord Śrī Kṛṣṇa heard these rumors spread by the people He decided to summon Akrūra from the kingdom of Kāśī. Akrūra was Kṛṣṇa's uncle; therefore, when he came back to Dvārakā Lord Kṛṣṇa first of all welcomed him as befitting a superior person. Kṛṣṇa is the Supersoul in everyone's heart; He knows everything going on in everyone's heart. He knew everything that had happened in connection with Akrūra's conspiracy with Śatadhanvā. Therefore, He smilingly began to address Akrūra.

Addressing him as the chief among magnificent men, Kṛṣṇa said, "My dear uncle, it is already known to Me that the Syamantaka jewel was left by Śatadhanvā with you. Presently there is no direct claimant of the Syamantaka jewel, for King Satrājit has no male issue. His daughter Satyabhāmā is not very anxious for this jewel, yet her expected son, as grandson of Satrājit, would, after performing the regulative principles of inheritance, be the legal claimant of the jewel." Lord Kṛṣṇa indicated by this statement that Satyabhāmā was already pregnant and that her son would be the real claimant for the jewel and would certainly take the jewel from him.

Kṛṣṇa continued, "This jewel is so powerful that no ordinary man is able to keep it. I know that you are very pious in activities, so there is no objection to the jewel being kept with you. There is one difficulty, and that is that My elder brother, Śrī Balarāma, does not believe My version that the jewel is with you. I therefore request you, O large-hearted one, to show Me the jewel before My other relatives so that they may be pacified. You cannot deny that the jewel is with you because from various kinds of rumors we can understand that you have enhanced your opulence and are performing sacrifices on an altar made of solid gold." The properties of the jewel were known: wherever the jewel remained, it would produce for the keeper almost nine *mounds* of pure gold daily. Akrūra was getting gold in that proportion and was distributing it very profusely at sacrificial performances. Lord Kṛṣṇa cited Akrūra's lavishly spending in gold as positive evidence of his possessing the Syamantaka jewel.

When Lord Kṛṣṇa, in friendly terms and in sweet language, impressed Akrūra about the real fact and Akrūra understood that nothing could be concealed from the knowledge of Śrī Kṛṣṇa, he brought the valuable jewel, shining like the sun and covered by cloth, and presented it before Kṛṣṇa. Lord Kṛṣṇa took the Syamantaka jewel in His hand and showed it to all His relatives and friends present there and then again returned the jewel to Akrūra in their presence so that they would know that the jewel was actually being kept by Akrūra in Dvārakā City.

This story of the Syamantaka jewel is very significant. In the *Śrīmad-Bhāgavatam* it is said that anyone who hears the story of the Syamantaka jewel or describes it or simply remembers it will be free from all kinds of defamation and the reactions of all impious activities and thus will attain the highest perfectional condition of peace.

Thus ends the Bhaktivedanta purport of the Second Volume, Twenty-second Chapter of* Kṛṣṇa, *"The Killing of Satrājit and Śatadhanvā."

23 / Five Queens Married by Kṛṣṇa

There was a great rumor that the five Pāṇḍava brothers, along with their mother Kuntī, had, under the plan of Dhṛtarāṣṭra, died in a fire accident in the house of shellac in which they were living. But then the five brothers were detected at the marriage ceremony of Draupadī; so again another rumor spread that the Pāṇḍavas and their mother were not dead. It was a rumor, but actually it was so; they returned to their capital city, Hastināpura, and people saw them face to face. When this news was carried to Kṛṣṇa and Balarāma, Kṛṣṇa wanted to see them personally, and therefore Kṛṣṇa decided to go to Hastināpura.

This time, Kṛṣṇa visited Hastināpura in state, as a royal prince, accompanied by His commander-in-chief, Yuyudhāna, and by many other soldiers. He had not actually been invited to visit the city, yet He went to see the Pāṇḍavas out of His affection for His great devotees. He visited the Pāṇḍavas without warning, and all of them got up from their respective seats as soon as they saw Him. Kṛṣṇa is called Mukunda because as soon as one comes in constant touch with Kṛṣṇa or sees Him in full Kṛṣṇa consciousness, one immediately becomes freed from all material anxieties. Not only that, but he immediately becomes blessed with all spiritual bliss.

On receiving Kṛṣṇa, the Pāṇḍavas became very enlivened, just as if awakened from unconsciousness or from loss of life. When a man is lying unconscious, his senses and the different parts of his body are not active, but when he regains his consciousness, the senses immediately become active. Similarly, the Pāṇḍavas received Kṛṣṇa as if they had just regained their consciousness, and so they became very much enlivened. Lord Kṛṣṇa embraced every one of them, and by the touch of the Supreme Personality of Godhead, the Pāṇḍavas immediately became freed from all reactions of material contamination, and therefore they were smiling in spiritual bliss. By seeing the face of Lord Kṛṣṇa, everyone was transcendentally satisfied.

Lord Kṛṣṇa, although the Supreme Personality of Godhead, was playing the part of an ordinary human being, and thus He immediately touched the feet of Yudhiṣṭhira and Bhīma because they were His two older cousins. Arjuna embraced Kṛṣṇa as a friend of the same age, whereas the two younger brothers, namely Nakula and Sahadeva, touched the lotus feet of Kṛṣṇa to show Him respect. After an exchange of greetings according to the social etiquette befitting the position of the Pāṇḍavas and Lord Kṛṣṇa, Kṛṣṇa was offered an exalted seat. When He was comfortably seated, the newly married Draupadī, young and very beautiful in her natural feminine gracefulness, came before Lord Kṛṣṇa to offer her respectful greetings. The Yādavas who accompanied Kṛṣṇa to Hastināpura were also very respectfully received; specifically, Sātyaki, or Yuyudhāna, was also offered a nice seat. In this way, when everyone else was properly seated, the five brothers took their seats nearby Lord Kṛṣṇa.

After meeting with the five brothers, Lord Kṛṣṇa personally went to visit Śrīmatī Kuntīdevī, the mother of the Pāṇḍavas, who was also the paternal aunt of Kṛṣṇa. In offering His respects to His aunt, Kṛṣṇa also touched her feet. Kuntīdevī's eyes became wet, and, in great love, she feelingly embraced Lord Kṛṣṇa. She then inquired from Him about the well-being of her paternal family members—her brother Vasudeva, his wife, and other members of the family. Similarly, Kṛṣṇa also inquired from His aunt about the welfare of the Pāṇḍava families. Although Kuntīdevī was related to Kṛṣṇa by family ties, she knew immediately after meeting Him that He was the Supreme Personality of Godhead. She remembered the past calamities of her life and how by the grace of Kṛṣṇa the Pāṇḍavas and their mother had been saved. She knew perfectly well that no one, without Kṛṣṇa's grace, could have saved them from the fire accident designed by Dhṛtarāṣṭra and his sons. In a choked up voice, she began to narrate before Kṛṣṇa the past history of their life.

Śrīmatī Kuntī said: "My dear Kṛṣṇa, I remember the day when You sent my brother Akrūra to gather information about us. This means that You always remember us automatically. When You sent Akrūra, I could understand that there was no possibility of our being put into danger. All good fortune in our life began when You sent Akrūra to us. Since then, I have been convinced that we are not without protection. We may be put into various types of dangerous conditions by our family members, the Kurus, but I am confident that You remember us and that You always keep us safe and sound. Devotees who simply think of You are always immune from all kinds of material dangers, and what to speak of ourselves, who are personally remembered by You. So, my dear Kṛṣṇa, there is no question of bad luck; we are always in an auspicious position because of Your grace. But because You have bestowed a special favor on us, people should not mistakenly think that You are partial to some and inattentive to others. You make no such distinction. No one is Your favorite and no one is Your enemy. As the Supreme Personality of Godhead, You are equal to everyone, and everyone can take advantage of Your special protection. The fact is that although You are equal to everyone, You are especially inclined to the devotees who always think of You. The devotees are related to You by ties of love. As such, they cannot forget You even for a moment. You are present in everyone's heart, but because the devotees always remember You, You also respond accordingly. Although the mother has affection for all the children, she takes special care of the one who is fully dependent. I know certainly, my dear Kṛṣṇa, that being seated in everyone's heart, You always create auspicious situations for Your unalloyed devotees."

Then King Yudhiṣṭhira also praised Kṛṣṇa as the Supreme Personality and universal friend of everyone, but because Kṛṣṇa was taking special care of the Pāṇḍavas, King Yudhiṣṭhira said: "My dear Kṛṣṇa, we do not know what sort of pious activities we have executed in our past lives that have made You so kind and graceful to us. We know very well that the great mystics who are always engaged in meditation to capture You do not find it easy to obtain such grace, nor can they draw any personal attention from You. I cannot understand why You are so kind upon us. We are not *yogīs*, but, on the contrary, we are attached to material contaminations. We are householders dealing in politics, worldly affairs. I do not know why You are so kind upon us."

Being requested by King Yudhiṣṭhira, Kṛṣṇa agreed to stay in Hastināpura for four months during the rainy season. The four months of the rainy season are called *Cāturmāsya.* During this period, the generally itinerant preachers and *brāhmaṇas* stop at a certain place and live under rigid regulative principles. Although Lord Kṛṣṇa is above all regulative principles, He agreed to stay at Hastināpura out of affection for the Pāṇḍavas. Taking this opportunity of Kṛṣṇa's residence in Hastināpura, all the citizens of the town got the privilege of seeing Him now and then, and thus they merged into transcendental bliss simply by seeing Lord Kṛṣṇa eye to eye.

One day while Kṛṣṇa was staying with the Pāṇḍavas, He and Arjuna prepared themselves to go to the forest to hunt. Both of them sat down on the chariot, which flew a flag with a picture of Hanumān. Arjuna's special chariot is always marked with the picture of Hanumān, and therefore his name is also Kapidhvaja. (*Kapi* means Hanumān, and *dhvaja* means "flag.")

Thus Arjuna went to the forest with his bow and infallible arrows. He dressed himself with suitable protective garments, for he was to practice killing many enemies. He specifically entered that part of the forest where there were many tigers, deer and various other animals. Kṛṣṇa did not go with Arjuna to practice animal killing because He doesn't have to practice anything; He is self-sufficient. He accompanied Arjuna to see how he was practicing because in the future he would have to kill many enemies. After entering the forest, Arjuna killed many tigers, boars, bison, *gavayas* (a kind of wild animal), rhinoceroses, deer, hares, porcupines and similar other animals, which he pierced with his arrows. Some of the dead animals, which were fit to be offered in the sacrifices, were carried by the servants and sent to King Yudhiṣṭhira. Other ferocious animals, such as tigers and rhinoceroses, were killed only to stop disturbances in the forest. Since there are many sages and saintly persons who are residents of the forests, it is the duty of the *kṣatriya* kings to keep even the forest in a peaceful condition for living.

Arjuna felt tired and thirsty from hunting, and therefore he went to the bank of the Yamunā along with Kṛṣṇa. When both the Kṛṣṇas, namely Kṛṣṇa and Arjuna (Arjuna is sometimes called Kṛṣṇa, as is Draupadī), reached the bank of the Yamunā, they washed their hands and feet and mouths and drank the clear water of the Yamunā. While they were resting and drinking water, they saw a beautiful girl of marriageable age walking alone on the bank of the Yamunā. Kṛṣṇa asked His friend Arjuna to go forward and ask the girl who she was. By the order of Kṛṣṇa, Arjuna immediately approached the girl, who was very beautiful. She had an attractive body and nice glittering teeth and smiling face. Arjuna inquired, "My dear girl, you are so beautiful with your raised breasts–may I ask you who you are? We are surprised to see you loitering here alone. What is your purpose in coming here? We can guess only that you are searching after a suitable husband. If you don't mind, you can disclose your purpose. I shall try to satisfy you."

The beautiful girl was the river Yamunā personified. She replied, "Sir, I am the daughter of the sun-god, and I am now performing penance and austerity to have Lord Viṣṇu as my husband. I think He is the Supreme Person and just suitable to become my husband. I disclose my desire thus because you wanted to know it."

The girl continued, "My dear sir, I know you are the hero Arjuna; so I may further say that I'll not accept anyone as my husband besides Lord Viṣṇu, because He is the only protector of all living entities and the bestower of liberation for all conditioned souls. I shall be thankful unto you if you pray to Lord Viṣṇu to become pleased with me." The girl Yamunā knew it well that Arjuna was a great devotee of Lord Kṛṣṇa and that if he would pray, Kṛṣṇa would never deny his request. To approach Kṛṣṇa directly may sometimes be futile, but to approach Kṛṣṇa through His devotee is sure to be successful. She further told Arjuna, "My name is Kālindī, and I live within the water of the Yamunā. My father was kind enough to construct a special house for me within the waters of the Yamunā, and I have vowed to remain in the water as long as I cannot find Lord Kṛṣṇa." The message of the girl Kālindī was duly carried to Kṛṣṇa by Arjuna although Kṛṣṇa, as the Supersoul of everyone's heart, knew everything. Without further discussion, Kṛṣṇa immediately accepted Kālindī and asked her to sit down on the chariot. Then all of them approached King Yudhiṣṭhira.

After this, Kṛṣṇa was asked by King Yudhiṣṭhira to help in constructing a suitable house to be planned by the great architect Viśvakarmā, the celestial engineer in the heavenly kingdom. Kṛṣṇa immediately called for Viśvakarmā, and He made him construct a wonderful city according to the desire of King Yudhiṣṭhira. When this city was constructed, Mahārāja Yudhiṣṭhira requested Kṛṣṇa to live with them a few days more in order to give them the pleasure of His association. Lord Kṛṣṇa accepted the request of Mahārāja Yudhiṣṭhira and remained there for many days more.

In the meantime, Kṛṣṇa engaged in the pastime of offering Khāṇḍava Forest, which belonged to King Indra. Kṛṣṇa wanted to give it to Agni, the fire-god. Khāṇḍava Forest contained many varieties of drugs, and Agni required to eat them for rejuvenation. Agni, however, did not touch Khāṇḍava Forest directly, but requested Kṛṣṇa to help him. Agni knew that Kṛṣṇa was very much pleased with him because he had formerly given Him the Sudarśana disc. So in order to satisfy Agni, Kṛṣṇa became the chariot driver of Arjuna, and both went to the Khāṇḍava Forest. After Agni had eaten up the Khāṇḍava Forest, he was very much pleased. This time, he offered a specific bow known as Gāṇḍīva, four white horses, one chariot, and an invincible quiver with two specific arrows considered to be talismans, which had so much power that no warrior could counteract them. When the Khāṇḍava Forest was being devoured by the fire-god, Agni, there was a demon of the name Maya who was saved by Arjuna from the devastating fire. For this reason, that former demon became a great friend of Arjuna, and in order to please Arjuna he constructed a nice assembly house within the city constructed by Viśvakarmā. This assembly house had some corners so puzzling that when Duryodhana came to visit this house he was misdirected, accepting water as land and land as water.

Duryodhana thus became insulted by the opulence of the Pāṇḍavas, and he became their determined enemy.

After a few days, Kṛṣṇa took permission from King Yudhiṣṭhira to return to Dvārakā. When he got permission, he went to his country, accompanied by Sātyaki, the leader of the Yadus who were living in Hastināpura with Him. Kālindī also returned with Kṛṣṇa to Dvārakā. After returning, Kṛṣṇa consulted many learned astrologers to find the suitable moment at which to marry Kālindī, and then He married her with great pomp. This marriage ceremony gave much pleasure to the relatives of both parties, and all of them enjoyed the great occasion.

The kings of Avantīpura (now known as Ujjain) were named Vinda and Anuvinda. Both kings were under the control of Duryodhana. They had one sister named Mitravindā, who was a very qualified, learned and elegant girl. She was the daughter of one of Kṛṣṇa's aunts. She was to select her husband in the assembly of princes, but she strongly desired to have Kṛṣṇa as her husband. During the assembly for selecting her husband, however, Kṛṣṇa was present, and He forcibly carried away Mitravindā in the presence of all other royal princes. Being unable to resist Kṛṣṇa, the princes were left simply looking at each other.

After this incident, Kṛṣṇa married the daughter of the King of Kośala. The King of Kośala Province was called Nagnajit. He was very pious and was a follower of the Vedic ritualistic ceremonies. His most beautiful daughter was named Satyā. Sometimes Satyā was called Nāgnajitī, for she was the daughter of King Nagnajit. King Nagnajit wanted to give the hand of his daughter to any prince who could defeat seven very strong, stalwart bulls maintained by him. No one in the princely order could defeat the seven bulls, and therefore no one could claim the hand of Satyā. The seven bulls were very strong, and they could hardly bear even the smell of any prince. Many princes approached this kingdom and tried to subdue these bulls, but instead of controlling them, they themselves were defeated. This news was spread all over the country, and when Kṛṣṇa heard that the girl Satyā could be achieved only by defeating the seven bulls, He prepared Himself to go to the kingdom of Kośala. With many soldiers, He approached that part of the country, known as Ayodhyā, making a regular state visit.

When it was known to the King of Kośala that Kṛṣṇa had come to ask the hand of his daughter, he became very pleased. With great respect and pomp, he welcomed Kṛṣṇa to the kingdom. When Kṛṣṇa approached him, he offered Him a suitable sitting place and articles for reception. Everything appeared to be very elegant. Kṛṣṇa also offered him respectful obeisances, thinking him to be His future father-in-law.

When Satyā, the daughter of King Nagnajit, understood that Kṛṣṇa Himself had come to marry her, she was very much pleased that the husband of the goddess of fortune had so kindly come there to accept her. She had cherished the idea of marrying Kṛṣṇa for a long time and was following the principles of austerities in order to obtain her desired husband. She then began to think, "If I have performed any pious activities to the best of my capacity and if I have sincerely thought all along to have Kṛṣṇa as my husband, then Kṛṣṇa may be pleased to fulfill my long-cherished desire." She began to offer prayers to Kṛṣṇa mentally, thinking, "I do not know how the Supreme Personality of Godhead can be pleased upon me. He is the master and Lord of everyone. Even the goddess of fortune, whose place is next to the Supreme Personality of Godhead, and Lord Śiva, Lord Brahmā and many other demigods of different planets always offer their respectful obeisances unto the Lord. The Lord also sometimes descends on this earth in different incarnations in order to fulfill the desire of His devotees. He is so exalted and great that I do not know how to satisfy Him." She thought that the Supreme Personality of Godhead could be pleased only out of His own causeless mercy upon the devotee; otherwise, there was no other means to please Him. Lord Caitanya, in the same way, prayed in His *Śikṣāṣṭaka* verses, "My Lord, I am Your eternal servant. Somehow or other I have fallen into this material existence. If You kindly pick me up and fix me as an atom of dust at Your lotus feet, it will be a great favor to Your eternal servant." The Lord can be pleased only by a humble attitude in the service spirit. The more we render service unto the Lord under the direction of the spiritual master, the more we make advancement on the path of approaching the Lord. We cannot demand any grace or mercy from the Lord because of our service rendered to Him. He may accept or not accept our service, but the only means to satisfy the Lord is through the service attitude, and nothing else.

King Nagnijit was already a pious king, and having Kṛṣṇa in his palace, he began to worship Him to the best of his knowledge and capacity. He presented himself before the Lord thus: "My dear Lord, You are the proprietor of the whole cosmic manifestation, and You are Nārāyaṇa, the rest of all living creatures. You are self-sufficient and pleased with Your personal opulences, so how can I offer You anything? And how could I please You by such offering? It is not possible, because I am an insignificant living being. Actually I have no capacity to render any service unto You."

Kṛṣṇa is the Supersoul of all living creatures, so He could understand the mind of Satyā, the daughter of King Nagnajit. He was also very much pleased with the respectful worship of the King in offering Him a sitting place, eatables, residence, etc. He was appreciative, therefore, that both the girl and the father of the girl were anxious to have Him as their intimate relative. He began to smile and in a great voice said, "My dear King Nagnajit, you know very well that anyone in the princely order who is regular in his position will never ask anything from anyone, however exalted he may be. Such requests by a *kṣatriya* king from another person have been deliberately forbidden by the learned Vedic followers. If a *kṣatriya* breaks this regulation, his action is condemned by learned scholars. But in spite of this rigid regulative principle, I am asking you for the hand of your beautiful daughter just to establish our relationship in return for your great reception of Me. You may also be pleased to be informed that in our family tradition there is no scope for our offering anything in exchange for accepting your daughter. We cannot pay any price which you may impose for delivering her." In other words, Kṛṣṇa wanted the hand of Satyā from the King without fulfilling the condition of defeating the seven bulls.

After hearing the statement of Lord Kṛṣṇa, King Nagnajit said, "My dear Lord, You are the reservoir of all pleasure, all opulences and all qualities. The goddess of fortune, Lakṣmījī, always lives on Your chest. Under these circumstances, who can be a better husband for my daughter? Both myself and my daughter have always prayed for this opportunity. You are the chief of the Yadu dynasty. You may kindly know that from the very beginning I have made a vow to marry my daughter to a suitable candidate, one who can come out victorious in the test I have devised. I have imposed this test just to understand the prowess and position of my intended son-in-law. You are Lord Kṛṣṇa, and You are the chief of all heroes. I am sure You shall be able to bring these seven bulls under control without any difficulty. Until now they have never been subdued by any prince; anyone who has attempted to bring them under control has simply had his limbs broken."

King Nagnajit continued his request: "Kṛṣṇa, if You'll kindly bridle the seven bulls and bring them under control, then undoubtedly You will be selected as the desired husband of my daughter, Satyā." After hearing this statement, Kṛṣṇa could understand that the King did not want to break his vow. Thus, in order to fulfill his desire, He tightened His belt and prepared to fight with the bulls. He immediately divided Himself into seven Kṛṣṇas, and each one of Them immediately caught hold of a bull and bridled its nose, thus bringing it under control as if it were a plaything.

Kṛṣṇa's dividing Himself into seven is very significant. It was known to Satyā, the daughter of King Nagnajit, that Kṛṣṇa had already married many other wives, and still she was attached to Kṛṣṇa. In order to encourage her, He immediately expanded Himself into seven. The purport is that Kṛṣṇa is one, but He has unlimited forms of expansions. He married many hundreds of thousands of wives, but this does not mean that while He was with one wife the others were bereft of His association. Kṛṣṇa could associate with each and every wife by His expansions.

When Kṛṣṇa brought the bulls under His control by bridling their noses, their strength and pride were immediately smashed. The name and fame which the bulls had attained was thus vanquished. When the bulls had been bridled by Kṛṣṇa, He pulled them strongly, just as a child pulls a toy wooden bull. Upon seeing this advantage of Kṛṣṇa, King Nagnajit became very much astonished and immediately, with great pleasure, brought his daughter Satyā before Kṛṣṇa and handed her over to Him. Kṛṣṇa also immediately accepted Satyā as His wife. Then there was a marriage ceremony with great pomp. The queens of King Nagnajit also were very much pleased because their daughter Satyā got Kṛṣṇa as her husband. Since the King and queens were very pleased on this auspicious occasion, there was a celebration all over the city in honor of the marriage. Everywhere was heard the sounds of the conchshell and kettledrum and various other vibrations of music and song. The learned *brāhmaṇas* began to shower their blessings upon the newly married couple. In jubilation, all the inhabitants of the city dressed themselves with colorful garments and ornaments. King Nagnajit was so pleased that he began to give a dowry to the daughter and son-in-law, as follows.

First of all he gave them ten thousand cows and three thousand well-dressed young maidservants, ornamented up to their necks. This system of dowry is still current in India especially for the *kṣatriya* princes. Also, when a *kṣatriya* prince is married, at least a dozen maidservants of similar age are given along with the bride. After giving the cows and maidservants, the King also enriched the dowry by giving 9,000 elephants and a hundred times more chariots than elephants. This means that he gave 900,000 chariots. And he gave a hundred times more horses than chariots, or 90,000,000 horses, and a hundred times more slaves than horses. Such slaves and maidservants were maintained by the royal princes with all provisions, as if they were their own children or family members. After giving this dowry as described, the King of the Kośala Province bade his daughter and great son-in-law be seated on a chariot. He allowed them to go to their home, guarded by a division of well-equipped soldiers. When they were travelling fast to their new home, his heart became enlivened with affection for them.

Before this marriage of Satyā with Kṛṣṇa, there had been many competitive engagements with the bulls of King Nagnajit, and many other princes of the Yadu dynasty and of other dynasties as well had tried to win the hand of Satyā. When the frustrated princes of the other dynasties heard that Kṛṣṇa was successful in getting the hand of Satyā by subduing the bulls, naturally they became envious. While Kṛṣṇa was travelling to Dvārakā, all the frustrated and defeated princes encircled Him and began to shower their arrows on the bridal party. When they attacked Kṛṣṇa's party and threw arrows like incessant torrents of rain, Arjuna, the best friend of Kṛṣṇa, took charge of the challenge, and he alone drove them off very easily to please his great friend Kṛṣṇa on the occasion of His marriage. He immediately took up his bow of the name Gāṇḍīva and chased away all the princes; exactly as a lion drives away all other small animals simply by chasing them, Arjuna drove away all the princes without killing even one of them. After this, the chief of the Yadu dynasty, Lord Kṛṣṇa, along with His newly married wife and a huge dowry, entered the city of Dvārakā with great pomp. Kṛṣṇa then lived there with His wife very peacefully.

Kṛṣṇa had another aunt, His father's sister, whose name was Śrutakīrti, and who was married and lived in the Kekaya province. She had a daughter whose name was Bhadrā. Bhadrā also wanted to marry Kṛṣṇa, and her brother handed her over to Him unconditionally. Kṛṣṇa also accepted her as His bona fide wife. Thereafter, Kṛṣṇa married a daughter of the king of the Madras Province, and her name was Lakṣmaṇā. Lakṣmaṇā had all good qualities. She was also forcibly married by Kṛṣṇa, who took her in the same way that Garuḍa snatched the jar of nectar from the hands of the demons. Kṛṣṇa kidnapped this girl in the presence of many other princes in the assembly of her *svayaṁvara. Svayaṁvara* is a ceremony in which the bride can select her own husband from an assembly of many princes

The description of Kṛṣṇa's marriage with the five girls mentioned in this chapter is not sufficient. He had many other thousands of wives besides them. The other thousands of wives were accepted by Kṛṣṇa after killing one demon named Bhaumāsura. All these thousands of girls were held captive in the palace of Bhaumāsura, and Kṛṣṇa released them and married them.

Thus ends the Bhaktivedanta purport of the Second Volume, Twenty-third Chapter of* Kṛṣṇa, *"Five Queens Married by Kṛṣṇa."

24 / Deliverance of the Demon Bhaumāsura

The story of Bhaumāsura—how he kidnapped and made captive 16,000 princesses by collecting them from the palaces of various kings and how he was killed by Kṛṣṇa, the Supreme Lord of wonderful character—is all described by Śukadeva Gosvāmī to King Parīkṣit in the *Śrīmad-Bhāgavatam.* Generally, the demons are always against the demigods. This demon, Bhaumāsura, having become very powerful, took by force the umbrella from the throne of the demigod Varuṇa. He also took the earrings of Aditi, the mother of the demigods. He conquered a portion of heavenly Mount Meru and occupied the portion which was known as Maṇiparvata. The King of the heavenly planets, Indra, therefore came to Dvārakā to complain about Bhaumāsura before Lord Kṛṣṇa.

Hearing this complaint by Indra, the King of heaven, Lord Kṛṣṇa, accompanied by His wife Satyabhāmā, immediately started for the abode of Bhaumāsura. Both of them rode on the back of Garuḍa, who flew them to Prāgjyotiṣapura, the capital city of Bhaumāsura. It was not a very easy task to enter into the city of Prāgjyotiṣapura, because it was very well fortified. First of all, there were four formidable forts guarding the four directions of the city, and it was well-protected on all sides by formidable military strength. The next boundary was a water canal all around the city, and in addition the whole city was surrounded with electric wires. The next fortification was of *anila,* a gaseous substance. After this, there was a network of barbed wiring constructed by a demon of the name Mura. It appeared that the city was well-protected even in terms of today's scientific advancements.

When Kṛṣṇa arrived, He broke all the forts to pieces by the strokes of His club, and the military strength scattered here and there by the constant onslaught of the arrows of Kṛṣṇa. With His celebrated Sudarśana-cakra He counteracted the electrified boundary; the channels of water and the gaseous boundary were made null and void, and He cut to pieces the electrified network fabricated by the demon Mura. By the vibration of His conchshell, He not only broke the hearts of great fighters, but also the fighting machines which were there. Similarly, the walls around the city were broken by His invincible club.

The vibration of His conchshell sounded like the thunderbolt at the time of the dissolution of the whole cosmic situation. The demon Mura heard the vibration of the conchshell, awakened from his sleep, and personally came out to see what had happened. He had five heads and had long been living within the water. The Mura demon was as brilliant as the sun at the time of the dissolution of the cosmic manifestation, and his temper was like blazing fire. The effulgence of his body was so dazzling that it was difficult to see him with open eyes. When he came out, he first of all took out his trident and began to rush the Supreme Personality of Godhead. The onslaught of the demon Mura was like a big snake attacking Garuḍa. His angry mood was very severe, and he appeared ready to devour the three worlds. First of all he attacked the carrier of Kṛṣṇa, Garuḍa, by whirling his trident and he began to vibrate sounds through his five faces like the roaring of a lion. The roaring produced by the vibration of his mouths spread all over the atmosphere until it extended not only all over the world, but also into outer space, up and down and out to the ten directions. In this way, the sound was rumbling throughout the whole universe.

Lord Kṛṣṇa saw that the trident of the Mura demon was gradually rushing toward His carrier, Garuḍa. Immediately, by a trick of His hand, He took two arrows and threw them toward the trident, cutting it to pieces. Simultaneously, using many arrows, He pierced the mouths of the demon Mura. When he saw himself outmaneuvered by the Supreme Personality of Godhead, the Mura demon immediately began to strike Him in great anger with his club. But Lord Kṛṣṇa, with His own club, broke the club of Mura to pieces before it could reach Him. The demon, bereft of his weapon, decided to attack Kṛṣṇa with his strong arms, but by the aid of His Sudarśana-cakra, Kṛṣṇa immediately separated the demon's five heads from his body. The demon then fell into the water, just as the peak of a mountain falls into the ocean after being struck by the thunderbolt of Indra.

This demon Mura had seven sons, named Tāmra, Antarikṣa, Śravaṇa, Vibhāvasu, Vasu, Nabhasvān and Aruṇa. All of them became puffed up and vengeful because of the death of their father, and in order to retaliate, they prepared in great anger to fight with Kṛṣṇa. They equipped themselves with necessary weapons and situated Pīṭha, another demon, to act as commander in the battle. By the order of Bhaumāsura, all of them combinedly attacked Kṛṣṇa.

When they came before Lord Kṛṣṇa, they began to shower Him with many kinds of weapons, like swords, clubs, lances, arrows and tridents. But they did not know that the strength of the Supreme Personality of Godhead is unlimited and invincible. Kṛṣṇa, with His arrows, cut all the weapons of the men of Bhaumāsura into pieces, like grains. Kṛṣṇa then threw His weapons, and Bhaumāsura's commander-in-chief, Pīṭha, along with his assistants, fell down, their military dress cut off and their heads, legs, arms and thighs severed. All of them were sent to the superintendent of death, Yamarāja.

Bhaumāsura was also known as Narakāsura, for he happened to be the son of the earth personified. When he saw that all his soldiers, commanders and fighters were killed on the battlefield by the strokes of the weapons of the Personality of Godhead, he became exceedingly angry at the Lord. He then came out of the city with a great number of elephants who had all been born and brought up on the seashore. All of them were highly intoxicated. When they came out, they saw that Lord Kṛṣṇa and His wife were beautifully situated high in outer space just like a blackish cloud about the sun, glittering with the light of electricity. The demon Bhaumāsura immediately released a weapon called Śataghnī, by which he could kill hundreds of warriors with one stroke, and simultaneously all his assistants also threw their respective weapons at the Supreme Personality of Godhead. Lord Kṛṣṇa began to counteract all these weapons by releasing His feathered arrows. The result of this fight was that all the soldiers and commanders of Bhaumāsura fell to the ground, their arms, legs and heads separated from their trunks, and all their horses and elephants also fell with them. In this way, all the weapons released by Bhaumāsura were cut to pieces by the reaction of the Lord's arrows.

The Lord was fighting on the back of Garuḍa, and Garuḍa was also helping the Lord by striking the horses and the elephants with his wings and scratching their heads with his nails and sharpened beak. The elephants were feeling much pain by Garuḍa's attack on them, and they were all dispersing from the battlefield. Bhaumāsura alone remained on the battlefield, and he engaged himself in fighting with Kṛṣṇa. He saw that Kṛṣṇa's carrier, Garuḍa, was causing great disturbance to his soldiers and elephants, and in great anger he struck Garuḍa with all his strength, which defied the strength of the thunderbolt. Fortunately, Garuḍa was not an ordinary bird, and he felt the strokes given by Bhaumāsura just as a great elephant feels the impact of a garland of flowers.

Bhaumāsura thus came to see that none of his tricks would act upon Kṛṣṇa, and he became aware that all his attempts to kill Kṛṣṇa would be frustrated. Yet he attempted for the last time, taking a trident in his hand to strike Him. Kṛṣṇa was so dexterous that before Bhaumāsura could touch his trident, his head was cut off by the sharp Sudarśana-cakra. His head, illuminated by earrings and helmets, fell down on the battlefield. On the occasion of Bhaumāsura's being killed by Lord Kṛṣṇa, all the demon's relatives began to scream in disappointment, and the saintly persons began to glorify the chivalrous activities of the Lord. Taking this opportunity, the denizens of the heavenly planets began to shower flowers on the Lord.

At this time, the earth personified appeared before Lord Kṛṣṇa and greeted Him with a garland of *vaijayantī* jewels. She also returned the dazzling earrings of Aditi, bedecked with jewels and gold. She also returned the umbrella of Varuṇa, along with another valuable jewel, which she presented to Kṛṣṇa. After this, the earth personified began to offer her prayers to Kṛṣṇa, the Supreme Personality and master of the world, who is always worshiped by very exalted demigods. She fell down in obeisances and, in great devotional ecstasy, began to speak.

"Let me offer my respectful obeisances unto the Lord, who is always present with four kinds of symbols, namely His conchshell, disc, lotus and club, and who is the Lord of all demigods. Please accept my respectful obeisances unto You. My dear Lord, You are the Supersoul, and in order to satisfy the aspiration of Your devotees, You descend on the earth in Your various transcendental incarnations, which are just appropriate to the devotees' worshipful desires. Kindly accept my respectful obeisances.

"My dear Lord, the lotus flower is grown out of Your navel, and You are always decorated with a garland of lotus flowers. Your eyes are always spread like the petals of the lotus flower, and therefore they are all-pleasing to the eyes of others. Your lotus feet are so soft and delicate that they are always worshiped by Your unalloyed devotees, and they pacify their lotus-like hearts. I therefore repeatedly offer my respectful obeisances unto You.

"You possess all kinds of religions, fame, property, knowledge and renunciation; You are the shelter of all five opulences. Although You are all-pervading, You have nevertheless appeared as the son of Vasudeva. Please, therefore, accept my respectful obeisances. You are the original Supreme Personality of Godhead and the supreme cause of all causes. Only Your Lordship is the reservoir of all knowledge. Let me offer my respectful obeisances unto You. Personally You are unborn; still, You are the father of the whole cosmic manifestation. You are the reservoir and shelter of all kinds of energies. The manifestive appearance of this world is caused by You, and You are both the cause and effect of this cosmic manifestation. Please therefore accept my respectful obeisances.

"My dear Lord, as for the three gods—Brahmā, Viṣṇu and Śiva—they are also not independent of You. When there is necessity of creating this cosmic manifestation, You create Your passionate appearance of Brahmā, and when You want to maintain this cosmic manifestation, You expand Yourself as Lord Viṣṇu, the reservoir of all goodness. Similarly, You appear as Lord Śiva, master of the modes of ignorance, and thus dissolve the whole creation. Your transcendental position is always maintained, in spite of creating these three modes of material nature. You are never entangled like the ordinary living entities with these modes of material nature.

"Actually, my Lord, You are the material nature, You are the father of the universe, and You are the eternal time that has caused the combination of nature and the material creator. Still, You are always transcendental to all these material activities. My dear Lord, O Supreme Personality of Godhead, I know that earth, water, fire, air, sky, the five sense objects, mind, the senses and their deities, egotism, as well as the total material energy—everything animate and inanimate in this phenomenal world is resting upon You. Since everything is produced of You, nothing can be separated from You. Yet, since You are transcendentally situated, neither can anything material be identified with Your personality. Everything is, therefore, simultaneously one and different from You, and the philosophers who try to separate everything from you are certainly mistaken in their viewpoint.

"My dear Lord, may I inform You that this boy, whose name is Bhagadatta, is the son of my son, Bhaumāsura. He has been very much affected by the ghastly situation created by the death of his father and has become very much confused, being afraid of the present situation. I have therefore brought him to surrender unto Your lotus feet. I request Your Lordship to give shelter to this boy and bless him with Your lotus feet. I am bringing him to You so that he may become relieved from the reactions of all the sinful activities of his father."

When Lord Kṛṣṇa heard the prayers of mother Earth, He immediately assured her of immunity from all fearful situations. He said to Bhagadatta, "Don't be afraid." Then He entered the palace of Bhaumāsura, which was equipped with all kinds of opulences. In the palace of Bhaumāsura Lord Kṛṣṇa saw 16,100 young princesses, who had been kidnapped and held captive there. When the princesses saw the Supreme Personality of

Godhead, Kṛṣṇa, enter the palace, they immediately became captivated by the beauty of the Lord and prayed for His causeless mercy. Within their minds, they decided to accept Lord Kṛṣṇa as their husband without any hesitation. Each one of them began to pray to providence that Kṛṣṇa might become her husband. Sincerely and seriously, they offered their hearts to the lotus feet of Kṛṣṇa with an unalloyed devotional attitude. As the Supersoul in everyone's heart, Kṛṣṇa could understand their uncontaminated desire, and He agreed to accept them as His wives. Thus, He arranged for suitable dresses and ornaments for them, and each of them, seated on a palanquin, was dispatched to Dvārakā City. Kṛṣṇa also collected unlimited wealth from the palace, along with chariots, horses, jewels and treasure. He took from the palace fifty white elephants, each with four tusks, and all of them were dispatched to Dvārakā.

After this incident, Lord Kṛṣṇa and Satyabhāmā entered Amarāvatī, the capital city of the heavenly planet, and they immediately entered the palace of King Indra and his wife, Śacīdevī, who welcomed them. Kṛṣṇa then presented Indra with the earrings of Aditi.

When Kṛṣṇa and Satyabhāmā were returning from the capital city of Indra, Satyabhāmā remembered Kṛṣṇa's promise to give her the plant of the *pārijāta* flower. Taking the opportunity of having come to the heavenly kingdom, she plucked a *pārijāta* plant and kept it on the back of Garuḍa. Once Nārada took a *pārijāta* flower and presented it to Kṛṣṇa's senior wife, Śrī Rukmiṇīdevī. On account of this, Satyabhāmā developed an inferiority complex; she also wanted a flower from Kṛṣṇa. Kṛṣṇa could understand the competitive womanly nature of His co-wives, and He smiled. He immediately asked Satyabhāmā, "Why are you asking for only one flower? I would like to give you a whole tree of *pārijāta* flowers."

Actually, Kṛṣṇa had purposely taken His wife Satyabhāmā with Him so she could collect the *pārijāta* with her own hand. But the denizens of the heavenly planet, including Indra, became very irritated. Without their permission, Satyabhāmā had plucked a *pārijāta* plant, which is not to be found on the earth planet. Indra, along with other demigods, offered opposition to Kṛṣṇa and Satyabhāmā for taking away the plant, but in order to please His favorite wife Satyabhāmā, Kṛṣṇa became determined and adamant, so there was a fight between the demigods and Kṛṣṇa. As, usual, Kṛṣṇa came out victorious, and He triumphantly brought the *pārijāta* plant chosen by His wife to this earth planet, to Dvārakā. After this, the plant was installed in the palace garden of Satyabhāmā. On account of this extraordinary tree, the garden house of Satyabhāmā became extraordinarily beautiful. As the *pārijāta* plant came down to the earthly planet, the fragrance of the flower also came down, and the celestial swans also migrated to this earth in search of its fragrance and honey.

King Indra's behavior toward Kṛṣṇa was not very much appreciated by great sages like Śukadeva Gosvāmī. Out of His causeless mercy, Kṛṣṇa had gone to the heavenly kingdom, Amarāvatī, to present King Indra with his mother's earrings, which had been lost to Bhaumāsura, and Indra had been very glad to receive them. But when a flower plant from the heavenly kingdom was taken by Kṛṣṇa, Indra offered to fight with Him. This was self-interest on the part of Indra. He offered his prayer, tipping down his head to the lotus feet of Kṛṣṇa, but as soon as his purpose was served, he became a different creature. That is the way of the dealings of materialistic men. Materialistic men are always interested in their own profit. For this purpose they can offer any kind of respect to anyone, but when their personal interest is over, they are no longer friends. This selfish nature is not only found among the richer class of men on this planet, but is present even in personalities like Indra and other demigods. Too much wealth makes a man selfish. A selfish man is not prepared to take to Kṛṣṇa consciousness and is condemned by great devotees like Śukadeva Gosvāmī. In other words, possession of too many worldly riches is a disqualification for advancement in Kṛṣṇa consciousness.

After defeating Indra, Kṛṣṇa arranged to marry the 16,100 girls brought from the custody of Bhaumāsura. By expanding Himself in 16,100 forms, He simultaneously married them all in different palaces in one auspicious moment. He thus established the truth that Kṛṣṇa and no one else is the Supreme Personality of Godhead. There is nothing impossible, for Kṛṣṇa is the Supreme Personality of Godhead; He is all-powerful, omnipresent and imperishable, and as such there is nothing wonderful in this pastime. All the palaces of the more than 16,000 queens of Kṛṣṇa were full with suitable gardens, furniture and other paraphernalia, of which there is no parallel in this world. There is no exaggeration in this story from *Śrīmad-Bhāgavatam.* The queens of Kṛṣṇa were all expansions of the goddess of fortune, Lakṣmījī. Kṛṣṇa used to live with them in different palaces, and He treated them in exactly the same way as an ordinary man treats his wife.

We should always remember that the Supreme Personality of Godhead Kṛṣṇa was playing exactly like a human being; although He showed His extraordinary opulences by simultaneously marrying more than 16,000 wives in more than 16,000 palaces, He behaved with them just like an ordinary man, and He strictly followed the relationship between husband and wife required in ordinary homes. Therefore, it is very difficult to understand the characteristics of the Supreme Brahman, the Personality of Godhead. Even demigods like Brahmā and others are unable to probe into the transcendental pastimes of the Lord. The wives of Kṛṣṇa were so fortunate that they got the Supreme Personality of Godhead as their husband, although their husband's personality was unknown even to the demigods like Brahmā.

In their dealings as husband and wife, Kṛṣṇa and His queens would smile, talk, joke, embrace, and so on, and their conjugal relationship ever increasingly developed. In this way, both Kṛṣṇa and the queens enjoyed transcendental happiness in their household life. Although each and every queen had thousands of maidservants engaged for her service, the queens were all personally attentive in serving Kṛṣṇa. Each one of them used to receive Kṛṣṇa personally when He entered the palace. They engaged in getting Him seated on a nice couch, presenting Him with all kinds of worshipable paraphernalia, washing His lotus feet with Ganges water, offering Him betel nuts and massaging His legs. In this way, they were giving Him relief from the fatigue of being away from home. They saw to fanning Him nicely, offering Him fragrant essential floral oil, decorating Him with flower garlands, dressing His hair, asking Him to lie down to take rest, bathing Him personally and feeding Him nice palatable dishes. All these things were done by each queen herself. They did not wait for the maidservants. In other words, Kṛṣṇa and His different queens displayed on this earth an ideal household life.

Thus ends the Bhaktivedanta purport of the Second Volume, Twenty-fourth Chapter of Kṛṣṇa, *"Deliverance of the Demon Bhaumāsura."*

25 / Talks Between Kṛṣṇa and Rukmiṇī

Once upon a time, Lord Kṛṣṇa the Supreme Personality of Godhead, the bestower of all knowledge to all living entities from Brahmā to the insignificant ant, was sitting in the bedroom of Rukmiṇī, who was engaged in the service of the Lord along with her assistant maidservants. Kṛṣṇa was sitting on the bedstead of Rukmiṇī, and the maidservants were engaged in fanning Him with *cāmaras* (yak-tail fly-whisks).

Lord Kṛṣṇa's dealings with Rukmiṇī as a perfect husband are a perfect manifestation of the supreme perfection of the Personality of Godhead. There are many philosophers who propound a concept of the Absolute Truth in which God cannot do this or that. They deny the incarnation of God, or the Supreme Absolute Truth in human form. But actually, the fact is different: God cannot be subjected to our imperfect sensual activities. He is the all-powerful, omnipresent Personality of Godhead, and by His supreme will, He can not only create, maintain and annihilate the whole cosmic manifestation, but He can also descend as an ordinary human being in order to execute the highest mission. As stated in the *Bhagavad-gītā,* whenever there are discrepancies in the discharge of human occupational duties, He descends. He is not forced to appear by any external agency, but descends by His own internal potency in order to reestablish the standard functions of human activities as well as to simultaneously annihilate the disturbing elements in the progressive march of human civilization. In accordance with this principle of the transcendental pastimes of the Supreme Personality of Godhead, He descended in His eternal form of Śrī Kṛṣṇa in the dynasty of the Yadus.

The palace of Rukmiṇī was wonderfully finished. There were many canopies hanging on the ceiling with laces bedecked with pearl garlands, and the whole palace was illuminated by the effulgence of valuable jewels. There were many flower orchards of *baela* and *cāmeli,* which are considered to be the most fragrant flowers in India. There were many clusters of these plants, with blooming flowers enhancing the beauty of the palace. And because of the exquisite fragrance of the flowers, little groups of humming bees were gathered around the trees, and at night the pleasing moonshine glittered through the network of holes in the windows. There were many heavily flowered trees of *pārijāta,* and the mild wind stirred the flavor of the flowers all around. Within the walls of the palace, there was incense burning, and the fragrant smoke was leaking out of the window shutters. Within the room there were mattresses covered with white bedsheets resembling the foam of milk; the bedding was as soft and white as milk foam. In this situation, Lord Śrī Kṛṣṇa was very comfortably sitting and enjoying the service of Rukmiṇījī assisted by her maidservants.

Rukmiṇī was also very eager to get the opportunity of serving the Supreme Personality of Godhead as her husband. She therefore wanted to serve the Lord personally and took the handle of the *cāmara* from the hand of the maidservant and began to move the fan. The handle of the *cāmara* was made of gold, decorated and bedecked with valuable jewels, and it became more beautiful when it was taken by Rukmiṇī, because all of her fingers were beautifully set with jeweled rings. Her legs were decorated with ankle bells and jewels, which rang very softly between the pleats of her sari. Rukmiṇī's raised breasts were smeared with *kuṅkuma* and saffron; thus her beauty was enhanced by the reflection of the reddish color emanating from her covered breasts. The highly raised lower part of her buttocks was decorated with a jeweled lace girdle, and a locket of great effulgence hung on her neck. Above all, because she was engaged in the service of Lord Kṛṣṇa—although at that time she was old enough to have grown-up sons—her beautiful body was beyond compare in the three worlds. When we take account of her beautiful face, it appears that the curling hair on her head, the beautiful earrings on her ears, her smiling mouth, and her necklace of gold, all combined to shower rains of nectar; and it was definitely proved that Rukmiṇī was none other than the original goddess of fortune who is always engaged in the service of the lotus feet of Nārāyaṇa.

The pastimes of Kṛṣṇa and Rukmiṇī in Dvārakā are accepted by great authorities as manifestations of those of Nārāyaṇa and Lakṣmī, which are of an exalted opulence. The pastimes of Rādhā and Kṛṣṇa in Vṛndāvana are simple and rural, distinguished from the polished urban characteristics of those of Dvārakā. The characteristics of Rukmiṇī were unusually bright, and Kṛṣṇa was very much satisfied with her behavior.

Kṛṣṇa had experienced that when Rukmiṇī was offered a *pārijāta* flower by Nārada Muni, Satyabhāmā had become envious of her co-wife and had immediately demanded a similar flower from Kṛṣṇa. In fact, she could not be pacified until she was promised the whole tree. That was actually done by Kṛṣṇa; the tree was brought down to the earth planet from the heavenly kingdom. After this episode, Kṛṣṇa expected that because Satyabhāmā had been rewarded by a full tree of *pārijāta,* Rukmiṇī would also demand something. Rukmiṇī did not mention anything of the incident, however, for she was grave and simply satisfied in her service. Kṛṣṇa wanted to see her a bit irritated, and therefore He schemed in order to see the beautiful face of Rukmiṇī in an irritated condition. Although Kṛṣṇa had more than 16,100 wives, He used to behave with each of them with familial affection; He would create a particular situation between Himself and His wife in which the wife would criticize Him in the irritation of love, and Kṛṣṇa would enjoy this. In this case, because Kṛṣṇa could not find any fault with Rukmiṇī, for she was very great and always engaged in His service, He smilingly, in great love, began to speak to her. Rukmiṇī was the daughter of King Bhīṣmaka, a powerful king. Thus Kṛṣṇa did not address her as Rukmiṇī; He addressed her this time as the princess. "My dear princess, it is very surprising. Many great personalities in the royal order wanted to marry you. Although not all of them were kings, all possessed the opulence and riches of the kingly order; they were well-behaved, learned, famous among kings, beautiful in their bodily features and personal qualifications, liberal, very powerful in strength, and advanced in every respect. They were not unfit in any way, and over and above that, your father and your brother had no objection to such marriages. On the contrary, they gave their word of honor that you would be married with Śiśupāla; the marriage was sanctioned by your parents. Śiśupāla was a great king and was so lusty and mad after your beauty that if he had married you, I think he would always have remained with you just like your faithful servant.

"In comparison to Śiśupāla, with his personal qualities, I am nothing. And you may personally realize it. I am surprised that you rejected the marriage with Śiśupāla and accepted Me, who am inferior in comparison to Śiśupāla. I think myself completely unfit to be your husband because you are so beautiful, sober, grave and exalted. May I inquire from you the reason that induced you to accept Me? Now, of course, I can address you as My beautiful wife, but still I may inform you of My actual position—that I am inferior to all those princes who wanted to marry you.

"First of all, you may know that I was so much afraid of Jarāsandha that I could not dare to live on the land, and thus I have constructed this house within the water of the sea. It is not my business to disclose this secret to others, but you must know that I am not very heroic; I am a coward and am afraid of them. Still I am not safe, because all the great kings of the land are inimical to Me. I have personally created this inimical feeling by fighting with them in many ways. Another fault is that although I am on the throne of Dvārakā, I have no immediate claim. Although I got a kingdom by killing My maternal uncle, Kaṁsa, the kingdom was to go to My grandfather; so actually I have no possession of a kingdom. Besides that, I have no fixed aim in life. People cannot understand Me very well. What is the ultimate goal of My life? They know very well that I was a cowherd boy in Vṛndāvana. People expected that I would follow the footsteps of My foster father, Nanda Mahārāja, and be faithful to Śrīmatī Rādhārāṇī and all Her friends in the village of Vṛndāvana. But all of a sudden I left them. I wanted to become a famous prince. Still I could not have any kingdom, nor could I rule as a prince. People are bewildered about My ultimate goal of life; they do not know whether I am a cowherd boy or a prince, whether I am the son of Nanda Mahārāja or the son of Vasudeva. Because I have no fixed aim in life, people may call Me a vagabond. Therefore, I am surprised that you could select such a vagabond husband.

"Besides this, I am not very much polished, even in social etiquette. A person should be satisfied with one wife, but you see I have married many times, and I have more than 16,000 wives. I cannot please all of them as a polished husband. My behavior with them is not very nice, and I know you are very much conscious of it. I sometimes create a situation with My wives which is not very happy. Because I was trained in a village in My childhood, I am not well acquainted with the etiquette of urban life. I do not know the way to please a wife with nice words and behavior. And from practical experience it is found that any woman who follows My way or who becomes attracted by Me is ultimately left to cry for the rest of her life. In Vṛndāvana, many *gopīs* were attracted to Me, and now I have left them, and they are living but are simply crying for Me in separation. I have heard from Akrūra and Uddhava that since I left Vṛndāvana, all my cowherd boy friends, the *gopīs* and Rādhārāṇī, and My foster father Nanda Mahārāja are simply crying constantly for Me. I have left Vṛndāvana for good and am now engaged with the queens in Dvārakā, but I am not well-behaved with any of you. So you can very easily understand that I have no steadiness of character; I am not a very reliable husband. The net result of being attracted to Me is to acquire a life of bereavement only.

"My dear beautiful princess, you may also know that I am always penniless. Just after My birth, I was carried penniless to the house of Nanda Mahārāja, and I was raised just like a cowherd boy. Although My foster father possessed many hundreds of thousands of cows, I was not proprietor of even one of them. I was simply entrusted to take care of them and tender them, but I was not the proprietor. Here also, I am not proprietor of anything, but am always penniless. There is no cause to lament for such a penniless condition; I possessed nothing in the past, so why should I lament that I do not possess anything at present? You may note also that My devotees are not very opulent persons; they also are very poor in worldly goods. Those who are very rich, possessing worldly wealth, are not interested in devotion to Me or Kṛṣṇa consciousness. On the contrary, when a person becomes penniless, whether by force or by circumstances, he may become interested in Me if he gets the proper opportunity. Persons who are proud of their riches, even if they are offered association with My devotees, do not take advantage of consciousness of Me. In other words, the poorer class of men may have some interest in Me, but the richer class of men have no interest. I think, therefore, that your selection of Me was not very intelligent. You appear to be very intelligent, trained by your father and brother, but ultimately you have made a great mistake in selecting your life's companion.

"But there is no harm; it is better late than never. You are at liberty to select a suitable husband who is actually an equal to you in opulence, family tradition, wealth, beauty, education–in all respects. Whatever mistakes you may have made may be forgotten. Now you may chalk out your own lucrative path of life. Usually a person does not establish a marital relationship with a person who is either higher or lower than his position. My dear daughter of the King of Vidarbha, I think you did not consider very sagaciously before your marriage. Thus you made a wrong selection by choosing Me as your husband. You mistakenly heard about My having very exalted character, although factually I was nothing more than a beggar. Without seeing Me and My actual position, simply by hearing about Me, you selected Me as your husband. That was not very rightly done. Therefore I advise you that it is better late than never; you can now select one of the great *kṣatriya* princes and accept him as your life's companion, and you can reject Me."

Kṛṣṇa was proposing that Rukmiṇī divorce Him at a time when Rukmiṇī already had many grown-up children. Therefore Kṛṣṇa's whole proposition to Rukmiṇī appeared to be something unexpected, because according to Vedic culture there was no such thing as separation of husband and wife by divorce. Nor was it possible for Rukmiṇī to do so in advanced age, when she had many married sons. Each and every one of Kṛṣṇa's proposals appeared to Rukmiṇī to be crazy, and she was surprised that Kṛṣṇa could say such things. Simple as she was, her anxiety was increasing more and more at the thought of separation from Kṛṣṇa.

Kṛṣṇa continued: "After all, you have to prepare yourself for your next life. I therefore advise that you select someone who can help you both in this life and the next life, for I am completely unable to help. My dear beautiful princess, you know that all the members of the princely order, including Śiśupāla, Śālva, Jarāsandha, Dantavakra and even your elder brother Rukmī, are all My enemies; they do not like Me at all. They hate Me from the core of their hearts. All these princes were very much puffed up with their worldly possessions, and they did not care a fig for anyone who came before them. In order to teach them some lessons, I agreed to kidnap you according to your desire; otherwise I actually have no love for you, although you loved Me even before the marriage.

"As I have already explained, I am not very much interested in family life or love between husband and wife. By nature, I am not very fond of family life, wife, children, home and opulences. As My devotees are always neglectful of all these worldly possessions, I am also like that. Actually, I am interested in self-realization; that gives Me pleasure, and not this family life." After submitting His statement, Lord Kṛṣṇa suddenly stopped.

The great authority Śukadeva Gosvāmī remarks that Kṛṣṇa almost always passed His time with Rukmiṇī, and Rukmiṇī was a bit proud to be so fortunate that Kṛṣṇa never left her even for a moment. Kṛṣṇa, however, does not like any of His devotees to be proud. As soon as a devotee becomes so, by some tactic He cuts down that pride. In this case also, Kṛṣṇa said many things which were hard for Rukmiṇī to hear. She could only conclude that although she was proud of her position, Kṛṣṇa could be separated from her at any moment.

Rukmiṇī was conscious that her husband was not an ordinary human being. He was the Supreme Personality of Godhead, the master of the three worlds. By the way He was speaking, she was afraid of being separated from the Lord, for she had never heard such harsh words from Kṛṣṇa before. Thus she became perplexed with fear of separation, and her heart began to palpitate. Without replying to a word of Kṛṣṇa's statement, she simply cried in great anxiety, as if being drowned in an ocean of grief. She silently scratched the ground with the nails of her toes, which were reflecting reddish light on the ground. The tears from her eyes were pink, mixed with the black cosmetic ointment from her eyelids, and the waters were dropping down, washing the *kuṅkuma* and saffron from her breasts. Choked up on account of great anxiety, unable to speak even a word, she kept her head downward and remained standing just like a stick. Due to extremely painful fearfulness and lamentation, she lost all her reasoning powers and became so weak that immediately her body lost so much weight that the bangles on her wrists became slackened. The *cāmara* rod with which she was serving Kṛṣṇa immediately fell from her hand. Her brain and memory became puzzled, and she lost consciousness. The nicely combed hair on her head scattered here and there, and she fell down straight, like a banana tree cut down by a whirlwind.

Lord Kṛṣṇa immediately realized that Rukmiṇī had not taken His words in a joking spirit. She had taken them very seriously, and in her extreme anxiety over immediate separation from Him, she had fallen into this condition. Lord Śrī Kṛṣṇa is naturally very affectionate toward His devotees, and seeing Rukmiṇī's condition, His heart immediately became softened. At once He became merciful to her. The relationship between Kṛṣṇa and Rukmiṇī was as Lakṣmī-Nārāyaṇa; therefore, He appeared before her in His four-handed manifestation of Nārāyaṇa. He got down from the bedstead, brought her up by her hands, and, placing His cooling hands on her face, smoothed the scattered hairs on her head. Lord Kṛṣṇa dried the wet breast of Rukmiṇījī with His hand. Understanding the seriousness of Rukmiṇī's love for Him, He embraced her to His chest.

The Supreme Personality is very expert in putting a thing reasonably for one's understanding, and thus He tried to retract all that He said before. He is the only resort for all the devotees, and so He knows very well how to satisfy His pure devotees. Kṛṣṇa understood that Rukmiṇī could not follow the statements which He had made in a joking way. To counteract her confusion, He again began to speak, as follows.

"My dear daughter of King Vidarbha, My dear Rukmiṇī, please do not misunderstand Me. Don't be unkind unto Me like this. I know you are sincerely and seriously attached to Me; you are My eternal companion. The words which have affected you so much are not factual. I wanted to irritate you a bit, and I was expecting you to make counter answers to those joking words. Unfortunately, you have taken them seriously; I am very sorry for it. I expected that your red lips would tremble in anger on hearing My statement and you would chastise Me in many words. O perfection of love, I never expected that your condition would be like this. I expected that you would put your blinking eyes upon Me in retaliation, and in that way, I would be able to see your beautiful face in that angry mood.

"My dear beautiful wife, you know that we are householders. We are always busy in many household affairs, so we long for a time that we can enjoy some joking words between us. That is our ultimate game in household life. Actually, the householders work very hard day and night, but all fatigue of the day's labor becomes minimized as soon as they meet, husband and wife together, and enjoy life in many ways." Lord Kṛṣṇa wanted to exhibit Himself just as an ordinary householder who delights himself by exchanging joking words with his wife. He therefore repeatedly requested Rukmiṇī not to take those words very seriously.

In this way, when Lord Kṛṣṇa pacified Rukmiṇī by His sweet words, she could understand that what was formerly spoken by Him was not actually meant, but was spoken to evoke some joking pleasure between themselves. She was therefore pacified by hearing the words of Kṛṣṇa. Gradually she was freed from all fearfulness of separation from Him, and she began to look on His face very cheerfully with her naturally smiling face. She said, "My dear lotus-eyed Lord, Your statement that we are not a fit combination is completely right. It is not possible for me to come to an equal level with You because You are the reservoir of all qualities, the unlimited Supreme Personality of Godhead. How can I be a fit match for You? There is no possibility of comparison with You, who are the master of all greatness, controller of the three qualities and the object of worship for great demigods like Brahmā and Lord Śiva. As far as I am concerned, I am a production of the three modes of material nature. The three modes of material nature are impediments towards the progressive advancement of devotional service. When and where can I be a fit match for You? My dear husband, You have rightly said also that being afraid of the kings, You have taken shelter in the water of the sea. But who is the king of this material world? I do not think that the so-called royal families are kings of the material world. The kings of the material world are the three modes of material nature. They are actually the controllers of this material world. You are situated in the core of everyone's heart, where You remain completely aloof from the touch of the three modes of material nature, and there is not doubt about it.

"You say You always maintain enmity with the worldly kings. But who are the worldly kings? I think the worldly kings are the senses. They are most formidable, and they control everyone. Certainly You maintain enmity with these material senses. You are never under the control of the senses; rather, You are the controller of the senses, Hṛṣīkeśa. My dear Lord, You have said that You are bereft of all royal power, and that is also correct. Not only are You bereft of material world supremacy, but even Your servants, those who have some attachment to Your lotus feet, also give up the material world supremacy because they consider the material position to be the darkest region, which checks the progress of spiritual enlightenment. Your servants do not like material supremacy, so what to speak of You? My dear Lord, Your statement that You do not act as an ordinary person with a particular aim in life is also perfectly correct. Even Your great devotees and servants, known as great sages and saintly persons, remain in such a state that no one can get any clue to the aim of their lives. They are considered by the human society to be crazy and cynical. Their aim of life remains a mystery to the common human being; the lowest of the mankind can know neither You nor Your servant. A contaminated human being cannot even imagine the pastimes of You and Your devotees. O unlimited one, when the activities and endeavors of Your devotees remain a mystery to the common human being, how can they understand Your motive and endeavor? All kinds of energies and opulences are engaged in Your service, but still they are resting at Your shelter.

"You have described Yourself as penniless, but this condition is not poverty. Since there is nothing in existence but Yourself, You do not require to possess anything–You Yourself are everything. Unlike others, You do not require to purchase anything extraneously. With You all contrary things can be adjusted because You are absolute. You do not possess anything, but no one is richer than You. In the material world no one can be rich without possessing. Since Your Lordship is absolute, You can adjust the contradiction of possessing nothing but at the same time being the richest. In the *Vedas* it is stated that although You have no material hands and legs, You accept everything which is offered in devotion by the devotees. You have no material eyes and ears, but still You can see everything everywhere, and You can hear everything everywhere. Although You do not possess anything, the great demigods who accept prayers and worship from others come and worship You to solicit Your mercy. How can You be categorized among the poor?

"My dear Lord, You have also stated that the richest section of human society does not worship You. This is also correct, because persons who are puffed up with material possessions think of utilizing their property for sense gratification. When a poverty-stricken man becomes rich, he makes a program for sense gratification. This is due to his ignorance of how to utilize his hard-earned money. Under the spell of the external energy, he thinks that his money is properly employed in sense gratification, and thus he neglects to render transcendental service. My dear Lord, You have stated that persons who possess nothing are very dear to You; renouncing everything, Your devotee wants to possess You only. I see, therefore, that a great sage like Nārada Muni who does not possess any material property is still very dear to You. And such persons do not care for anything but Your Lordship.

"My dear Lord, You have stated that a marriage between persons equal in status of social standing, beauty, riches, strength, influence and renunciation can be a suitable match. But this status of life can only be possible by Your grace. You are the supreme perfectional source of all opulences. Whatever opulent status of life one may have is all derived from You. As described in the *Vedānta-sūtra, janmādyasya yataḥ:* You are the supreme source from which everything emanates, the reservoir of all pleasures. Therefore, persons who are endowed with knowledge desire only to achieve You, and nothing else. To achieve Your favor, they give up everything—even the transcendental realization of Brahman. You are the supreme ultimate goal of life. You are the reservoir of all interests of the living entities. Those who are actually well-motivated desire only You, and for this reason they give up everything to attain success. They therefore deserve to be associated with You. In the society of the servitors and served in Kṛṣṇa consciousness, one is not subjected to the pains and pleasures of material society, which functions according to sex attraction. Therefore, everyone, man or woman, should seek to be an associate in Your society of servitors and served. You are the Supreme Personality of Godhead; no one can excel You, nor can anyone come up to an equal level with You. The perfect social system is that in which You remain in the center, being served as the Supreme, and all others engage as Your servitors. In such a perfectly constructed society, everyone can remain eternally happy and blissful.

"My Lord, You have stated that only the beggars praise Your glories, and that is also perfectly correct. But who are those beggars? Those beggars are all exalted devotees, liberated personalities and those in the renounced order of life. They are all great souls and devotees who have no other business than to glorify You. Such great souls forgive even the worst offender. These so-called beggars execute their spiritual advancement of life, tolerating all kinds of tribulations in the material world. My dear husband, do not think that out of my inexperience I accepted You as my husband; actually, I followed all these great souls. I followed the path of these great beggars and decided to surrender my life unto Your lotus feet.

"You have said that You are penniless, and that is correct. You distribute Yourself completely to these great souls and devotees. Knowing this fact perfectly well, I rejected even such great personalities like Lord Brahmā and King Indra. My Lord, the great time factor acts under Your direction only. The time factor is so great and powerful that within moments it can effect devastation anywhere within the creation. Considering all these factors, I thought Jarāsandha, Śiśupāla and similar other princes who wanted to marry Me to be no more important than ordinary insects.

"My dear all-powerful son of Vasudeva, Your statement that You have taken shelter within the water of the ocean, being afraid of all the great princes, is quite suitable, but my experience with You contradicts this. I have actually seen that You kidnapped me forcibly in the presence of all these princes. At the time of my marriage ceremony, simply by giving a jerk to the string of Your bow, You very easily drove the others away and kindly gave me shelter at Your lotus feet. I still remember vividly that You kidnapped me in the same way as a lion forcibly takes his share of hunted booty, driving away all other small animals within the twinkling of an eye.

"My dear lotus-eyed Lord, I cannot understand Your statement that women and other persons who have taken shelter under Your lotus feet pass their days only in bereavement. From the history of the world we can see that princes like Aṅga, Pṛthu, Bharata, Yayāti and Gaya were all great emperors of the world, and there were no competitors to their exalted positions. But in order to achieve the favor of Your lotus feet, they renounced their exalted positions and entered into the forest to practice penances and austerities. When they voluntarily accepted such a position, accepting Your lotus feet as all in all, does it mean that they were in lamentation and bereavement?

"My dear Lord, You have advised me that I can still select another from the princely order and divorce myself of Your companionship. But, my dear Lord, it is perfectly well-known to me that You are the reservoir of all good qualities. Great saintly persons like Nārada Muni are always engaged simply in glorifying Your transcendental characteristics. If someone simply takes shelter of such a saintly person, he immediately becomes freed from all material contamination. And by coming in direct contact with Your service the goddess of fortune agrees to bestow all her blessings. Under the circumstances, what woman who has once heard of Your glories from authoritative sources and somehow or other has tasted the nectarean flavor of Your lotus feet can be foolish enough to agree to marry someone of this material world who is always afraid of death, disease, old age and rebirth? I have therefore accepted Your lotus feet, not without consideration, but after mature and deliberate decision. My dear Lord, You are the master of the three worlds. You can fulfill all the desires of all Your devotees in this world and the next, because You are the Supreme Soul of everyone. I have therefore selected You as my husband, considering You to be the only fit personality. You may throw me in any species of life according to the reaction of my fruitive activities, and I haven't the least concern for this. My only ambition is that I may always remain fast to Your lotus feet, because You can deliver Your devotees from the illusory material existence and are always prepared to distribute Yourself to Your devotees.

"My dear Lord, You have advised me to select one of the princes such as Śiśupāla, Jarāsandha or Dantavakra, but what is their position in this world? They are always engaged in hard labor to maintain their household life, just like the bulls working hard day and night with the oil-pressing machine. They are compared to asses, beasts of burden. They are always dishonored like the dogs, and they are miserly like the cats. They have sold themselves like slaves to their wives. Any unfortunate woman who has never heard of Your glories may accept such a man as her husband, but a woman who has learned about You—that You are praised not only in this world, but in the halls of the great demigods like Lord Brahmā and Lord Śiva—will not accept anyone besides Yourself as her husband. A man within this material world is just a dead body. In fact, superficially, the living entity is covered by this body, which is nothing but a bag of skin decorated with beards and moustaches, hairs on the body, nails on the fingers and hairs on the head. Within this decorated bag there are bunches of muscles, bundles of bones, and pools of blood, always mixed up with stool, urine, mucus, bile and polluted air, and enjoyed by different kinds of insects and germs. A foolish woman accepts such a dead body as her husband and, in sheer misunderstanding, loves him as her dear companion. This is only possible because such a woman has never tasted the ever-blissful flavor of Your lotus feet.

"My dear lotus-eyed husband, You are self-satisfied. You do not care whether or not I am beautiful or qualified; You are not at all concerned about it. Therefore Your nonattachment for me is not at all astonishing; it is quite natural. You cannot be attached to any woman, however exalted her position and beauty. Whether You are attached to me or not, may my devotion and attention be always engaged at Your lotus feet. The material mode of passion is also Your creation, so when You passionately glance upon me, I accept it as the greatest boon of my life. I am ambitious only for such auspicious moments."

After hearing Rukmiṇī's statement and her clarification of each and every word which He had used to arouse her anger of love toward Him, Kṛṣṇa addressed Rukmiṇī as follows: "My dear chaste wife, My dear princess, I was expecting such an explanation from you, and for this purpose only I spoke all those joking words, so that you might be cheated of the real point of view. Now My purpose has been served. The wonderful explanation that you have given to each and every word of Mine is completely factual and approved by Me. O most beautiful Rukmiṇī, You are My dearmost wife. I am greatly pleased to understand how much love you have for Me. Please take it for granted that no matter what ambition and desire you might have and no matter what you might expect from Me, I am always at your service. And it is a fact also that My devotees, My dearmost friends and servitors, are always free from material contamination, even though they are not inclined to ask from Me such liberation. My devotees never desire anything from Me except to be engaged in My service. And yet because they are completely dependent upon Me, even if they are found to ask something from Me, that is not material. Such ambitions and desires, instead of becoming the cause of material bondage, become the source of liberation from this material world.

"My dear chaste and pious wife, I have tested, on the basis of strict chastity, your love for your husband, and you have passed the examination most successfully. I have purposely agitated you by speaking many words which were not applicable to your character, but I am surprised to see that not a pinch of your devotion to Me has been deviated from its fixed position. My dear wife, I am the bestower of all benedictions, even up to the standard of liberation from this material world, and it is I only who can stop the continuation of material existence and call one back to home, back to Godhead. One whose devotion for Me is adulterated worships Me for some material benefit, just to keep himself in the world of material happiness, culminating in the pleasure of sex life. One who engages himself in severe penance and austerities just to attain this material happiness is certainly under the illusion of My external energy. Persons who are engaged in My devotional service simply for the purpose of material gains and sense gratification certainly are very foolish. Material happiness based on sex life is available in the most abominable species of life, such as the hogs and dogs. No one should try to approach Me for such happiness, because it is available even if one is put into a hellish condition of life. It is better, therefore, for persons who are simply after material happiness and not after Me to remain in that hellish condition."

Material contamination is so strong that everyone is working very hard day and night for material happiness. The show of religiousness, austerity, penance, humanitarianism, philanthropy, politics, science–everything is aimed at realizing some material benefit. For the immediate success of material benefit, the materialistic persons generally worship different demigods, and under the spell of material propensities they sometimes take to the devotional service of the Lord. Sometimes it so happens that if a person sincerely serves the Lord and at the same time maintains material ambition, the Lord very kindly removes the sources of material happiness. Without finding any recourse in material happiness, the devotee then engages himself absolutely in pure devotional service.

Lord Kṛṣṇa continued, "My dear best of the queens, it is clearly understood by Me that you have no material ambition; your only purpose is to serve Me, and you have long been engaged in unalloyed service. Exemplary unalloyed devotional service not only can bestow upon the devotee liberation from this material world, but it also promotes him to the spiritual world for being eternally engaged in My service. Persons who are too addicted to material happiness cannot render such service. Women whose hearts are polluted and full of material desires devise various means of sense gratification while outwardly showing themselves to be great devotees.

"My dear honored wife, although I have thousands of wives, I do not think that any one of them can love Me more than you. The practical proof of your extraordinary position is that you had never seen Me before your marriage; you had simply heard about Me from a third person, and still your faith in Me was so fixed that even in the presence of many qualified, rich and beautiful men of the royal order, you did not select any one of them as your husband, but insisted on having Me. You neglected all the princes present, and very politely you sent Me a confidential letter inviting Me to kidnap you. While I was kidnapping you, your elder brother Rukmī violently protested and fought with Me. As a result of the fight, I defeated him mercilessly and disfigured his body. At the time of Aniruddha's marriage, when we were all engaged in playing chess, there was another fight with your brother Rukmī on a controversial verbal point, and My elder brother Balarāma finally killed him. I was surprised to see that you did not utter even a word of protest over this incidence. Because of your great anxiety that you might be separated from Me, you suffered all the consequences without speaking even a word. As the result of this great silence, My dear wife, you have purchased Me for all time; I have become eternally under your control. You sent your messenger to Me inviting Me to kidnap you, and when you found that there was a little delay in My arriving on the spot, you began to see the whole world as vacant. At that time you concluded that your beautiful body was not fit to be touched by anyone else; therefore, thinking that I was not coming, you decided to commit suicide and immediately end that body. My dear Rukmiṇī, such great and exalted love for Me will always remain within My soul. As far as

I am concerned, it is not within My power to repay you for your unalloyed devotion to Me."

The Supreme Personality of Godhead Kṛṣṇa certainly has no business being anyone's husband or son or father, because everything belongs to Him and everyone is under His control. He does not require anyone's help for His satisfaction. He is *ātmārāma,* self-satisfied; He can derive all pleasure by Himself, without anyone's help. When the Lord descends to play the part of a human being, He plays a role either as a husband, son, friend or enemy, in full perfection. As such, when He was playing as the perfect husband of the queens, especially of Rukmiṇījī, He enjoyed conjugal love in complete perfection.

According to Vedic culture, although polygamy is allowed, none of the wives should be ill-treated. In other words, one may take many wives only if he is able to satisfy all of them equally as an ideal householder; otherwise it is not allowed. Lord Kṛṣṇa is the world-teacher; therefore, even though He had no need for a wife, He expanded Himself into as many forms as He had wives, and He lived with them as an ideal householder, observing the regulative principles, rules and commitments in accordance with the Vedic injunctions and the social laws and customs of society. For each of His 16,108 wives, He simultaneously maintained different palaces, different establishments and different atmospheres. Thus the Lord, although one, exhibited Himself as 16,108 ideal householders.

Thus ends the Bhaktivedanta purport of the Second Volume, Twenty-fifth Chapter of Kṛṣṇa, *"Talks Between Kṛṣṇa and Rukmiṇī."*

26 / The Genealogical Table of the Family of Kṛṣṇa

Kṛṣṇa had 16,108 wives, and in each of them He begot ten sons, all of them equal to their father in the opulences of strength, beauty, wisdom, fame, wealth and renunciation. "Like father like son." All the 16,108 wives of Kṛṣṇa were princesses, and when each saw that Kṛṣṇa was always present in her respective palace and did not leave home, they considered Kṛṣṇa to be a henpecked husband who was very much attached to them. Every one of them thought that Kṛṣṇa was her very obedient husband, but actually Kṛṣṇa had no attraction for any of them. Although each thought that she was the only wife of Kṛṣṇa and was very, very dear to Him, Lord Kṛṣṇa, since He is *ātmārāma,* self-sufficient, was neither dear nor inimical to any one of them; He was equal to all the wives and treated them as a perfect husband just to please them. For Him, there was no need for even a single wife. In fact, since they were women, the wives could not understand the exalted position of Kṛṣṇa nor the truths about Him.

All the princesses who were wives of Kṛṣṇa were exquisitely beautiful, and each one of them was attracted by Kṛṣṇa's eyes, which were just like lotus petals, and by His beautiful face, long arms, broad ears, pleasing smile, humorous talk and sweet words. Influenced by these features of Kṛṣṇa, they all used to dress themselves very attractively, desiring to attract Kṛṣṇa by their feminine bodily appeal. They used to exhibit their feminine characteristics by smiling and moving their eyebrows, thus throwing sharpened arrows of conjugal love just to awaken Kṛṣṇa's lusty desires for them. Still, they could not arouse the mind of Kṛṣṇa or His sex appetite. This means that Kṛṣṇa never had any sex relations with any of His many wives, save and except to beget children.

The queens of Dvārakā were so fortunate that they got Lord Śrī Kṛṣṇa as their husband and personal companion, although He is not approachable by exalted demigods like Brahmā. They remained together as husband and wife, and Kṛṣṇa, as an ideal husband, treated them in such a way that at every moment there was an increase of transcendental bliss in their smiling exchanges, talking and mixing together. Each and every wife had hundreds and thousands of maidservants, yet when Kṛṣṇa entered the palaces of His thousands of wives, each one of them used to receive Kṛṣṇa personally by seating Him in a nice chair, worshiping Him with all requisite paraphernalia, personally washing His lotus feet, offering Him betel nuts, massaging His legs to relieve them from fatigue, fanning Him to make Him comfortable, offering all kinds of scented sandalwood pulp, oils and aromatics, putting flower garlands on His neck, dressing His hair, getting Him to lie down on the bed and assisting Him in taking His bath. Thus they served always in every respect, especially when Kṛṣṇa was eating. They were always engaged in the service of the Lord.

Of the 16,108 queens of Kṛṣṇa, each of whom had ten sons, there is the following list of the sons of the first eight queens. By Rukmiṇī, Kṛṣṇa had ten sons: Pradyumna, Cārudeṣṇa, Sudeṣṇa, Cārudeha, Sucāru, Cārugupta, Bhadracāru, Cārucandra, Vicāru, and Cāru. None of them were inferior in their qualities to their divine father, Lord Kṛṣṇa. Similarly, Satyabhāmā had ten sons, and their names are as follows: Bhānu, Subhānu, Svarbhānu, Prabhānu, Bhānumān, Candrabhānu, Bṛhadbhānu, Atibhānu, Śrībhānu and Pratibhānu. The next queen, Jāmbavatī, had ten sons, headed by Sāmba. Their names are as follows: Sāmba, Sumitra, Purujit, Śatajit, Sahasrajit, Vijaya, Citraketu, Vasumān, Draviḍa and Kratu. Lord Kṛṣṇa was specifically very affectionate to the sons of Jāmbavatī. By His wife Satyā, the daughter of King Nagnajit, Lord Kṛṣṇa had ten sons. They are as follows: Vīra, Candra, Aśvasena, Citragu, Vegavān, Vṛṣa, Āma, Śaṅku, Vasu and Kunti. Amongst all of them, Kunti was very powerful. Kṛṣṇa had ten sons by Kālindī, and they are as follows: Śruta, Kavi, Vṛṣa, Vīra, Subāhu, Bhadra, Śānti, Darśa, Pūrṇamāsa and the youngest, Somaka. For His next wife, Lakṣmaṇā, the daughter of the King of Madras Province, He begot ten sons, of the names Praghoṣa, Gātravān, Siṁha, Bala, Prabala, Ūrdhvaga, Mahāśakti, Saha, Oja and Aparājita. Similarly, His next wife, Mitravindā, had ten sons. They are as follows: Vṛka, Harṣa, Anila, Gṛdhra, Vardhana, Annāda, Mahāṁsa, Pāvana, Vahni and Kṣudhi. His next wife, Bhadrā, had ten sons, of the names Saṅgrāmajit, Bṛhatsena, Śūra, Praharaṇa, Arijit, Jaya, Subhadra, Vāma, Āyu and Satyaka. Besides these eight chief queens, Kṛṣṇa had 16,100 other wives, and all of them had ten sons each.

The eldest son of Rukmiṇī, Pradyumna, was married with Māyāvatī from his very birth, and afterwards he was again married with Rukmavatī, the daughter of his maternal uncle, Rukmī. From this Rukmavatī, Pradyumna had a son named Aniruddha. In this way, Kṛṣṇa's family—Kṛṣṇa and His wives, along with their sons and grandsons and even great-grandsons—all combined together to include very nearly one billion family members.

Rukmī, the elder brother of Kṛṣṇa's first wife, Rukmiṇī, was greatly harassed and insulted in his fight with Kṛṣṇa, but on the request of Rukmiṇī his life was saved. Since then Rukmī had held a great grudge against Kṛṣṇa and was always inimical toward Him. Nevertheless, his daughter was married with Kṛṣṇa's son, and his granddaughter was married with Kṛṣṇa's grandson, Aniruddha. This fact appeared to be a little astonishing to Mahārāja Parīkṣit when he heard it from Śukadeva Gosvāmī. "I am surprised that Rukmī and Kṛṣṇa, who were so greatly inimical to one another, could again be united by marital relationships between their descendants." Parīkṣit Mahārāja was curious about the mystery of this incident, and therefore he inquired further from Śukadeva Gosvāmī. Because Śukadeva Gosvāmī was a practical *yogī,* nothing was hidden from his power of insight. A perfect *yogī* like Śukadeva Gosvāmī can see past, present and future in all details. Therefore, from such *yogīs* or mystics there can be nothing concealed. When Parīkṣit Mahārāja inquired from Śukadeva Gosvāmī, Śukadeva Gosvāmī answered as follows.

Pradyumna, the eldest son of Kṛṣṇa, born of Rukmiṇī, was Cupid himself. He was so beautiful and attractive that the daughter of Rukmī, namely Rukmavatī, could not select any husband other than Pradyumna during her *svayaṁvara.* Therefore, in that selection meeting, she garlanded Pradyumna in the presence of all other princes. When there was a fight among the princes, Pradyumna came out victorious, and therefore Rukmī was obliged to offer his beautiful daughter to him. Although a far-off enmity was always blazing in the heart of Rukmī because of his being insulted by Kṛṣṇa's kidnapping of his sister Rukmiṇī, when his daughter selected Pradyumna as her husband Rukmī could not resist consenting to the marriage ceremony just to please his sister, Rukmiṇī. And so Pradyumna became the nephew of Rukmī. Besides the ten sons described above, Rukmiṇī had one beautiful daughter with big eyes, and she was married to the son of Kṛtavarmā, whose name was Balī.

Although Rukmī was a veritable enemy of Kṛṣṇa, he had great affection for his sister, Rukmiṇī, and he wanted to please her in all respects. On this account, when Rukmiṇī's grandson Aniruddha was to be married, Rukmī offered his granddaughter Rocanā to Aniruddha. Such marriage between immediate cousins is not very much sanctioned by the Vedic culture, but in order to please Rukmiṇī, Rukmī offered his daughter and granddaughter to the son and grandson of Kṛṣṇa. In this way, when the negotiation of the marriage of Aniruddha with Rocanā was complete, a big marriage party accompanied Aniruddha and started from Dvārakā. They travelled until they reached Bhojakaṭa, which Rukmī had colonized after his sister had been kidnapped by Kṛṣṇa. This marriage party was led by the grandfather, namely Lord Kṛṣṇa, accompanied by Lord Balarāma, as well as Kṛṣṇa's first wife, Rukmiṇī, His son Pradyumna, Jāmbavatī's son Sāmba and many other relatives and family members. They reached the town of Bhojakaṭa, and the marriage ceremony was peacefully performed.

The King of Kaliṅga was a friend of Rukmī's, and he gave him the ill advice to play with Balarāma and thus defeat Him in a bet. Amongst the *kṣatriya* kings, betting and gambling in chess was not uncommon. If someone challenged a friend to play on the chessboard, the friend could not deny the challenge. Śrī Balarāmajī was not a very expert chess player, and this was known to the King of Kaliṅga. So Rukmī was advised to retaliate against the family members of Kṛṣṇa by challenging Balarāma to play chess. Although not a very expert chess player, Śrī Balarāmajī was very enthusiastic in sporting activities. He accepted the challenge of Rukmī and sat down to play. Betting was with gold coins, and Balarāma first of all challenged with one hundred coins, then 1,000 coins, then 10,000 coins. Each time, Balarāma lost, and Rukmī became victorious.

Śrī Balarāma's losing the game was an opportunity for the King of Kaliṅga to criticize Kṛṣṇa and Balarāma. Thus the King of Kaliṅga was talking jokingly and purposefully showing his teeth to Balarāma. Because Balarāma was the loser in the game, He was a little intolerant of the sarcastic joking words. He became a little agitated, and when Rukmī again challenged Balarāma, he made a bet of 100,000 gold coins. Fortunately, this time Balarāma won. Although Balarāmajī had won, Rukmī, out of his cunningness, began to claim that Balarāma was the loser and that he himself had won. Because of this lie, Balarāmajī became most angry with Rukmī. His agitation was so sudden and great that it appeared like a tidal wave in the ocean on a full moon day. Balarāma's eyes are naturally reddish, and when He became agitated and angry His eyes became more reddish. This time He challenged and made a bet of a hundred million coins.

Again Balarāma was the winner according to the rules of chess, but Rukmī again cunningly began to claim that he had won. Rukmī appealed to the princes present, and He especially mentioned the name of the King of Kaliṅga. At that time there was a voice from the air during the dispute, and it announced that for all honest purposes Balarāma, the actual winner of this game, was being abused and that the statement of Rukmī that he had won was absolutely false.

In spite of this divine voice, Rukmī insisted that Balarāma had lost, and by his persistence it appeared that he had death upon his head. Falsely puffed up by the ill advice of his friend, he did not give much importance to the oracle, and he began to criticize Balarāmajī. He said, "My dear Balarāmajī, You two brothers, cowherd boys only, may be very expert in tending cows, but how can You be expert in playing chess or shooting arrows on the battlefield? These arts are well-known only to the princely order." Hearing this kind of pinching talk by Rukmī and hearing the loud laughter of all the other princes present there, Lord Balarāma became as agitated as burning cinders. He immediately took a club in His hand and, without any further talk, struck Rukmī on the head. From that one blow, Rukmī fell down immediately and was dead and gone. Thus Rukmī was killed by Balarāma on that auspicious occasion of Aniruddha's marriage.

These things are not very uncommon in *kṣatriya* society, and the King of Kaliṅga, being afraid that he would be the next to be attacked, fled from the scene. Before he could escape even a few steps, however, Balarāmajī immediately captured him and, because the King was always showing his teeth while criticizing Balarāma and Kṛṣṇa, broke all his teeth with His club. The other princes who were supporting the King of Kaliṅga and Rukmī were also captured, and Balarāma beat them with His club, breaking their legs and hands. They did not try to retaliate but thought it wise to run away from the bloody scene.

During this strife between Balarāma and Rukmī, Lord Kṛṣṇa did not utter a word, for He knew that if He supported Balarāma, Rukmiṇī would be unhappy, and if He said that the killing of Rukmī was unjust, then Balarāma would be unhappy. Therefore, Lord Kṛṣṇa was silent on the death of His brother-in-law, Rukmī, on the occasion of His grandson's marriage. He did not disturb either His affectionate relationship with Balarāma or with Rukmiṇī. After this, the bride and the bridegroom were ceremoniously seated on the chariot, and they started for Dvārakā, accompanied by the bridegroom's party. The bridegroom's party was always protected by Lord Kṛṣṇa, the killer of the Madhu demon. Thus they left Rukmī's kingdom, Bhojakaṭa, and happily started for Dvārakā.

Thus ends the Bhaktivedanta purport of the Second Volume, Twenty-sixth Chapter of* Kṛṣṇa, *"The Genealogical Table of the Family of Kṛṣṇa."

27 / The Meeting of Uṣā and Aniruddha

The meeting of Aniruddha and Uṣā, which caused a great fight between Lord Kṛṣṇa and Lord Śiva, is very mysterious and interesting. Mahārāja Parīkṣit was anxious to hear the whole story from Śukadeva Gosvāmī, and thus Śukadeva narrated it. "My dear King, you must have heard the name of King Bali. He was a great devotee who gave away in charity all that he had—namely, the whole world—to Lord Vāmana, the incarnation of Viṣṇu as a dwarf *brāhmaṇa.* King Bali had one hundred sons, and the eldest of all of them was Bāṇāsura."

This great hero Bāṇāsura, born of Mahārāja Bali, was a great devotee of Lord Śiva and was always ready to render service unto him. Because of his devotion, he achieved a great position in society, and he was honored in every respect. Actually, he was very intelligent and liberal also, and his activities are all praiseworthy because he never deviated from his promise and word of honor; he was very truthful and fixed in his vow. In those days, he was ruling over the city of Śonitapura. By the grace of Lord Śiva Bāṇāsura had one thousand hands, and he became so powerful that even demigods like King Indra were serving him as most obedient servants.

Long ago, when Lord Śiva was dancing in his celebrated fashion called *tāṇḍava-nṛtya,* for which he is known as Naṭarāja, Bāṇāsura helped Lord Śiva in his dancing by rythmically beating drums with his one thousand hands. Lord Śiva is well-known as Āśutoṣa, very easily pleased, and he is also very affectionate to his devotees. He is a great protector for persons who take shelter of him and is the master of all living entities in this material world. Being pleased with Bāṇāsura, he said, "Whatever you desire you can have from me because I am very much pleased with you." Bāṇāsura replied, "My dear lord, if you please, you can remain in my city just to protect me from the hands of my enemies."

Once upon a time, Bāṇāsura came to offer his respects to Lord Śiva. By touching the lotus feet of Lord Śiva with his helmet, which was shining like the sun globe, he offered his obeisances unto him. While offering his respectful obeisances, Bāṇāsura said, "My dear lord, anyone who has not fulfilled his ambition will be able to do so by taking shelter of your lotus feet, which are just like desire trees—one can take from them anything he desires. My dear lord, you have given me one thousand arms, but I do not know what to do with them. Please pardon me, but it appears that I cannot use them properly in fighting. I cannot find anyone competent to fight with me except your lordship, the original father of the material world. Sometimes I feel a great tendency to fight with my arms, and I go out to find a suitable warrior. Unfortunately, everyone flees, knowing my extraordinary power. Being baffled at not finding a match, I simply satisfy the itching of my arms by beating them against the mountains. In this way, I tear many great mountains to pieces."

Lord Śiva realized that his benediction had become troublesome for Bāṇāsura and addressed him, "You rascal! You are very eager to fight, but since you have no one to fight with, you are distressed. Although you think that there is no one in the world to oppose you except me, I say that you will eventually find such a competent person. At that time your days will come to an end, and your flag of victory will no longer fly. Then you will see your false prestige smashed to pieces!"

After hearing Lord Śiva's statement, Bāṇāsura became very puffed up with his power. He was elated that he would meet someone who would be able to smash him to pieces. Bāṇāsura then returned home with great pleasure, and he always waited for the day when the suitable fighter would come to cut down his strength. He was such a foolish demon. It appears that foolish, demonic human beings, when unnecessarily overpowered with material opulences, want to exhibit these opulences, and such foolish people feel satisfaction when these opulences are exhausted. The idea is that they do not know how to expend their energy for right causes, being unaware of the benefit of Kṛṣṇa consciousness. Actually, there are two classes of men—one is Kṛṣṇa conscious, the other is non-Kṛṣṇa conscious. The non-Kṛṣṇa conscious men are generally devoted to the demigods, whereas the Kṛṣṇa conscious men are devoted to the Supreme Personality of Godhead. Kṛṣṇa conscious persons utilize everything for the service of the Lord. The non-Kṛṣṇa conscious persons utilize everything for sense gratification, and Bāṇāsura is a perfect example of such a person. He was very anxious to utilize for his own satisfaction his extraordinary power to fight. Not finding any combatant, he struck his powerful hands against the mountains, breaking them into pieces. In contrast to this, Arjuna also possessed extraordinary powers for fighting, but he utilized them only for Kṛṣṇa.

Bāṇāsura had a very beautiful daughter, whose name was Uṣā. When she had attained the age of marriage and was sleeping amongst her many girl friends, she dreamt one night that Aniruddha was by her side and that she was enjoying a conjugal relationship with him, although she had never actually seen him nor heard of him before. She awoke from her dream exclaiming very loudly, "My dear beloved, where are you?" Being exposed to her other friends in this way, she became a little bit ashamed. One of Uṣā's girl friends was Citralekhā, who was the daughter of Bāṇāsura's prime minister. Citralekhā and Uṣā were intimate friends, and out of great curiosity Citralekhā asked, "My dear beautiful princess, as of yet you are not married to any young boy, nor have you seen any boys until now; so I am surprised that you are exclaiming like this. Who are you searching after? Who is your suitable match?"

On hearing Citralekhā's inquiries, Uṣā replied, "My dear friend, in my dream I saw a nice young man who is very, very beautiful. His complexion is swarthy, his eyes are just like lotus petals, and he is dressed in yellow garments. His arms are very long, and his general bodily features are so pleasing that any young girl would be attracted. I feel much pride in saying that this beautiful young man was kissing me, and I was very much enjoying the nectar of his kissing. I am sorry to inform you that just after this he disappeared, and I have been thrown into the whirlpool of disappointment. My dear friend, I am very anxious to find this wonderful young man, the desired lord of my heart."

After hearing Uṣā's words, Citralekhā immediately replied, "I can understand your bereavement, and I assure you that if this boy is within these three worlds—the upper, middle, and lower planetary systems—I must find him for your satisfaction. If you can identify him from your dream, I shall bring you peace of mind. Now, let me draw some pictures for you to inspect, and as soon as you find the picture of your desired husband, let me know. It doesn't matter where he is; I know the art of bringing him here. So, as soon as you identify him, I shall immediately arrange for it."

Citralekhā, while talking, began to draw many pictures of the demigods inhabiting the higher planetary systems, then pictures of the Gandharvas, Siddhas, Cāraṇas, Pannagas, Daityas, Vidyādharas and Yakṣas, as well as many human beings. (The statements of *Śrīmad-Bhāgavatam* and other Vedic literature prove definitely that on each and every planet there are living entities of different varieties. Therefore, it is foolish to assert that there are no living entities but those on this earth.) Citralekhā painted many pictures. Among those of the human beings was the Vṛṣṇi dynasty, including Vasudeva, the father of Kṛṣṇa, Śūrasena, the grandfather of Kṛṣṇa, Śrī Balarāmajī, Lord Kṛṣṇa and many others. When Uṣā saw the picture of Pradyumna, she became a little bashful, but when she saw the picture of Aniruddha, she became so bashful that she immediately lowered her head and smiled, having found the man she was seeking. She identified the picture to Citralekhā as that of the man who had stolen her heart.

Citralekhā was a great mystic *yoginī*, and as soon as Uṣā identified the picture, although neither of them had ever seen him nor knew his name, Citralekhā could immediately understand that the picture was of Aniruddha, a grandson of Kṛṣṇa. That very night she traveled in outer space and within a very short time reached the city of Dvārakā, which was well-protected by Kṛṣṇa. She entered the palace and found Aniruddha sleeping in his bedroom on a very opulent bed. Citralekhā, by her mystic power, immediately brought Aniruddha, in that sleeping condition, to the city of Śonitapura so that Uṣā might see her desired husband. Uṣā immediately bloomed in happiness and began to enjoy the company of Aniruddha with great satisfaction.

The palace in which Uṣā and Citralekhā lived was so well fortified that it was impossible for any male to either enter or see inside. Uṣā and Aniruddha lived together in the palace, and day after day the love of Uṣā for Aniruddha grew four times upon four times. Uṣā pleased Aniruddha with her valuable dresses, flowers, garlands, scents and incense. By his bedside sitting place were other paraphernalia for residential purposes—nice drinks such as milk and sherbet and nice eatables which could be chewed or swallowed. Above all, she pleased him with sweet words and very obliging service. Aniruddha was worshiped by Uṣā as if he were the Supreme Personality of Godhead. By her excellent service, Uṣā made Aniruddha forget all other things and was able to draw his attention and love upon her without deviation. In such an atmosphere of love and service, Aniruddha practically forgot himself and could not recall how many days he had been away from his real home.

In due course of time, Uṣā exhibited some bodily symptoms by which it could be understood that she was having intercourse with a male friend. The symptoms were so prominent that her actions could no longer be concealed from anyone. Uṣā was always cheerful in the association of Aniruddha, but she did not know the bounds of her satisfaction. The housekeeper and the watchmen of the palace could guess very easily that she was having relations with a male friend, and without waiting for further development, all of them informed their master, Bāṇāsura. In Vedic culture, an unmarried girl having association with a male is the greatest disgrace to the family, and so the caretaker cautiously informed his master that Uṣā was developing symptoms indicating a disgraceful association. The servants informed their master that they were not at all neglectful in guarding the house, being alert day and night against any young man who might enter. They were so careful that a male could not even see what was going on there, and so they were surprised that she had become contaminated. Since they could not trace out the reason for it, they submitted the whole situation before their master.

Bāṇāsura was shocked to understand that his daughter Uṣā was no longer a virgin maiden. This weighed heavily on his heart, and without delay he rushed towards the palace where Uṣā was living. There he saw that Uṣā and Aniruddha were sitting together and talking. Uṣā and Aniruddha looked very beautiful together, Aniruddha being the son of Pradyumna, who was Cupid himself. Bāṇāsura saw his daughter and Aniruddha as a suitable match, yet for family prestige, he did not like the combination at all. Bāṇāsura could not understand who the boy actually was. He appreciated the fact that Uṣā could not have selected anyone in the three worlds more beautiful. Aniruddha's complexion was brilliant and swarthy. He was dressed in yellow garments and had eyes just like lotus petals. His arms were very long, and he had nice, curling, bluish hair. The glaring rays of his glittering earrings and the beautiful smile on his lips were certainly captivating. Still, Bāṇāsura was very angry.

When Bāṇāsura saw him, Aniruddha was engaged in playing with Uṣā. Aniruddha was nicely dressed, and Uṣā had garlanded him with various beautiful flowers. The reddish *kuṅkuma* powder put on the breasts of women was spotted here and there on the garland, indicating that Uṣā had embraced him. Bāṇāsura was struck with wonder that, even in his presence, Aniruddha was peacefully sitting in front of Uṣā. Aniruddha knew, however, that his would-be father-in-law was not at all pleased and that he was gathering many soldiers in the palace to attack him.

Thus, not finding any other weapon, Aniruddha took hold of a big iron rod and stood up before Bāṇāsura and his soldiers. He firmly took a posture indicating that if he were attacked he would strike all of the soldiers down to the ground with the iron rod. Bāṇāsura and his company of soldiers saw that the boy was standing before them just like the superintendent of death with his invincible rod. Now, under the order of Bāṇāsura, the soldiers from all sides attempted to capture and arrest him. When they dared to come before him, Aniruddha struck them with the rod, breaking their heads, legs, arms and thighs, and one after another, they began to fall to the ground. He killed them just as the leader of a flock of hawks kills barking dogs, one after another. In this way, Aniruddha was able to escape the palace.

Bāṇāsura knew various arts of fighting, and by the grace of Lord Śiva, he knew how to arrest his opposing enemy by the use of a *nāgapāśa*, snake-noose, and so Aniruddha was seized as he came out of the palace. When Uṣā received the news that her father had arrested Aniruddha, she became overwhelmed with grief and confusion. Tears began to glide down her eyes, and being unable to check herself, she began to cry very loudly.

Thus ends the Bhaktivedanta purport of the Second Volume, Twenty-seventh Chapter of* Kṛṣṇa, *"The Meeting of Uṣā and Aniruddha."

28 / Lord Kṛṣṇa Fights with Bāṇāsura

When the four months of the rainy season passed and still Aniruddha had not returned home, all the members of the Yadu family became much perturbed. They could not understand how the boy was missing. Fortunately, one day the great sage Nārada came and informed the family about Aniruddha's disappearance from the palace. He explained how Aniruddha had been carried to the city of Śonitapura, the capital of Bāṇāsura's empire, and how Bāṇāsura had arrested him with the *nāgapāśa,* even though Aniruddha had defeated his soldiers. This news was given in detail, and the whole story was disclosed. Then the members of the Yadu dynasty, all of whom had great affection for Kṛṣṇa, prepared to attack the city of Śonitapura. Practically all the leaders of the family, including Pradyumna, Sātyaki, Gada, Sāmba, Sāraṇa, Nanda, Upananda and Bhadra, combined together and gathered eighteen *akṣauhiṇī* military divisions into phalanxes. Then they all went to Śonitapura and surrounded it with soldiers, elephants, horses and chariots.

Bāṇāsura heard that the soldiers of the Yadu dynasty were attacking the whole city, tearing down various walls, gates and nearby gardens. Becoming very angry, he immediately ordered his soldiers, who were of equal caliber, to go and face them. Lord Śiva was so kind to Bāṇāsura that he personally came as the commander-in-chief of the military force, assisted by his heroic sons Kārttikeya and Gaṇapati. Seated on his favorite bull, Nandīśvara, Lord Śiva led the fighting against Lord Kṛṣṇa and Balarāma. We can simply imagine how fierce the fighting was—Lord Śiva with his valiant sons on one side and Lord Kṛṣṇa, the Supreme Personality of Godhead, and His elder brother, Śrī Balarāmajī, on the other. The fighting was so fierce that those who saw the battle were struck with wonder, and the hairs on their bodies stood up. Lord Śiva was engaged in fighting directly with Lord Kṛṣṇa, Pradyumna was engaged with Kārttikeya, and Lord Balarāma was engaged with Bāṇāsura's commander-in-chief, Kumbhāṇḍa, who was assisted by Kūpakarṇa. Sāmba, the son of Kṛṣṇa, was engaged in fighting with the son of Bāṇāsura, and Bāṇāsura was engaged in fighting with Sātyaki, commander-in-chief of the Yadu dynasty. In this way the fighting was waged.

News of the fighting spread all over the universe. Demigods such as Lord Brahmā, from higher planetary systems, along with great sages and saintly persons, Siddhas, Cāraṇas and Gandharvas—all being very curious to see the fight between Lord Śiva, Lord Kṛṣṇa and their assistants—were hovering over the battlefield in their airplanes. Lord Śiva is called the *bhūta-nātha,* being assisted by various types of powerful ghosts and denizens of the inferno—*bhūtas, pretas, pramathas, guhyakas, ḍākinīs, piśācas, kūṣmāṇḍas, vetālas, vināyakas,* and *brahma-rākṣasas.* (Of all kinds of ghosts, the *brahma-rākṣasas* are very powerful. *Brāhmaṇas* transferred to the role of ghosts become *brahma-rākṣasas.)*

The Supreme Personality of Godhead Śrī Kṛṣṇa simply drove all these ghosts away from the battlefield, beating them with His celebrated bow, Śārṅgadhanu. Lord Śiva then began to release all his selected weapons upon the Personality of Godhead. Lord Śrī Kṛṣṇa, without any difficulty, counteracted all these weapons with counter-weapons. He counteracted the *brahmāstra,* similar to the atomic bomb, by another *brahmāstra,* and an air weapon by a mountain weapon. When Lord Śiva released a particular weapon bringing about a violent hurricane on the battlefield, Lord Kṛṣṇa presented just the opposing element, a mountain weapon which checked the hurricane on the spot. Similarly when Lord Śiva released his weapon of devastating fire, Kṛṣṇa counteracted it with torrents of rain.

At last, when Lord Śiva released his personal weapon, called *pāśupata-śastra,* Kṛṣṇa immediately counteracted it by the *nārāyaṇa-śastra.* Lord Śiva then became exasperated in fighting with Lord Kṛṣṇa. Kṛṣṇa then took the opportunity to release His yawning weapon. When this weapon is released, the opposing party becomes tired, stops fighting, and begins to yawn. Consequently, Lord Śiva became so fatigued that he refused to fight anymore and began to yawn. Kṛṣṇa was now able to turn His attention from the attack of Lord Śiva to the efforts of Bāṇāsura, and He began to kill his personal soldiers with swords and clubs. Meanwhile, Lord Kṛṣṇa's son Pradyumna was fighting fiercely with Kārttikeya, the commander-in-chief of the demigods. Kārttikeya was wounded, and his body was bleeding profusely. In this condition, he left the battlefield and, without fighting anymore, rode away on the back of his peacock carrier. Similarly, Lord Balarāma was smashing Bāṇāsura's commander-in-chief, Kumbhāṇḍa, with the strokes of his club. Kūpakarṇa was also wounded in this way, and both he and Kumbhāṇḍa fell on the battlefield, the commander-in-chief being fatally wounded. Without guidance, all of Bāṇāsura's soldiers scattered here and there.

When Bāṇāsura saw that his soldiers and commanders had been defeated, his anger only increased. He thought it wise to stop fighting with Sātyaki, Kṛṣṇa's commander-in-chief, and instead directly attacked Lord Kṛṣṇa. Now having the opportunity to use his one thousand hands, he rushed towards Kṛṣṇa, simultaneously working 500 bows and 2,000 arrows. Such a foolish person could never measure Kṛṣṇa's strength. Immediately, without any difficulty, Kṛṣṇa cut each of Bāṇāsura's bows into two pieces and, to check him from going further, made his chariot horses lay on the ground. The chariot then broke to pieces. After doing this, Kṛṣṇa blew His conchshell, Pāñcajanya.

There was a demigoddess named Koṭarā who was worshiped by Bāṇāsura, and their relationship was as mother and son. Mother Koṭarā was upset that Bāṇāsura's life was in danger, so she appeared on the scene. With naked body and scattered hair, she stood before Lord Kṛṣṇa. Śrī Kṛṣṇa did not like the sight of this naked woman, and to avoid seeing her, He turned His face. Bāṇāsura, getting this chance to escape Kṛṣṇa's attack, left the battlefield. All the strings of his bows were broken, and there was no chariot or driver, so he had no alternative than to return to his city. He lost everything in the battle.

Being greatly harassed by the arrows of Kṛṣṇa, all the associates of Lord Śiva, the hobgoblins and ghostly *bhūtas, pretas* and *kṣatriyas,* left the battlefield. Lord Śiva then took to his last resort. He released his greatest death weapon, known as Śivajvara, which destroys by excessive temperature. It is said that at the end of this creation the sun becomes twelve times more scorching than usual. This twelve-times-hotter temperature is called Śivajvara. When the Śivajvara personified was released, he had three heads and three legs, and as he came toward Kṛṣṇa it appeared that he was burning everything into ashes. He was so powerful that he made blazing fire appear in all directions, and Kṛṣṇa observed that he was specifically coming toward Him.

As there is a Śivajvara weapon, there is also a Nārāyaṇajvara weapon. Nārāyaṇajvara is represented by excessive cold. When there is excessive heat, one can somehow or other tolerate it, but when there is excessive cold, everything collapses. This is actually experienced by a person at the time of death. At the time of death, the temperature of the body first of all increases to 107 degrees, and then the whole body collapses and immediately becomes as cold as ice. To counteract the scorching heat of the Śivajvara, there was no other weapon but Nārāyaṇajvara.

When Lord Kṛṣṇa saw that the Śivajvara had been released by Lord Śiva, He had no other recourse than to release Nārāyaṇajvara. Lord Śrī Kṛṣṇa is the original Nārāyaṇa and the controller of the Nārāyaṇajvara weapon. When the Nārāyaṇajvara was released, there was a great fight between the two *jvaras*. When excessive heat is counteracted by extreme cold, it is natural for the hot temperature to gradually reduce, and this is what occurred in the fight between Śivajvara and Nārāyaṇajvara. Gradually, Śivajvara's temperature diminished, and Śivajvara began to cry for help from Lord Śiva, but Lord Śiva was unable to help him in the presence of the Nārāyaṇajvara. Unable to get any help from Lord Śiva, the Śivajvara could understand that he had no means of escape outside surrendering unto Nārāyaṇa, Lord Kṛṣṇa Himself. Lord Śiva, the greatest of the demigods, could not help him, what to speak of the lesser demigods, and therefore Śivajvara ultimately surrendered unto Kṛṣṇa, bowing before Him and offering a prayer so that the Lord might be pleased and give him protection.

By this incidence of the fight between the ultimate weapons of Lord Śiva and Lord Kṛṣṇa it is proved that if Kṛṣṇa gives someone protection, no one can kill him. But if Kṛṣṇa does not give one any protection, then no one can save him. Lord Śiva is called Mahādeva, greatest of all demigods, although sometimes Lord Brahmā is considered the greatest of all demigods, because he can create, whereas Lord Śiva can annihilate the creations of Brahmā. But both Lord Brahmā and Lord Śiva act only in one capacity. Lord Brahmā can create, and Lord Śiva can annihilate, but neither of them can maintain. Lord Viṣṇu, however, not only maintains, but He creates, and annihilates also. Factually, the creation is not effected by Brahmā, because Brahmā himself is created by Lord Viṣṇu. Lord Śiva is created, or born, of Brahmā. The Śivajvara thus understood that without Kṛṣṇa or Nārāyaṇa, no one could help him. He therefore rightly took shelter of Lord Kṛṣṇa and, with folded hands, began to pray as follows.

"My dear Lord, I offer my respectful obeisances unto You because You have unlimited potencies. No one can surpass Your potencies, and thus You are the Lord of everyone. Generally people consider Lord Śiva to be the most powerful personality in the material world, but Lord Śiva is not all-powerful; You are all-powerful. This is factual. You are the original consciousness or knowledge. Without knowledge or consciousness, nothing can be powerful. A material thing might be very powerful, but without the touch of knowledge or consciousness it cannot act. A material machine may be very gigantic and wonderful, but without the touch of someone conscious and in knowledge, the material machine is useless for all purposes. My Lord, You are complete knowledge, and there is not a pinch of material contamination in Your personality. Lord Śiva may be a powerful demigod because of his specific power to annihilate the whole creation, and similarly, Lord Brahmā may be very powerful because he can create the entire universe, but actually neither Brahmā nor Lord Śiva is the original cause of this cosmic manifestation. You are the Absolute Truth, the Supreme Brahman, and You are the original cause. The original cause of the cosmic manifestation is not the impersonal Brahman effulgence. That impersonal Brahman effulgence is resting on Your personality. As is confirmed in the *Bhagavad-gītā,* the cause of the impersonal Brahman is Lord Kṛṣṇa. This Brahman effulgence is likened to the sunshine which emanates from the sun globe. Therefore, impersonal Brahman is not the ultimate cause. The ultimate cause of everything is the supreme eternal form of Kṛṣṇa. All material actions and reactions are taking place in the impersonal Brahman, but in the personal Brahman, the eternal form of Kṛṣṇa, there is no action and reaction. My Lord, Your body is therefore completely peaceful, completely blissful and is devoid of material contamination.

"In the material body there are actions and reactions of the three modes of material nature. The time factor is the most important element and is above all others, because the material manifestation is effected by time agitation. Thus natural phenomena come into existence, and as soon as there is the appearance of phenomena, fruitive activities are visible. As the result of these fruitive activities, a living entity takes his form. He acquires a particular type of nature which is packed up in a subtle body and gross body formed by the life air, the ego, the ten sense organs, the mind and the five gross elements. These then create the type of body which later becomes the root or cause of various other bodies, which are acquired one after another by the transmigration of the soul. All these phenomenal manifestations are the combined actions of Your material energy. Unaffected by the action and reaction of different elements, You are the cause of this external energy, and because You are transcendental to such compulsions of material energy, You are the supreme tranquility. You are the last word in freedom from material contamination. I am therefore taking shelter at Your lotus feet, giving up all other shelter.

"My dear Lord, Your appearance as the son of Vasudeva in Your role as a human being is one of the pastimes of Your complete freedom. To benefit Your devotees and to vanquish the nondevotees, You appear in multi-incarnations. All such incarnations descend in fulfillment of Your promise in the *Bhagavad-gītā* that You appear as soon as there are discrepancies in the system of progressive life. When there are disturbances by irregular principles, my dear Lord, You appear by Your internal potency. Your main business is to protect and maintain the demigods and spiritually inclined persons and maintain the standard of material law and order. Simultaneous to the maintenance of such law and order, Your violence to the miscreants and demons is quite befitting. This is not the first time You have incarnated; it is to be understood that You have done so many, many times before.

"My dear Lord, I beg to submit that I have been very greatly chastised by the release of Your Nārāyaṇajvara. It is certainly very cooling, yet at the same time very severely dangerous and unbearable for all of us. My dear Lord, as long as one is forgetful of Kṛṣṇa consciousness, driven by the spell of material desires and ignorant of the ultimate shelter at Your lotus feet, one who has accepted this material body becomes disturbed by the three miserable conditions of material nature. Because one does not surrender unto You, he therefore continues to suffer perpetually."

After hearing the Śivajvara, Lord Kṛṣṇa replied, "O three-headed one, I am pleased with your statement. Be assured there is no more suffering for you from the Nārāyaṇajvara. Not only are you now free from fear of Nārāyaṇajvara, but anyone in the future who simply recollects this fight between Śivajvara and Nārāyaṇajvara will also be freed from all kinds of fearfulness." After hearing the Supreme Personality of Godhead, the Śivajvara offered his respectful obeisances unto His lotus feet and left.

In the meantime Bāṇāsura somehow or other recovered from his setbacks and, with rejuvenated energy, returned to fight. This time Bāṇāsura appeared before Lord Kṛṣṇa, who was seated on His chariot, with different kinds of weapons in his one thousand hands. Bāṇāsura was very much agitated. He began to splash his different weapons, like torrents of rain, upon the body of Lord Kṛṣṇa. When Lord Kṛṣṇa saw the weapons of Bāṇāsura coming at Him, like water coming out of a strainer, He took His sharp-edged Sudarśana disc and began to cut off the demon's one thousand hands one after another, just as a gardener trims the twigs of a tree with sharp cutters. When Lord Śiva saw that his devotee Bāṇāsura could not be saved even in his presence, he came to his senses and personally came before Lord Kṛṣṇa and began to pacify Him by offering the following prayers.

Lord Śiva said, "My dear Lord, You are the worshipable object of the Vedic hymns. One who does not know You considers the impersonal *brahmajyoti* to be the ultimate Supreme Absolute Truth, without any knowledge that You are existing behind Your spiritual effulgence in Your eternal abode. My dear Lord, You are therefore called *Parambrahman.* This word, *Parambrahman,* has been used in the *Bhagavad-gītā* to identify You. Saintly persons who have completely cleansed their hearts of all material contamination can realize Your transcendental form, although You are all-pervading like the sky, unaffected by any material thing. Only the devotees can realize You, and no one else. In the impersonalists' conception of Your supreme existence, the sky is just like Your navel, the fire is Your mouth, and the water is Your semina. The heavenly planets are Your head, all the directions are Your ears, the Urvī planet is Your lotus feet, the moon is Your mind, and the sun is Your eye. As far as I am concerned, I act as Your ego. The ocean is Your abdomen, and the King of heaven, Indra, is Your arm. Trees and plants are the hairs of Your body, the cloud is the hair on Your head, and Lord Brahmā is Your intelligence. All the great progenitors, known as Prajāpatis, are Your symbolic representatives. And religion is Your heart. The impersonal feature of Your supreme body is conceived of in this way, but You are ultimately the Supreme Person. The impersonal feature of Your supreme body is only a small expansion of Your energy. You are likened to the original fire, and the expansions are Your light and heat."

Lord Śiva continued: "My dear Lord, although You are manifested universally, different parts of the universe are the different parts of Your body, and by Your inconceivable potency You can simultaneously be both localized and universal. In the *Brahma-saṁhitā* we also find it stated that although You always remain in Your abode, Goloka Vṛndāvana, You are nevertheless present everywhere. As stated in the *Bhagavad-gītā,* You appear to protect the devotees, which indicates good fortune for all the universe. All of the demigods are directing different affairs of the universe by Your grace only. Thus the seven upper planetary systems are being maintained by Your grace. At the end of this creation, all manifestations of Your energies, whether in the shape of demigods, human beings or lower animals, enter into You, and all immediate and remote causes of cosmic manifestation rest in You without distinctive features of existence. Ultimately, there is no possibility of distinction between Yourself and any other thing on an equal level with You or subordinate to You. You are simultaneously the cause of this cosmic manifestation and its ingredients as well. You are the Supreme Whole, one without a second. In the phenomenal manifestation there are three stages: the stage of consciousness, the stage of semiconsciousness in dreaming, and the stage of unconsciousness.

But Your Lordship is transcendental to all these different material stages of existence. You exist, therefore, in a fourth dimension, and Your appearance and disappearance do not depend on anything beyond Yourself. You are the supreme cause of everything, but for Yourself there is no cause. You Yourself cause Your own appearance and disappearance. Despite Your transcendental position, my Lord, in order to show Your six opulences and advertise Your transcendental qualities, You have appeared in Your different incarnations—fish, tortoise, boar, Nṛsiṁha, Keśava, etc.—by Your personal manifestation; and You have appeared as different living entities by Your separated manifestations. By Your internal potency, You appear as the different incarnations of Viṣṇu, and by Your external potency You appear as the phenomenal world.

"Because it is a cloudy day to the common man's eyes, the sun appears to be covered. But the fact is that because the sunshine creates the cloud, even though the whole sky is cloudy, the sun can never actually be covered. Similarly, the less intelligent class of men claims that there is no God, but when the manifestation of different living entities and their activities is visible, enlightened persons see You present in every atom and through the via media of Your external and marginal energies. Your unlimited potential activities are experienced by the most enlightened devotees, but those who are bewildered by the spell of Your external energy identify themselves with this material world and become attached to society, friendship and love. Thus they embrace the threefold miseries of material existence and are subjected to the dualities of pain and pleasure. They are sometimes drowned in the ocean of attachment and sometimes taken out of it.

"My dear Lord, only by Your mercy and grace can the living entity get the human form of life, which is a chance to get out of the miserable condition of material existence. However, a person who possesses a human body but who cannot bring the senses under control is carried away by the waves of sensual enjoyment. As such, he cannot take shelter of Your lotus feet and thus engage in Your devotional service. The life of such a person is very unfortunate, and anyone living such a life of darkness is certainly cheating himself and thus cheating others also. Therefore, human society without Kṛṣṇa consciousness is a society of cheaters and the cheated.

"My Lord, You are actually the dearmost Supersoul of all living entities and the supreme controller of everything. The human being who is always illusioned is afraid of ultimate death. A man who is simply attached to sensual enjoyment voluntarily accepts the miserable material existence and thus wanders after the will-o'-the-wisp of sense pleasure. He is certainly the most foolish man, for he drinks poison and puts aside the nectar. My dear

Lord, all the demigods, including myself and Lord Brahmā, as well as great saintly persons and sages who have cleansed their hearts of this material attachment, have, by Your grace, wholeheartedly taken shelter of Your lotus feet. We have all taken shelter of You, because we have accepted You as the Supreme Lord and the dearmost life and soul of all of us. You are the original cause of this cosmic manifestation, You are its supreme maintainer, and You are the cause of its dissolution also. You are equal to everyone, the most peaceful supreme friend of every living entity. You are the supreme worshipable object for every one of us. My dear Lord, let us always be engaged in Your transcendental loving service so that we may get free from this material entanglement.

"Lastly, my Lord, I may inform You that this Bāṇāsura is very dear to me. He has rendered very valuable service unto me; therefore I want to see him always happy. Being pleased with him, I have given him the assurance of safety. I pray to You, my Lord, that as You were pleased upon his forefathers King Prahlāda and Bali Mahārāja, You will also be pleased with him."

After hearing Lord Śiva's prayer, Lord Kṛṣṇa addressed him also as lord and said, "My dear Lord Śiva, I accept your statements, and your desire for Bāṇāsura is also accepted by Me. I know that this Bāṇāsura is the son of Bali Mahārāja, and as such I cannot kill him because that is My promise. I gave a benediction to King Prahlāda that all the demons who would appear in his family would never be killed by Me. Therefore, without killing this Bāṇāsura, I have simply cut off his arms to deprive him of his false prestige. The large number of soldiers which he was maintaining became a burden on this earth, and I have killed them all in order to minimize the burden. Now he has four remaining arms, and he will remain immortal, without being affected by the material pains and pleasures. I know that he is one of the chief devotees of your lordship, so you can now rest assured that henceforward he need have no fear from anything."

When Bāṇāsura was benedicted by Lord Kṛṣṇa in this way, he came before the Lord and bowed down before Him, touching his head to the earth. He immediately arranged to bring Aniruddha along with his daughter Uṣā, seated on a nice chariot, and presented them before Lord Kṛṣṇa. After this, Lord Kṛṣṇa took charge of Aniruddha and Uṣā, who had become very opulent materially because of the blessings of Lord Śiva. Thus, keeping forward a division of one *akṣauhiṇī* of soldiers, Kṛṣṇa began to proceed toward Dvārakā. In the meantime, all the people at Dvārakā, having received the news that Lord Kṛṣṇa was returning with Aniruddha and Uṣā in great opulence, decorated every corner of the city with flags, festoons and garlands. All the big roads and crossings were carefully cleansed and sprinkled with sandalwood pulp mixed with water. Everywhere there was the flavor of sandalwood. All the citizens, accompanied by their friends and relatives, welcomed Lord Kṛṣṇa with great pomp and jubilation. At that time, there was a tumultuous vibration of conchshells and drums and bugles to receive the Lord. In this way the Supreme Personality of Godhead Kṛṣṇa entered His capital, Dvārakā.

Śukadeva Gosvāmī assured King Parīkṣit that the narration of the fight between Lord Śiva and Lord Kṛṣṇa is not at all inauspicious like ordinary fights. On the contrary, if one remembers the narration of this fight between Lord Kṛṣṇa and Lord Śiva in the morning and takes pleasure in the victory of Lord Kṛṣṇa, he will never experience defeat anywhere in his struggle of life.

This episode of Bāṇāsura's fighting with Kṛṣṇa and later on being saved by the grace of Lord Śiva is confirmation of the statement in the *Bhagavad-gītā* that the worshipers of demigods cannot achieve any benediction without its being sanctioned by the Supreme Lord, Kṛṣṇa. Here, in this narration, we find that although Bāṇāsura was a great devotee of Lord Śiva, when he faced death by Kṛṣṇa, Lord Śiva was not able to save him. But Lord Śiva appealed to Kṛṣṇa to save his devotee, and it was thus sanctioned by the Lord. This is the position of Lord Kṛṣṇa. The exact words used in this connection in the *Bhagavad-gītā* are *mayaiva vihitān hi tān.* This means that without the sanction of the Supreme Lord, no demigod can award any benediction to the worshiper.

Thus ends the Bhaktivedanta purport of the Second Volume, Twenty-eighth Chapter of Kṛṣṇa, *"Lord Kṛṣṇa Fights with Bāṇāsura."*

29 / The Story of King Nṛga

Once the family members of Lord Kṛṣṇa, such as Sāmba, Pradyumna, Cārubhānu and Gada, all princes of the Yadu dynasty, went for a long picnic in the forest near Dvārakā. In the course of their excursion, all of them became thirsty, and so they began to try to find out where water was available in the forest. When they approached a well, they found that there was no water in it, but on the contrary, within the well was a wonderful living entity. It was a large lizard, and all of them became astonished to see such a wonderful animal. They could understand that the animal was trapped and could not escape by its own effort, so out of compassion they tried to take the large lizard out of the well. Unfortunately, they could not get the lizard out, even though they tried to do so in many ways.

When the princes returned home, their story was narrated before Lord Kṛṣṇa. Lord Kṛṣṇa is the friend of all living entities. Therefore, after hearing the appeal from His sons, He personally went to the well and easily got the great lizard out simply by extending His left hand. Immediately upon being touched by the hand of Lord Kṛṣṇa, that great lizard gave up its former shape and appeared as a beautiful demigod, an inhabitant of the heavenly planets. His bodily complexion glittered like molten gold. He was decorated with fine garments, and he wore costly ornaments around his neck.

How the demigod had been obliged to accept the body of a lizard was not a secret to Lord Kṛṣṇa, but still, for others' information, the Lord inquired, "My dear fortunate demigod, now I see that your body is so beautiful and lustrous. Who are you? We can guess that you are one of the best demigods in the heavenly planets. All good fortune to you. I think that you are not meant to be in this situation. It must be due to the results of your past activities that you have been put into the species of lizard life. Still, I want to hear from you how you were put in this position. If you think that you can disclose this secret, then please tell us your identity."

Actually this large lizard was King Nṛga, and when he was questioned by the Supreme Personality of Godhead he immediately bowed down before the Lord, touching to the ground the helmet on his head, which was as dazzling as the sunshine. In this way, he first of all offered his respectful obeisances unto the Supreme Lord. He then said, "My dear Lord, I am the son of King Ikṣvāku, and am King Nṛga. If you have ever taken account of all charitably disposed men, I am sure that You must have heard my name. My Lord, You are the witness. You are aware of every bit of work done by the living entities—past, present and future. Nothing can be hidden from Your eternal cognizance. Still, You have ordered me to explain my history, and I shall therefore narrate the full story."

King Nṛga proceeded to narrate the history of his degradation, caused by his *karma-kāṇḍa* activities. He was very charitably disposed and had given away so many cows that he said the number was equal to the amount of dust on the earth, the stars in the sky and the rainfall. According to the Vedic ritualistic ceremonies, a man who is charitably disposed is commanded to give cows to the *brāhmaṇas.* From King Nṛga's statement, it appears that he followed this principle earnestly; however, as a result of a slight discrepancy in his action, he was forced to take birth as a lizard. Therefore it is recommended by the Lord in the *Bhagavad-gītā* that one who is charitably disposed and desires to derive the benefit of his charity should offer his gifts to please Kṛṣṇa. To give in charity means to perform pious activities. As a result of pious activities one may be elevated to the higher planetary systems; but promotion to the heavenly planets is no guarantee that one will never fall down. Rather, from the example of King Nṛga, it is definitely proved that fruitive activities, even if they are very pious, cannot give us eternal blissful life. As stated in the *Bhagavad-gītā,* the result of work, either pious or impious, is sure to bind a man unless it is discharged as *yajña* on behalf of the Supreme Personality of Godhead.

King Nṛga continued to say that the cows given in charity were not ordinary cows. Each one was very young and had given birth to only one calf. They were full of milk, very peaceful and healthy. All the cows were purchased with money that had been earned legally. Furthermore, their horns were gold-plated, their hooves were bedecked with silver plates, and they were covered with silken wrappers which were embroidered with pearls and necklaces. He stated that these valuably decorated cows were not given to any worthless person, but were distributed to the first-class *brāhmaṇas,* whom he had also decorated with nice garments and gold ornaments. The *brāhmaṇas* were well qualified, none of them were rich, and their family members were always in want for the necessities of life. A real *brāhmaṇa* never hoards money for a luxurious life, like the *kṣatriyas* or the *vaiśyas,* but always keeps himself in a poverty-stricken condition, knowing that money diverts the mind to materialistic ways of life. To live in this way is the vow of a qualified *brāhmaṇa,* and all of these *brāhmaṇas* were well situated in that exalted vow. They were well learned in Vedic knowledge. They executed the required austerities and penances in their lives, and were liberal, meeting the standard of qualified *brāhmaṇas.* They were equally friendly to everyone; above all, they were young and quite fit to act as qualified *brāhmaṇas.* Besides the cows, they were also given land, gold, houses, horses and elephants. Those who were not married were given wives, maidservants, grains, silver, utensils, garments, jewels, household furniture, chariots, etc. This charity was nicely performed as a sacrifice according to the Vedic rituals. The King also stated that not only had he bestowed gifts on the *brāhmaṇas,* but he had performed other pious activities, such as digging a well, planting trees on the roadside and installing ponds on the highways.

The King continued, "In spite of all this, unfortunately one of the *brāhmaṇa's* cows chanced to enter amongst my other cows. Not knowing this, I again gave it in charity to another *brāhmaṇa.* As the cow was being taken away by the *brāhmaṇa,* its former master claimed it as his own, stating, 'This cow was formerly given to me, so how is it that you are taking it away?' Thus there was arguing and fighting between the two *brāhmaṇas,* and they came before me and charged that I had taken back a cow that I had previously given in charity." To give something to someone and then to take it away is considered a great sin, especially in dealing with a *brāhmaṇa.* When both the *brāhmaṇas* charged the King with the same complaint, he was simply puzzled as to how it had happened. Thereafter, with great humility, the King offered each of them one hundred thousand cows in exchange for the one cow that was causing the fight between them. He prayed to them that he was their servant and that there had been some mistake. Thus, in order to rectify it, he prayed that they would be very kind upon him and accept his offer in exchange for the cow. The King fervently appealed to the *brāhmaṇas* not to cause his downfall into hell because of this mistake. A *brāhmaṇa's* property is called *brahma-sva,* and according to Manu's law, it cannot be acquired even by the government. Both *brāhmaṇas* insisted that the cow was theirs and could not be taken back under any condition; neither of them agreed to exchange it for the one hundred thousand cows. Thus disagreeing with the King's proposal, both *brāhmaṇas* left the palace in anger, thinking that their lawful position had been usurped.

After this incident, when the time came for the King to give up his body, he was taken before Yamarāja, the superintendent of death. Yamarāja asked him whether he wanted to first enjoy the results of his pious activities or first suffer the results of his impious activities. Yamarāja also hinted that since the King had executed so many pious activities and charities, the limit of Nṛga's enjoyment would be unknown to him. There was practically no end to the King's material happiness, but in spite of this hint, he was bewildered. He decided to first suffer the results of his impious activities and then to accept the results of his pious activities; therefore Yamarāja immediately turned him into a lizard.

King Nṛga had remained in a well as a big lizard for a very long time. He told Lord Kṛṣṇa: "In spite of being put into that degraded condition of life, I simply thought of You, my dear Lord, and my memory was never vanquished." It appears from these statements of King Nṛga that persons who follow the principles of fruitive activities and derive some material benefits are not very intelligent. Being given the choice by the superintendent of death, Yamarāja, King Nṛga could have first accepted the results of his pious activities. Instead he thought it would be better to first receive the effects of his impious activities and then enjoy the effects of his pious activities without disturbance. On the whole, he had not developed Kṛṣṇa consciousness. The Kṛṣṇa conscious person develops love of God, Kṛṣṇa, not love for pious or impious activities; therefore he is not subjected to the results of such action. As stated in the *Brahma-saṁhitā,* a devotee, by the grace of the Lord, does not become subjected to the resultant reactions of fruitive activities.

Somehow or other, as a result of his pious activities, King Nṛga had aspired to see the Lord. He continued to say: "My dear Lord, I had a great desire that someday I might be able to see You personally. I think that my tendency to perform ritualistic and charitable activities, combined with this great desire to see You personally, has enabled me to retain the memory of who I was in my former life, even though I became a lizard." (Such a person, who remembers his past life, is called *jāti-smara.*) "My dear Lord, You are the Supersoul seated in everyone's heart. There are many great mystic *yogīs* who have eyes to see You through the *Vedas* and *Upaniṣads.* In order to achieve the elevated position of being equal in quality with You, they always meditate on You within their hearts. Although such exalted saintly persons may see You constantly within their hearts, they still cannot see You eye to eye; therefore I am very much surprised that I am able to see You personally. I know that I was engaged in so many activities, especially as a king. Although I was in the midst of luxury and opulence and was subjected to so much of the happiness and misery of material existence, I am so fortunate to be seeing You personally. As far as I know, when one becomes liberated from material existence, he can see You in this way."

When King Nṛga elected to receive the results of his impious activities, he was given the body of a lizard because of the mistake in his pious activities; thus he could not be directly converted to a higher status of life like a great demigod. However, along with his pious activities, he thought of Kṛṣṇa, so he was quickly released from the body of a lizard and given the body of a demigod. By worshiping the Supreme Lord, those who desire material opulences are given the bodies of powerful demigods. Sometimes these demigods can see the Supreme Personality of Godhead eye to eye, but they are still not yet eligible to enter into the spiritual kingdom, the Vaikuṇṭha planets. However, if the demigods continue to become devotees of the Lord, the next chance they get they will enter into the Vaikuṇṭha planets.

Having attained the body of a demigod, King Nṛga, continuing to remember everything, said, "My dear Lord, You are the Supreme Lord and are worshiped by all the demigods. You are not one of the living entities, but You are the Supreme Person, Puruṣottama. You are the source of all happiness to all living entities; therefore You are known as Govinda. You are the Lord of those living entities who have accepted a material body and those who have not yet accepted a material body." (Among the living entities who have not accepted a material body are those who are hovering in the material world as evil spirits or living in the ghostly atmosphere. However, those who live in the spiritual kingdom, the Vaikuṇṭhalokas, have bodies that are not made of material elements.) "You are, my Lord, infallible. You are the Supreme, the purest of all living entities. You are living in everyone's heart. You are the shelter of all living entities, Nārāyaṇa. Being seated in the heart of all living entities, You are the supreme director of everyone's sensual activities; therefore, You are called Hṛṣīkeśa.

"My dear Supreme Lord Kṛṣṇa, because You have given me this body of a demigod, I will have to go to some heavenly planet; so I am taking this opportunity to beg for Your mercy, that I may have the benediction of never forgetting Your lotus feet, no matter to which form of life or planet I may be transferred. You are all-pervading, present everywhere as cause and effect. You are the cause of all causes, and Your potency and power are unlimited. You are the Absolute Truth, the Supreme Personality of Godhead and the Supreme Brahman. I therefore offer my respectful obeisances unto You again and again. My dear Lord, Your body is full of transcendental bliss and knowledge, and You are eternal. You are the master of all mystic powers; therefore You are known as Yogeśvara. Kindly accept me as insignificant dust at Your lotus feet."

Before entering the heavenly planets, King Nṛga circumambulated the Lord. He touched his helmet to the lotus feet of the Lord and bowed before Him. Seeing the airplane from the heavenly planets present before him, he was given permission by the Lord to board it. After the departure of King Nṛga, Lord Kṛṣṇa expressed His appreciation for the King's devotion to the *brāhmaṇas* as well as his charitable disposition and his performance of Vedic rituals. Therefore, it is recommended that if one cannot directly become a devotee of the Lord, one should follow the Vedic principles of life. This will enable him, one day, to see the Lord by being promoted either directly to the spiritual kingdom or indirectly to the heavenly kingdom, where he has hope of being transferred to the spiritual planets.

At this time, Lord Kṛṣṇa was present among His relatives who were members of the *kṣatriya* class. To teach them through the exemplary character of King Nṛga, He said: "Even though a *kṣatriya* king may be as powerful as fire, it is not possible for him to usurp the property of a *brāhmaṇa* and utilize it for his own purpose. If this is so, how can ordinary kings, who falsely think of themselves as the most powerful beings within the material world, usurp a *brāhmaṇa's* property? I do not think that taking poison is as dangerous as taking a *brāhmaṇa's* property. For ordinary poison there is treatment—one can be relieved from its effects; but if one drinks the poison of taking a *brāhmaṇa's* property, there is no remedy for the mistake. The perfect example was King Nṛga. He was very powerful and very pious, but due to the small mistake of unknowingly usurping a *brāhmaṇa's* cow, he was condemned to the abominable life of a lizard. Ordinary poison affects only those who drink it, and ordinary fire can be extinguished simply by pouring water on it; but the *araṇi* fire ignited by the spiritual potency of a *brāhmaṇa* can burn to ashes the whole family of a person who provokes such a *brāhmaṇa."* (Formerly, the *brāhmaṇas* used to ignite the fire of sacrifice not with matches or any other external fire but with their powerful *mantras*, called *araṇi.)* "If someone even touches a *brāhmaṇa's* property, he is ruined for three generations. However, if a *brāhmaṇa's* property is forcibly taken away, the taker's family for ten generations before him and for ten generations after him will become subject to ruination. On the other hand, if someone becomes a Vaiṣṇava or devotee of the Lord, ten generations of his family before his birth and ten generations after will become liberated."

Lord Kṛṣṇa continued: "If some foolish king who is puffed up by his wealth, prestige and power wants to usurp a *brāhmaṇa's* property, it should be understood that such a king is clearing his path to hell; he does not know how much he has to suffer for such unwise action. If someone takes away the property of a very liberal *brāhmaṇa* who is encumbered by a large dependent family, then such a usurper is put into the hell known as Kumbhīpāka; not only is he put into this hell, but his family members also have to accept such a miserable condition of life. A person who takes away property which has either been awarded to a *brāhmaṇa* or given away by him is condemned to live for at least 60,000 years as miserably as an insect in stool. Therefore I instruct you, all My boys and relatives present here, do not, even by mistake, take the possession of a *brāhmaṇa* and thereby pollute Your whole family. If someone even wishes to possess such property, let alone attempts to take it away by force, the duration of his life will be reduced. He will be defeated by his enemies, and after being bereft of his royal position, when he gives up his body he will become a serpent. A serpent gives trouble to all other living entities. My dear boys and relatives, I therefore advise you that even if a *brāhmaṇa* becomes angry with you and calls you by ill names or cuts you, still you should not retaliate. On the contrary, you should smile, tolerate him and offer your respects to the *brāhmaṇa.* You know very well that even I Myself offer My obeisances to the *brāhmaṇas* with great respect three times daily. You should therefore follow My instruction and example. I shall not forgive anyone who does not follow them, and I shall punish him. You should learn from the example of King Nṛga that even if someone unknowingly usurps the property of a *brāhmaṇa,* he is put into a miserable condition of life."

Thus Lord Kṛṣṇa, who is always engaged in purifying the conditioned living entities, gave instruction not only to His family members and the inhabitants of Dvārakā, but to all the members of human society. After this the Lord entered His palace.

Thus ends the Bhaktivedanta purport of the Second Volume, Twenty-ninth Chapter of Kṛṣṇa, *"The Story of King Nṛga."*

30 / Lord Balarāma Visits Vṛndāvana

Lord Balarāma became very anxious to see His father and mother, Mahārāja Nanda and Yaśodā. Therefore He started for Vṛndāvana on a chariot with great enthusiasm. The inhabitants of Vṛndāvana had been anxious to see Kṛṣṇa and Balarāma for a very long time. When Lord Balarāma returned to Vṛndāvana, all the cowherd boys and the *gopīs* had grown up; but still, on His arrival, they all embraced Him, and Balarāma embraced them in reciprocation. After this He came before Mahārāja Nanda and Yaśodā and offered His respectful obeisances unto them. In response, mother Yaśodā and Nanda Mahārāja offered their blessings unto Him. They addressed Him as Jagadīśvara, or the Lord of the universe who maintains everyone. The reason for this was that both Kṛṣṇa and Balarāma maintain all living entities, and yet Nanda and Yaśodā were put into such difficulties on account of Their absence. Feeling like this, they embraced Balarāma and, seating Him on their laps, began their perpetual crying, wetting Balarāma with their tears. Lord Balarāma then offered His respectful obeisances to the elderly cowherd men and accepted the obeisances of the younger cowherd men. Thus, according to their different ages and relationships, Lord Balarāma exchanged feelings of friendship with them. He shook hands with those who were His equals in age and friendship, and with loud laughing embraced each one of them.

After being received by the cowherd men and boys, the *gopīs,* and King Nanda and Yaśodā, Lord Balarāma sat down, feeling satisfied, and they all surrounded Him. First Lord Balarāma inquired from them about their welfare, and then, not having seen Him for such a long time, they began to ask Him different questions. The inhabitants of Vṛndāvana had sacrificed everything for Kṛṣṇa, simply being captivated by the lotus eyes of the Lord. Because of their great desire to love Kṛṣṇa, they never desired anything like elevation to the heavenly planets or merging into the effulgence of Brahman to become one with the Absolute Truth. They were not even interested in enjoying a life of opulence, but were satisfied in living a simple life in the village as cowherd men. They were always absorbed in thoughts of Kṛṣṇa and did not desire any personal benefits, and they were all so much in love with Him that in His absence their voices faltered when they began to inquire from Balarāmajī.

First Nanda Mahārāja and Yaśodāmayī inquired, "My dear Balarāma, are our friends like Vasudeva and others in the family doing well? Now You and Kṛṣṇa are grown-up married men with children. In the happiness of family life, do You sometimes remember Your poor father and mother, Nanda Mahārāja and Yaśodādevī? It is very good news that the most sinful King Kaṁsa has been killed by You and that our friends like Vasudeva and the others, who had been harassed by him, have now been relieved. It is also very good news that both You and Kṛṣṇa defeated Jarāsandha and Kālayavana, who now is dead, and that You are now living in a fortified residence in Dvārakā."

When the *gopīs* arrived, Lord Balarāma glanced over them with loving eyes. Being overjoyed, the *gopīs,* who had so long been mortified on account of Kṛṣṇa's and Balarāma's absence, began to ask about the welfare of the two brothers. They specifically asked Balarāma whether Kṛṣṇa was enjoying His life surrounded by the enlightened women of Dvārakā Purī. "Does He sometimes remember His father Nanda and His mother Yaśodā and the other friends with whom He so intimately behaved while He was in Vṛndāvana? Does Kṛṣṇa have any plans to come here to see His mother Yaśodā, and does He remember us *gopīs* who are now pitiably bereft of His company? Kṛṣṇa might have forgotten us in the midst of the cultured women of Dvārakā, but as far as we are concerned, we are still remembering Him by collecting flowers and sewing them into garlands. When He does not come, however, we simply pass our time by crying. If only He would come here and accept these garlands that we have made. Dear Lord Balarāma, descendant of Daśārha, You know that we would give up everything for Kṛṣṇa's friendship. Even in great distress one cannot give up the connection of family members, but although it might be impossible for others, we gave up our fathers, mothers, sisters and relatives without caring at all about our renunciation. Then, all of a sudden, Kṛṣṇa renounced us and went away. He broke off our intimate relationship without any serious consideration and left for a foreign country. But He was so clever and cunning that He manufactured very nice words. He said, 'My dear *gopīs,* please do not worry. The service that you have rendered Me is impossible for Me to repay.' After all, we are women, so how could we disbelieve Him? Now we can understand that His sweet words were simply for cheating us."

Another *gopī,* protesting Kṛṣṇa's absence from Vṛndāvana, began to say: "My dear Balarāmajī, we are of course village girls, so Kṛṣṇa could cheat us in that way, but what about the women of Dvārakā? Don't think they are as foolish as we are! We village women might be misled by Kṛṣṇa, but the women in the city of Dvārakā are very clever and intelligent. Therefore I would be surprised if such city women could be misled by Kṛṣṇa and could believe His words."

Then another *gopī* began to speak. "My dear friend," she said, "Kṛṣṇa is very clever in using words. No one can compete with Him in that art. He can manufacture such colorful words and talk so sweetly that the heart of any woman would be misled. Besides that, He has perfected the art of smiling very attractively, and by seeing His smile women become mad after Him and would give themselves to Him without any hesitation."

Another *gopī,* after hearing this, said, "My dear friends, what is the use in talking about Kṛṣṇa? If you are at all interested in passing away time by talking, let us talk on some subject other than Him. If cruel Kṛṣṇa can pass His time without us, why can't we pass our time without Kṛṣṇa? Of course, Kṛṣṇa is passing His days very happily without us, but the difference is that we cannot pass our days very happily without Him."

When the *gopīs* were talking in this way, their feelings for Kṛṣṇa became more and more intensified, and they were experiencing Kṛṣṇa's smiling, Kṛṣṇa's words of love, Kṛṣṇa's attractive features, Kṛṣṇa's characteristics and Kṛṣṇa's embraces. By the force of their ecstatic feelings, it appeared to them that Kṛṣṇa was personally present and dancing before them. Because of their sweet remembrance of Kṛṣṇa, they could not check their tears, and they began to cry without consideration.

Lord Balarāma could, of course, understand the ecstatic feelings of the *gopīs,* and therefore He wanted to pacify them. He was expert in presenting an appeal, and thus, treating the *gopīs* very respectfully, He began to narrate the stories of Kṛṣṇa so tactfully that the *gopīs* became satisfied. In order to keep the *gopīs* in Vṛndāvana satisfied, Lord Balarāma stayed there continually for two months, namely the months of Caitra (March-April) and Vaiśākha (April-May). For those two months He kept Himself among the *gopīs,* and He passed every night with them in the forest of Vṛndāvana in order to satisfy their desire for conjugal love. Thus Balarāma also enjoyed the *rāsa* dance with the *gopīs* during those two months. Since the season was springtime, the breeze on the bank of the Yamunā was blowing very mildly, carrying the aroma of different flowers, especially of the flower known as *kaumudī.* Moonlight filled the sky and spread everywhere, and thus the banks of the Yamunā appeared to be very bright and pleasing, and Lord Balarāma enjoyed the company of the *gopīs* there.

The demigod known as Varuṇa sent his daughter Vāruṇī in the form of liquid honey oozing from the hollows of the trees. Because of this honey the whole forest became aromatic, and the sweet aroma of the liquid honey, Vāruṇī, captivated Balarāmajī. Balarāmajī and all the *gopīs* became very much attracted by the taste of Vāruṇī, and all of them drank it together. While drinking this natural beverage, Vāruṇī, all the *gopīs* chanted the glories of Lord Balarāma, and Lord Balarāma felt very happy, as if He had become intoxicated by drinking that Vāruṇī beverage. His eyes rolled in a pleasing attitude. He was decorated with long garlands of forest flowers, and the whole situation appeared to be a great function of happiness because of this transcendental bliss. Lord Balarāma smiled beautifully, and the drops of perspiration decorating His face appeared to be soothing morning dew.

While Balarāma was in that happy mood, He desired to enjoy the company of the *gopīs* in the water of the Yamunā. Therefore He called Yamunā to come nearby. But Yamunā neglected the order of Balarāmajī, considering Him to be intoxicated. Lord Balarāma became very much displeased at Yamunā's neglecting His order. He immediately wanted to scratch the land near the river with His plowshare. Lord Balarāma has two weapons, a plow and a club, and He takes service from them when they are required. This time He wanted to bring the Yamunā by force, and He took the help of His plow. He wanted to punish Yamunā because she did not come in obedience to His order. He addressed Yamunā: "You wretched river! You did not care for My order. Now I shall teach you a lesson! You did not come to Me voluntarily. Now with the help of My plow I shall force you to come. I shall divide you into hundreds of scattered streams!"

When Yamunā was threatened like this, she became greatly afraid of the power of Balarāma and immediately came in person, falling at His lotus feet and praying thus: "My dear Balarāma, You are the most powerful personality, and You are pleasing to everyone. Unfortunately, I forgot Your glorious, exalted position, but now I have come to my senses, and I remember that You hold all the planetary systems on Your head merely by Your partial expansion as Śeṣa. You are the sustainer of the whole universe. My dear Supreme Personality of Godhead, You are full of six opulences. Because I forgot Your omnipotence, I have mistakenly disobeyed Your order, and thus I have become a great offender. But, my dear Lord, please know that I am a surrendered soul unto You. You are very much affectionate to Your devotees. Therefore please excuse my impudence and mistakes and, by Your causeless mercy, may You now release me."

Upon displaying this submissive attitude, Yamunā was forgiven, and when she came nearby, Lord Balarāma wanted to enjoy the pleasure of swimming within her water along with the *gopīs* in the same way an elephant enjoys himself along with his many she-elephants. After a long time, when Lord Balarāma had enjoyed to His full satisfaction, He came out of the water, and immediately a goddess of fortune offered Him a nice blue garment and a valuable necklace made of gold. After taking bath in the Yamunā, Lord Balarāma, dressed in blue garments and decorated with golden ornaments, looked very attractive to everyone. Lord Balarāma's complexion is white, and when He was properly dressed He looked exactly like the white elephant of King Indra in the heavenly planet. The River Yamunā still has many small branches due to being scratched by the plowshare of Lord Balarāma. And all these branches of the River Yamunā are still glorifying the omnipotency of Lord Balarāma.

Lord Balarāma and the *gopīs* enjoyed transcendental pastimes together every night for two months, and time passed away so quickly that all those nights appeared to be only one night. In the presence of Lord Balarāma, all the *gopīs* and inhabitants of Vṛndāvana became as cheerful as they had been before in the presence of both brothers, Lord Kṛṣṇa and Lord Balarāma.

Thus ends the Bhaktivedanta purport of the Second Volume, Thirtieth Chapter of Kṛṣṇa, *"Lord Balarāma Visits Vṛndāvana."*

31 / Deliverance of Pauṇḍraka and the King of Kāśī

The story of King Pauṇḍraka is very interesting because there have always been many rascals and fools who have considered themselves to be God. Even in the presence of the Supreme Personality of Godhead, Kṛṣṇa, there was such a foolish person. His name was Pauṇḍraka, and He wanted to declare himself to be God. While Lord Balarāma was absent in Vṛndāvana, this King Pauṇḍraka, the King of the Karūṣa province, being foolish and puffed up, sent a messenger to Lord Kṛṣṇa. Lord Kṛṣṇa is accepted as the Supreme Personality of Godhead, and King Pauṇḍraka directly challenged Kṛṣṇa through the messenger, who stated that Pauṇḍraka, and not Kṛṣṇa, was Vāsudeva. In the present day there are many foolish followers of such rascals. Similarly, in his day, many foolish men accepted Pauṇḍraka as the Supreme Personality of Godhead. Because he could not estimate his own position, Pauṇḍraka falsely thought himself to be Lord Vāsudeva. Thus the messenger declared to Kṛṣṇa that out of his causeless mercy, King Pauṇḍraka, the Supreme Personality of Godhead, had descended on the earth just to deliver all distressed persons.

Surrounded by many other foolish persons, this rascal Pauṇḍraka had actually concluded that he was Vāsudeva, the Supreme Personality of Godhead. This kind of conclusion is certainly childish. When children are playing, they sometimes create a king amongst themselves, and the child who is so selected thinks that he is the king. Similarly, many foolish persons, due to ignorance, select another fool as God, and then the rascal considers himself God, as if God could be created by childish play or by the votes of men. Under this false impression, thinking himself the Supreme Lord, Pauṇḍraka sent his messenger to Dvārakā to challenge the position of Kṛṣṇa. The messenger reached the royal assembly of Kṛṣṇa in Dvārakā and conveyed the message given by his master, Pauṇḍraka. The message contained the following statements.

"I am the only Supreme Personality of Godhead, Vāsudeva. There is no man who can compete with me. I have descended as King Pauṇḍraka, taking compassion on the distressed conditioned souls out of my unlimited causeless mercy. You have falsely taken the position of Vāsudeva without authority, but you should not propagate this false idea. You must give up Your position. O descendant of the Yadu dynasty, please give up all the symbols of Vāsudeva which You have falsely assumed. And after giving up this position, come and surrender unto me. If out of Your gross impudence You do not care for my words, then I challenge You to fight. I am inviting You to a battle in which the decision will be settled."

When all the members of the royal assembly, including King Ugrasena, heard this message sent by Pauṇḍraka, they laughed very loudly for a considerable time. After enjoying the loud laughter of all the members of the assembly, Kṛṣṇa replied to the messenger as follows. "O messenger of Pauṇḍraka, you may carry My message to your master: He is a foolish rascal. I directly call him a rascal, and I refuse to follow his instructions. I shall never give up the symbols of Vāsudeva, especially My disc. I shall use this disc to kill not only King Pauṇḍraka but all his followers also. I shall destroy this Pauṇḍraka and his foolish associates, who merely constitute a society ot cheaters and cheated. When this action is taken, foolish King, you will have to conceal your face in disgrace, and when your head is severed from your body by My disc, it will be surrounded by meat-eating birds like vultures, hawks and eagles. At that time, instead of becoming My shelter as you have demanded, you will be subjected to the mercy of these low-born birds. At that time your body will be thrown to the dogs, who will eat it with great pleasure."

The messenger carried the words of Lord Kṛṣṇa to his master, Pauṇḍraka, who patiently heard all these insults. Without waiting longer, Lord Śrī Kṛṣṇa immediately started out on His chariot to punish the rascal Pauṇḍraka. Because at that time the King of Karūṣa was living with his friend the King of Kāśī, Kṛṣṇa surrounded the whole city of Kāśī.

King Pauṇḍraka was a great warrior, and as soon as he heard of Kṛṣṇa's attack, he came out of the city along with two *akṣauhiṇī* divisions of soldiers. The King of Kāśī was also a friend to King Pauṇḍraka, and he came out with three *akṣauhiṇī* divisions. When the two kings came before Lord Kṛṣṇa to oppose Him, Kṛṣṇa saw Pauṇḍraka face to face for the first time. Kṛṣṇa saw that Pauṇḍraka had decorated himself with the symbols of the conchshell, disc, lotus and club. He carried the Śārṅga bow, and on his chest was the insignia of Śrīvatsa. His neck was decorated with a false Kaustubha jewel, and he wore a flower garland in exact imitation of Lord

Vāsudeva. He was dressed in yellow colored silken garments, and the flag on his chariot carried the symbol of Garuḍa, exactly imitating Kṛṣṇa's. He had a very valuable helmet on his head, and his earrings, like swordfish, glittered brilliantly. On the whole, however, his dress and makeup were clearly imitation. Anyone could understand that he was just like someone onstage playing the part of Vāsudeva in false dress. When Lord Śrī Kṛṣṇa saw Pauṇḍraka imitating His posture and dress, He could not check His laughter, and thus He laughed with great satisfaction.

The soldiers on the side of King Pauṇḍraka began to shower their weapons upon Kṛṣṇa. The weapons, including various kinds of tridents, clubs, poles, lances, swords, daggers and arrows, came flying in waves, and Kṛṣṇa counteracted them. He smashed not only the weapons but also the soldiers and assistants of Pauṇḍraka, just as during the dissolution of this universe the fire of devastation burns everything to ashes. The elephants, chariots, horses, and infantry belonging to the opposite party were scattered by the weapons of Kṛṣṇa. The whole battlefield became scattered with the bodies of animals and chariots. There were fallen horses, elephants, men, asses and camels. Although the devastated battlefield appeared like the dancing place of Lord Śiva at the time of the dissolution of the world, the warriors who were on the side of Kṛṣṇa were very much encouraged by seeing this, and they fought with greater strength.

At this time, Lord Kṛṣṇa told Pauṇḍraka, "Pauṇḍraka, you requested Me to give up the symbols of Lord Viṣṇu, specifically My disc. Now I will give it up to you. Be careful! You falsely declare yourself to be Vāsudeva, imitating Myself. Therefore no one is a greater fool than you." From this statement of Kṛṣṇa's it is clear that any rascal who advertises himself as God is the greatest fool in human society. Kṛṣṇa continued: "Now, Pauṇḍraka, I shall force you to give up this false representation. You wanted Me to surrender unto you. Now this is your opportunity. We shall now fight, and if I am defeated and you become victorious, I shall certainly surrender unto you." In this way, after chastising Pauṇḍraka very severely, He smashed his chariot to pieces by shooting an arrow. With the help of His disc He separated the head of Pauṇḍraka from his body, just as Indra shaves off the peaks of mountains by striking them with his thunderbolt. Similarly, He also killed the King of Kāśī with His arrows. Lord Kṛṣṇa specifically arranged to throw the head of the King of Kāśī into the city of Kāśī itself so that his relatives and family members could see it. This was done by Kṛṣṇa just as a hurricane carries a lotus petal here and there. Lord Kṛṣṇa killed Pauṇḍraka and his friend Kāśīrāja on the battlefield, and then He returned to His capital city, Dvārakā.

When Lord Kṛṣṇa returned to the city of Dvārakā, all the Siddhas from the heavenly planets were singing the glories of the Lord. As far as Pauṇḍraka was concerned, somehow or other he was always thinking of Lord Vāsudeva by falsely dressing himself in that way, and therefore Pauṇḍraka achieved *sārūpya,* one of the five kinds of liberation, and was thus promoted to the Vaikuṇṭha planets, where the devotees have the same bodily features as Viṣṇu, with four hands holding the four symbols. Factually, his meditation was concentrated on the Viṣṇu form, but because he thought himself to be Lord Viṣṇu, it was offensive. After being killed by Kṛṣṇa, however, that offense was also mitigated. Thus he was given *sārūpya* liberation, and he attained the same form as the Lord.

When the head of the King of Kāśī was thrown through the city gate, people gathered and were astonished to see that wonderful thing. When they found out that there were earrings on it, they could understand that it was someone's head. They conjectured as to whose head it might be. Some thought it was Kṛṣṇa's head because Kṛṣṇa was the enemy of Kāśīrāja, and they calculated that the King of Kāśī might have thrown Kṛṣṇa's head into the city so that the people might take pleasure that the enemy was killed. But it was finally detected that the head was not Kṛṣṇa's, but that of Kāśīrāja himself. When it was so ascertained, the queens of the King of Kāśī immediately approached and began to lament the death of their husband. "My dear lord," they cried, "upon your death, we have become just like dead bodies."

The King of Kāśī had one son whose name was Sudakṣiṇa. After observing the ritualistic funeral ceremonies, he took a vow that since Kṛṣṇa was the enemy of his father, he would kill Kṛṣṇa and in this way liquidate his debts to his father. Therefore, accompanied by a learned priest qualified to help him, he began to worship Mahādeva, Lord Śiva. The lord of the kingdom of Kāśī is Viśvanātha (Lord Śiva). The temple of Lord Viśvanātha is still existing in Vārāṇasī, and many thousands of pilgrims still gather daily in that temple. By the worship of Sudakṣiṇa, Lord Śiva was very much pleased, and he wanted to give a benediction to his devotee. Sudakṣiṇa's purpose was to kill Kṛṣṇa, and therefore he prayed for a specific power by which he could kill Him. Lord Śiva advised that Sudakṣiṇa, assisted by the *brāhmaṇas,* execute the ritualistic ceremony for killing one's enemy. This ceremony is also mentioned in some of the *Tantras.* Lord Śiva informed Sudakṣiṇa that if such a black ritualistic ceremony were performed properly then the evil spirit named Dakṣiṇāgni would appear to carry out any order given to him. He would have to be employed, however, to kill someone other than a qualified *brāhmaṇa.* In such a case he would be accompanied by Lord Śiva's ghostly companions, and the desire of Sudakṣiṇa to kill his enemy would be fulfilled.

When Sudakṣiṇa was encouraged by Lord Śiva in that way, he became assured that he would be able to kill Kṛṣṇa. With a determined vow of austerity, he began to execute the black art of chanting *mantras,* assisted by the priests. After this, out of the fire came a great demonic form, whose hair, beard and moustache were exactly the color of hot copper. This form was very big and fierce. As the demon arose from the fire, cinders of fire emanated from the sockets of his eyes. The giant fiery demon appeared still more fierce due to the movements of his eyebrows. He exhibited long sharp teeth and, sticking out his long tongue, licked both sides of his lips. He was naked, and he carried a big trident, which was blazing like fire. After appearing from the fire of sacrifice, he stood wielding the trident in his hand. Instigated by Sudakṣiṇa, the demon proceeded toward the capital city, Dvārakā, along with many hundreds of ghostly companions, and it appeared that he was going to burn all outer space to ashes. The surface of the earth trembled because of his striking steps. When he entered the city of Dvārakā, all the residents panicked, just like animals at the time of a forest fire.

At that time Kṛṣṇa was engaged in playing chess in the royal assembly council hall. All the residents of Dvārakā approached and addressed Him, "Dear Lord of the three worlds, there is a great fiery demon ready to burn the whole city of Dvārakā. Please save us." Thus, after approaching Lord Kṛṣṇa, all the inhabitants of Dvārakā began to appeal to Him for protection from the fiery demon who had just appeared in Dvārakā to devastate the whole city.

Lord Kṛṣṇa, who specifically protects His devotees, saw that the whole population of Dvārakā was most perturbed by the presence of the great fiery demon. He immediately began to smile and assured them, "Don't worry. I shall give you all protection." The Supreme Personality of Godhead, Kṛṣṇa, is all-pervading. He is within everyone's heart, and He is without also in the form of the cosmic manifestation. He could understand that the fiery demon was a creation of Lord Śiva, and in order to vanquish him He took His Sudarśana-cakra and ordered him to take the necessary steps. The Sudarśana-cakra appeared with the effulgence of millions of suns, his temperature being as powerful as that of the fire created at the end of the cosmic manifestation. By his own effulgence, the Sudarśana-cakra began to illuminate the entire universe, on the surface of the earth as well as in outer space. Then the Sudarśana-cakra began to freeze the fiery demon created by Lord Śiva. In this way, the fiery demon was checked by the Sudarśana-cakra of Lord Kṛṣṇa, and being defeated in his attempt to devastate the city of Dvārakā, he turned back.

Having failed to set fire to Dvārakā, he went back to Vārāṇasī, the kingdom of Kāśīrāja. As a result of his return, all the priests who had helped instruct the black art of *mantras,* along with their employer. Sudakṣiṇa were burned into ashes by the glaring effulgence of the fiery demon. According to the methods of black art *mantras* instructed in the *Tantra,* if the *mantra* fails to kill the enemy, then, because it must kill someone, it kills the original creator. Sudakṣiṇa was the originator, and the priests assisted him; therefore all of them were burned to ashes. This is the way of the demons: the demons create something to kill God, but by the same weapon the demons themselves are killed.

Following just behind the fiery demon, the Sudarśana-cakra also entered Vārāṇasī. This city of Vārāṇasī had been very opulent and great for a very long time. Even now, the city of Vārāṇasī is very opulent and famous, and it is one of the important cities of India. There were then many big palaces, assembly houses, marketplaces and gates, with very important large monuments by the palaces and gates. Lecturing platforms could be found at each and every crossing of the roads. There was a treasury house, and elephant heads, horse heads, chariots, granaries and places for distribution of foodstuff. The city of Vārāṇasī had been filled with all these material opulences for a very long time, but because the king of Kāśī and his son Sudakṣiṇa were against Lord Kṛṣṇa, the Viṣṇu-cakra Sudarśana (the disc weapon of Lord Kṛṣṇa) devastated the whole city by burning all these important places. This excursion was more ravaging than modern bombing. The Sudarśana-cakra, having thus finished his duty, came back to his Lord Śrī Kṛṣṇa at Dvārakā.

This narration of the devastation of Vārāṇasī by Kṛṣṇa's disc weapon, the Sudarśana-cakra, is transcendental and auspicious. Anyone who narrates this story or anyone who hears this story with faith and attention will be released from all reaction to sinful activities. This is the assurance of Śukadeva Gosvāmī who narrated this story to Parīkṣit Mahārāja.

Thus ends the Bhaktivedanta purport of the Second Volume, Thirty-first Chapter of Kṛṣṇa, *"Deliverance of Pauṇḍraka and the King of Kāśī.'*

32 / Deliverance of Dvivida Gorilla

While Śukadeva Gosvāmī continued to speak on the transcendental pastimes and characteristics of Lord Kṛṣṇa, King Parīkṣit, upon hearing him, became more and more enthusiastic and wanted to hear further. Śukadeva Gosvāmī next narrated the story of Dvivida, the gorilla who was killed by Lord Balarāma.

This gorilla was a great friend of Baumāsura's or Narakāsura's, who was killed by Kṛṣṇa in connection with his kidnapping sixteen thousand princesses from all over the world. Dvivida was the minister of King Sugrīva. His brother, Mainda, was also a very powerful gorilla king. When Dvivida gorilla heard the story of his friend Baumāsura's being killed by Lord Kṛṣṇa, he planned to create mischief throughout the country in order to avenge the death of Baumāsura. His first business was to set fires in villages, towns, and industrial and mining places, as well as the residential quarters of the mercantile men who were busy dairy farming and protecting cows. Sometimes he would uproot a big mountain and tear it to pieces. In this way he created great disturbances all over the country, especially in the province of Kathwar. The city of Dvārakā was situated in this Kathwar province, and because Lord Kṛṣṇa used to live in this city, Dvivida specifically made it his target of disturbance.

Dvivida was as powerful as 10,000 elephants. Sometimes he would go to the seashore, and with his powerful hands he would create so much disturbance in the sea that he would overflood the neighboring cities and villages. Often he would go to the hermitages of great saintly persons and sages and cause a great disturbance by smashing their beautiful gardens and orchards. Not only did he create disturbances in that way, but sometimes he would pass urine and stool on their sacred sacrificial arena. He would thus pollute the whole atmosphere. He also kidnapped both men and women, taking them away from their residential places to the caves of the mountains. Putting them within the caves, he would close the entrances with large chunks of stone, like the *bhṛṅgī* insect, which arrests and carries away many flies and other insects and puts them within the holes of the trees where he lives. He thus regularly defied the law and order of the country. Not only that, but he would sometimes pollute the female members of many aristocratic families by forcibly raping them.

While creating such great disturbance all over the country, sometimes he heard very sweet musical sounds from the Raivataka mountain, and so he entered that mountainous region. There he saw that Lord Balarāma was present in the midst of many beautiful young girls, enjoying their company while engaged in singing and dancing. He became captivated by the beautiful features of Lord Balarāma's body, each and every part of which was very beautiful, decorated as He was with a garland of lotus flowers. Similarly, all the young girls present, dressed and garlanded with flowers, exhibited much beauty. Lord Balarāma seemed to be fully intoxicated from drinking the Vāruṇī beverage, and His eyes appeared to be rolling in a drunken state. Lord Balarāma appeared just like the king of the elephants in the midst of many she-elephants.

This gorilla by the name of Dvivida could climb up on the trees and jump from one branch to another. Sometimes he would jerk the branches, creating a particular type of sound, "Kila, kila," so that Lord Balarāma was greatly distracted from the pleasing atmosphere. Sometimes Dvivida would come before the women and exhibit different types of caricatures. By nature young women are apt to enjoy everything with laughter and joking, and when the gorilla came before them they did not take him seriously, but simply laughed at him. However, the gorilla was so rude that even in the presence of Balarāma he began to show the lower part of his body to the women, and sometimes he would come forward to show his teeth while moving his eyebrows. He disrespected the women, even in the presence of Balarāma. Lord Balarāma's name suggests that He is not only very powerful, but that He takes pleasure in exhibiting extraordinary strength. So He took a stone and threw it at Dvivida. The gorilla, however, artfully avoided being struck by the stone. In order to insult Balarāma, the gorilla took away the earthen pot in which the Vāruṇī was kept. Dvivida, being thus intoxicated, with his limited strength began to tear off all the valuable clothes worn by Balarāma and the accompanying young girls. He was so puffed up that he thought that Balarāma could not do anything to chastise him, and he continued to offend Balarāmajī and His companions.

When Lord Balarāma personally saw the disturbances created by the gorilla and heard that he had already performed many mischievous activities all over the country, He became very angry and decided to kill him. Immediately He took His club in His hands. The gorilla could understand that now Balarāma was going to attack him. In order to counteract Balarāma, he immediately uprooted a big oak tree, and with great force he came and struck at Lord Balarāma's head. Lord Balarāma, however, immediately caught hold of the big tree and remained undisturbed, just like a great mountain. To retaliate, He took His club by the name of Sunanda and began to hit the gorilla with it. The gorilla's head was severely injured. Currents of blood flowed from his head with great force, but the stream of blood enhanced his beauty like a stream of liquid manganese coming out of a great mountain. The striking of Balarāma's club did not even slightly disturb him. On the contrary, he immediately uprooted another big oak tree, and after clipping off all its leaves, he began to strike Balarāma's head with it. But Balarāma, with the help of His club, tore the tree to pieces. Since the gorilla was very angry, he took another tree in his hands and began to strike Lord Balarāma's body. Again Lord Balarāma tore the tree to pieces, and the fighting continued. Each time the gorilla would bring out a big tree to strike Balarāma, Lord Balarāma would tear the tree to pieces by the striking of His club. The gorilla Dvivida would clutch another tree from another direction and again attack Balarāma in the same way. As a result of this continuous fighting, the forest became treeless. When no more trees were available, Dvivida took help from the hills and threw large pieces of stone, like rainfall, upon the body of Balarāma. Lord Balarāma, also in a great sporting mood, began to smash those big pieces of stone into mere pebbles. The gorilla, being bereft of all trees and stone slabs, now stood before Him and waved his strong fists. Then, with great force, he began to beat the chest of Lord Balarāma with his fists. This time Lord Balarāma became most angry. Since the gorilla was striking Him with his hands, He would not strike him back with His own weapons, the club or the plow. Simply with His fist He began to strike the collarbone of the gorilla. This striking proved to be fatal to Dvivida, who immediately vomited blood and fell unconscious upon the ground. When the gorilla fell, it appeared that all the hills and forests tottered.

After this horrible incident, all the Siddhas, great sages and saintly persons from the upper planetary system began to shower flowers on the person of Lord Balarāma, and sounds glorifying the supremacy of Lord Balarāma were vibrated. All of them began to chant, "All glories to Lord Balarāma! Let us offer our respectful obeisances unto Your lotus feet. By

Your killing this great demon, Dvivida, You have initiated an auspicious era for the world." All such jubilant sounds of victory were heard from outer space. After killing the great demon Dvivida and being worshiped by showers of flowers and glorious sounds of victory, Balarāma returned to His capital city, Dvārakā.

Thus ends the Bhaktivedanta purport of the Second Volume, Thirty-second Chapter of Kṛṣṇa, *"Deliverance of Dvivida Gorilla."*

33 / The Marriage of Sāmba

Duryodhana, the son of Dhṛtarāṣṭra, had a marriageable daughter by the name of Lakṣmaṇā. She was a very highly qualified girl of the Kuru dynasty, and many princes wanted to marry her. In such cases, the *svayaṁvara* ceremony is held so that the girl may select her husband according to her own choice. In Lakṣmaṇā's *svayaṁvara* assembly, when the girl was to select her husband, Sāmba appeared. He was the son of Kṛṣṇa by Jāmbavatī, one of the chief wives of Lord Kṛṣṇa. This son Sāmba is so named because he was a very bad child, and he always lived close to his mother. The name Sāmba indicates a son who is very much his mother's pet. *Ambā* means mother, and *sa* means with. So this special name was given to him because he always remained with his mother. He was also known as Jāmbavatīsuta for the same reason. As previously explained, all the sons of Kṛṣṇa were as qualified as their great father, Lord Kṛṣṇa. Sāmba wanted the daughter of Duryodhana, Lakṣmaṇā, although she was not inclined to have him. Therefore Sāmba kidnapped Lakṣmaṇā by force from the *svayaṁvara* assembly.

Because Sāmba took Lakṣmaṇā away from the assembly by force, all the members of the Kuru dynasty, namely, Dhṛtarāṣṭra, Bhīṣma, Vidura, Ujahan and Arjuna, thought it an insult to their family tradition that the boy, Sāmba, could possibly have kidnapped their daughter. All of them knew that Lakṣmaṇā was not at all inclined to select him as a husband and that she was not given the chance to select her own husband; instead she was forcibly taken away by this boy. Therefore, they decided that he must be punished. They unanimously declared that he was most impudent and that he had degraded the Kurus' family tradition. Therefore, all of them, under the counsel of the elderly members of the Kuru family, decided to arrest the boy but not kill him. They concluded that the girl could not be married to any boy other than Sāmba since she had already been touched by him. (According to the Vedic system, once being used by some boy, a girl cannot be married or given to any other boy. Nor would anyone agree to marry a girl who had already thus associated with another boy.) The elderly members of the family, such as Bhīṣma, wanted to arrest him. All the members of the Kuru dynasty, especially the great fighters, joined together just to teach him a lesson, and Karṇa was made the commander-in-chief for this small battle.

While the plan was being made to arrest Sāmba, the Kurus counciled amongst themselves that upon his arrest, the members of the Yadu dynasty would be very angry with them. There was every possibility of the Yadus' accepting the challenge and fighting with them. But they also thought, "If they came here to fight with us, what could they do? The members of the Yadu dynasty cannot equal the members of the Kuru dynasty because the kings of the Kuru dynasty are the emperors, whereas the kings of the Yadu dynasty are able to enjoy their landed property." The Kurus thought, "If they come here to challenge us because their son was arrested, we will nevertheless accept the fight. All of us will teach them a lesson, so that automatically they will become subdued under pressure, as the senses are subdued by the mystic *yoga* process, *prāṇāyāma*." (In the mechanical system of mystic *yoga*, the airs within the body are controlled, and the senses are subdued and checked from being engaged in anything other than meditation upon Lord Viṣṇu.)

After consultation and after receiving permission from the elderly members of the Kuru dynasty, such as Bhīṣma and Dhṛtarāṣṭra, six great warriors –Karṇa, Śala, Bhuriśravā, Yajñaketu, and Duryodhana, the father of the girl–all *mahā-rathīs* and guided by the great fighter Bhīṣmadeva, attempted to arrest the boy Sāmba. There are different grades of fighters, including *mahā-rathī, eka-rathī,* and *rathī,* classified according to their fighting capacity. These *mahā-rathīs* could fight alone with many thousands of men. All of them combined together to arrest Sāmba. Sāmba was also a *mahā-rathī,* but he was alone and had to fight with the six other *mahā-rathīs.* Still he was not deterred when he saw all the great fighters of the Kuru dynasty coming up behind him to arrest him.

Alone, he turned towards them and took his nice bow, posing exactly as a lion stands adamant in the face of other animals. Karṇa was leading the party, and he challenged Sāmba, "Why are you fleeing? Just stand, and we shall teach you a lesson!" When challenged by another *kṣatriya* to stand and fight, a *kṣatriya* cannot go away; he must fight. Therefore, as soon as Sāmba accepted the challenge and stood alone before them, he was overpowered by showers of arrows thrown by all the great warriors. As a lion is never afraid of being chased by many wolves and jackals, similarly, Sāmba, the glorious son of the Yadu dynasty, endowed with inconceivable potencies as the son of Lord Kṛṣṇa, became very angry at the warriors of the Kuru dynasty for improperly using arrows against him. He fought them with great talent. First of all, he struck each of the six charioteers with six separate arrows. Another four arrows were used to kill the charioteers' horses, four on each chariot. One arrow was used to kill the driver, and one arrow was used for Karṇa as well as the other celebrated fighters. While Sāmba was so diligently fighting alone with the six great warriors, they all appreciated the inconceivable potency of the boy. Even in the midst of fighting, they admitted frankly that this boy Sāmba was wonderful. But the fighting was conducted in the *kṣatriya* spirit, so all together, although it was improper, they obliged Sāmba to get down from his chariot, now broken to pieces. Of the six warriors, four took care to kill Sāmba's four horses, and one of them managed to cut the string of Sāmba's bow so that he could no longer fight with them. In this way, with great difficulty and after a severe fight, Sāmba was left bereft of his chariot, and they were able to arrest him. Thus, the warriors of the Kuru dynasty accepted their great victory and took their daughter, Lakṣmaṇā, away from him. Thereafter, they entered the city of Hastināpura in great triumph.

The great sage Nārada immediately carried the news to the Yadu dynasty that Sāmba was arrested and told them the whole story. The members of the Yadu dynasty became very angry at Sāmba's being arrested, and improperly so by six warriors. Now, with the permission of the head of the Yadu dynasty's king, Ugrasena, they prepared to attack the capital city of the Kuru dynasty.

Although Lord Balarāma knew very well that by slight provocation people are prepared to fight with one another in the age of Kali, He did not like the idea that the two great dynasties, the Kuru dynasty and the Yadu dynasty, would fight amongst themselves, even though they were influenced by Kali-yuga. "Instead of fighting with them," He wisely thought, "let Me go there and see the situation, and let Me try to see if the fight can be settled by mutual understanding." Balarāma's idea was that if the Kuru dynasty could be induced to release Sāmba along with his wife, Lakṣmaṇā, then the fight could be avoided. He therefore immediately arranged for a nice chariot to go to Hastināpura, accompanied by learned priests and *brāhmaṇas*, as well as by some of the elderly members of the Yadu dynasty. He was confident that the members of the Kuru dynasty would agree to this marriage and avoid fighting amongst themselves. As

Lord Balarāma proceeded towards Hastināpura in this chariot, accompanied by the learned *brāhmaṇas* and the elderly members of the Yadu dynasty, He looked like the moon shining in the clear sky amongst the glittering stars. When Lord Balarāma reached the precincts of the city of Hastināpura, He did not enter, but stationed Himself in a camp outside the city in a small garden house. Then He asked Uddhava to see the leaders of the Kuru dynasty and inquire from them whether they wanted to fight with the Yadu dynasty or to make a settlement. Uddhava went to see the leaders of the Kuru dynasty, and he met all the important members, including Bhīṣmadeva, Dhṛtarāṣṭra, Droṇācārya, Bali, Duryodhana and Bāhlīka. After offering them due respects, he informed them that Lord Balarāma had already arrived at the garden, outside the city door.

The leaders of the Kuru dynasty, especially Dhṛtarāṣṭra and Duryodhana, were very joyful because they knew very well that Lord Balarāma was a great well-wisher of their family. There were no bounds to their joy on hearing the news, and so immediately they welcomed Uddhava. In order to properly receive Lord Balarāma, they all took auspicious paraphernalia for His reception in their hands and went to see Him outside the city door. According to their respective positions, they welcomed Lord Balarāma by giving Him in charity nice cows and *argha* (an assortment of articles such as *ārātrika* water, sweet preparations of honey, butter, etc., and flowers, and garlands scented with pulp). Because all of them knew the exalted position of Lord Balarāma as the Supreme Personality of Godhead, they bowed their heads before the Lord with great respect. They all exchanged words of reception by asking one another of their welfare, and when such formality was finished, Lord Balarāma, in a great voice and very patiently, submitted before them the following words for their consideration. "My dear friends, this time I have come to you as a messenger with the order of the all-powerful King Ugrasena. Please, therefore, hear the order with attention and great care. Without wasting a single moment, please try to carry out the order. King Ugrasena knows very well that you warriors of the Kuru dynasty improperly fought with the pious Sāmba, who was alone, and that with great difficulty and tactics you have arrested him. We have all heard this news, but we are not very agitated because we are most intimately related to each other. I do not think we should disturb our good relationship; we should continue our friendship without any unnecessary fighting. Please, therefore, immediately release Sāmba and bring him, along with his wife, Lakṣmaṇā, before Me."

When Lord Balarāma spoke in a commanding tone full of heroic assertion, supremacy and chivalry, His statements were not appreciated by the leaders of the Kuru dynasty. Rather, all of them became agitated, and with great anger they said: "Hello! These words are very astonishing but quite befitting the age of Kali; otherwise how could Balarāma speak so vituperatively? The language and tone used by Balarāma are simply abusive, and due to the influence of this age, it appears that the shoes befitting the feet want to rise to the top of the head where the helmet is worn. We are connected with the Yadu dynasty by marriage, and because of this they have been given the chance to come live with us, dine with us, and sleep with us; now they are taking advantage of these privileges. They had practically no position before we gave them a portion of our kingdom to rule, and now they are trying to command us. We have allowed the Yadu dynasty to use the royal insignias like the whisk, fan, conchshell, white umbrella, crown, royal throne, sitting place, bedstead, and everything befitting the royal order. They should not have used such royal paraphernalia in our presence, but we did not check them due to our family relationships. Now they have the audacity to order us to do things. Well, this is enough of their impudence! We cannot allow them to do any more of these things, nor shall we allow them to use these royal insignias. It would be best to take all these things away; it is improper to feed a snake with milk, since such merciful activities simply increase his venom. The Yadu dynasty is now trying to go against those who have fed them so nicely. Their flourishing condition is due to our gifts and merciful behavior, and still they are so shameless that they are trying to order us. How regrettable are all these activities! No one in the world can enjoy anything if the members of the Kuru dynasty like Bhīṣma, Droṇācārya and Arjuna do not allow them to. Exactly as a lamb cannot enjoy life in the presence of a lion, without our desire it is not even possible for the demigods in heaven, headed by King Indra, to find enjoyment in life, not to speak of ordinary human beings!" Actually the members of the Kuru dynasty were very puffed up due to their opulence, kingdom, aristocracy, family tradition, great warriors, family members and vast expansive empire. They did not even observe common formalities of civilized society, and in the presence of Lord Balarāma they uttered insulting words about the Yadu dynasty. Speaking in this unmannerly way, they returned to their city of Hastināpura.

Although Lord Balarāma patiently heard their insulting words and simply observed their uncivil behavior, from His appearance it was clear that He was burning with anger and was thinking of retaliating with great vengeance. His bodily features became so agitated that it was difficult for anyone to look at Him. He laughed very loudly and said: "It is true that if a man becomes too puffed up because of his family, opulence, beauty and material advancement, he no longer wants a peaceful life but becomes belligerent toward all others. It is useless to give such a person good instruction for gentle behavior and peaceful life, but on the contrary, one should search out the ways and means to punish him." Generally, due to material opulence a man becomes exactly like an animal. To give an animal peaceful instructions is useless, and the only means is *argumentum vaculum.* In other words, the only means to keep animals in order is a stick. "Just see how impudent the members of the Kuru dynasty are! I wanted to make a peaceful settlement despite the anger of all the other members of the Yadu dynasty, including Lord Kṛṣṇa Himself. They were preparing to attack the whole kingdom of the Kuru dynasty, but I pacified them and took the trouble to come here to settle the affair without any fighting. Still these rascals behave like this! It is clear that they do not want a peaceful settlement, but that they are factually warmongers. With great pride they have repeatedly insulted Me by calling the Yadu dynasty ill names.

"Even the King of heaven, Indra, abides by the order of the Yadu dynasty; and you consider King Ugrasena, who is the head of the Bhojas, Vṛṣṇis, Andhakas and Yādavas, to be the leader of a small phalanx! Your conclusion is wonderful! You do not care for King Ugrasena, whose order is obeyed even by King Indra. Consider the exalted position of the Yadu dynasty. They have forcibly used both the assembly house and the *pārijāta* tree of the heavenly planet, and still you think that they cannot order you. Don't you even think that Lord Kṛṣṇa, the Supreme Personality of Godhead, can sit on the exalted royal throne and command everyone? All right! If your thinking is like that, then you deserve to be taught a very good lesson. You have thought it wise that the royal insignias like the whisk, fan, white umbrella, royal throne and other princely paraphernalia not be used by the Yadu dynasty. Does this mean that even Lord Kṛṣṇa, the Lord of the whole creation and the husband of the goddess of fortune, cannot use this royal paraphernalia? The dust of Kṛṣṇa's lotus feet is worshiped by all the great demigods. The Ganges water is inundating the whole world, and since it is emanating from His lotus feet, its banks have turned into great places of pilgrimage. The principal deities of all planets are engaged in His service, and they consider themselves most fortunate to take the dust of the lotus feet of Kṛṣṇa on their helmets. Great demigods like Lord Brahmā, Lord Śiva, and even the goddess of fortune and I are simply plenary parts of His spiritual identity, and still you think that He is not fit to use the royal insignia or even sit on the royal throne? Alas, how regrettable it is that these fools consider us, the members of the Yadu dynasty, to be like shoes and themselves like helmets. It is clear now that these leaders of the Kuru dynasty have become mad over their worldly possessions and opulence. Every statement they made was full of crazy proposals. I should immediately take them to task and bring them to their senses. If I do not take steps against them, it will be improper on My part. Therefore, on this very day, I shall rid the whole world of any trace of the Kuru dynasty. I shall finish them off immediately!" While talking like this, Lord Balarāma seemed so furious that He looked as if He could burn the whole cosmic creation to ashes. He stood up steadily, and taking His plow in His hand, began striking the earth with it. In this way the whole city of Hastināpura was separated from the earth. Lord Balarāma then began to drag the city toward the flowing water of the river Ganges. Because of this, there was a great tremor throughout Hastināpura, as if there had been an earthquake, and it seemed that the whole city would be dismantled.

When all the members of the Kuru dynasty saw that their city was about to fall into the water of the Ganges and when they heard their citizens howling in great anxiety, they immediately came to their senses and understood what was happening. Thus without waiting another second they brought forward their daughter Lakṣmaṇā. They also brought Sāmba, who had forcibly tried to take her away, keeping him in the forefront with Lakṣmaṇā at his back. All the members of the Kuru dynasty appeared before Lord Balarāma with folded hands just to beg the pardon of the Supreme Personality of Godhead. Now using good sense, they said: "O Lord Balarāma, You are the reservoir of all pleasures. You are the maintainer and support of the entire cosmic situation. Unfortunately we were all unaware of Your inconceivable potencies. Dear Lord, please consider us most foolish. Our intelligence was bewildered and not in order. Therefore we have come before You to beg Your pardon. Please excuse us. You are the original creator, sustainer and annihilator of the whole cosmic manifestation, and still Your position is always transcendental. O all-powerful Lord, great sages speak about You. You are the original puppeteer, and everything in the world is just like Your toys. O unlimited one, You have a hold on everything, and like child's play You hold all the planetary systems on Your head. When the time for dissolution comes, You close up the whole cosmic manifestation within Yourself. At that time nothing remains but Yourself lying in the Causal Ocean as Mahā-Viṣṇu. Our dear Lord, You have appeared on this earth in Your transcendental body just for the maintenance of the cosmic situation. You are above all anger, envy and enmity. Whatever You do, even in the form of chastisement, is auspicious for the whole material existence. We are offering our respectful obeisances unto You because You are the imperishable Supreme Personality of Godhead, the reservoir of all opulences and potencies. O creator of innumerable universes, let us fall down and offer You our respectful obeisances, again and again. We are now completely surrendered unto You. Please, therefore, be merciful upon us and give us Your protection." When the prominent members of the Kuru dynasty, beginning with grandfather Bhīṣmadeva down to Arjuna and Duryodhana, had offered their respectful prayers in that way, the Supreme Personality of Godhead, Lord Balarāma, immediately became softened and assured them there was no cause for fear and that they need not worry.

For the most part it was the practice of the *kṣatriya* kings to inaugurate some kind of fighting between the parties of the bride and bridegroom before the marriage. When Sāmba forcibly took away Lakṣmaṇā, the elderly members of the Kuru dynasty were pleased to see that he was actually the suitable match for her. In order to see his personal strength, however, they fought with him, and without any respect for the regulations of fighting, they all arrested him. When the Yadu dynasty decided to release Sāmba from the confinement of the Kurus, Lord Balarāma came personally to settle the matter, and as a powerful *kṣatriya,* He ordered them to free Sāmba immediately. The Kauravas became superficially insulted by this order, so they challenged Lord Balarāma's power. They simply wanted to see Him exhibit His inconceivable strength. Thus with great pleasure they handed over their daughter to Sāmba, and the whole matter was settled. Duryodhana, being affectionate towards his daughter Lakṣmaṇā, had her married to Sāmba in great pomp. For her dowry, he first gave 1,200 elephants, each of which were at least sixty years old; then he gave 10,000 nice horses, 6,000 chariots, which were dazzling just like the sunshine, and 1,000 maidservants who were decorated with golden ornaments. Lord Balarāma, the most prominent member of the Yadu dynasty, acted as guardian of the bridegroom Sāmba and very pleasingly accepted the dowry. Balarāma was very satisfied after His great reception from the side of the Kurus, and accompanied by the newly married couple, He started towards His capital city of Dvārakā.

Lord Balarāma triumphantly reached Dvārakā, where He met with many citizens who were all His devotees and friends. When they all assembled, Lord Balarāma narrated the whole story of the marriage, and they were astonished to hear how Balarāma had made the city of Hastināpura tremble. It is confirmed by Śukadeva Gosvāmī that the site of Hastināpura is now known as New Delhi, and the river flowing through the city is called the Yamunā, although in those days it was known as the Ganges. From authorities like Jīva Gosvāmī it is also confirmed that the Ganges and Yamunā are the same river flowing in different courses. The part of the Ganges which flows through Hastināpura to the area of Vṛndāvana is called the Yamunā because it is sanctified by the transcendental pastimes of Lord Kṛṣṇa. The part of Hastināpura which slopes towards the Yamunā becomes inundated during the rainy season and reminds everyone of Lord Balarāma's threatening to cast the city into the Ganges.

Thus ends the Bhaktivedanta purport of the Second Volume, Thirty-third Chapter of Kṛṣṇa, *"The Marriage of Sāmba."*

34 / The Great Sage Nārada Visits the Different Homes of Lord Kṛṣṇa

The great sage Nārada heard that Lord Kṛṣṇa had married 16,000 wives after He had killed the demon Narakāsura, sometimes called Bhaumāsura. Nārada became astonished that Lord Kṛṣṇa had expanded Himself into 16,000 forms and married these wives simultaneously in different palaces. Being inquisitive as to how Kṛṣṇa was managing His household affairs with so many wives, Nārada desired to see these pastimes and so set out to visit Kṛṣṇa's different homes. When Nārada arrived in Dvārakā, he saw that the gardens and parks were full of various flowers of different colors and orchards that were overloaded with a variety of fruits. Beautiful birds were chirping, and peacocks were delightfully crowing. There were tanks and ponds full of blue and red lotus flowers, and some of these sites were filled with varieties of lilies. The lakes were full of nice swans and cranes whose voices resounded everywhere. In the city there were as many as 900,000 great palaces built of first-class marble with gates and doors made of silver. The posts of the houses and palaces were bedecked with jewels such as touchstone, sapphires and emeralds, and the floors gave off a beautiful luster. The highways, lanes, streets, crossings and marketplaces were all beautifully decorated. The whole city was full of residential homes, assembly houses, and temples, all of different architectural beauty. All of this made Dvārakā a glowing city. The big avenues, crossings, lanes, streets, and also the thresholds of every residential house, were very clean. On both sides of every path there were bushes, and at regular intervals there were large trees that shaded the avenues so that the sunshine would not bother the passersby.

In this greatly beautiful city of Dvārakā, Lord Kṛṣṇa, the Supreme Personality of Godhead, had many residential quarters. The great kings and princes of the world used to visit these palaces just to worship Him. The architectural plans were made personally by Viśvakarmā, the engineer of the demigods, and in the construction of the palaces he exhibited all of his talents and ingenuity. These residential quarters numbered more than 16,000, and a different queen of Lord Kṛṣṇa resided in each of them. The great sage Nārada entered one of these houses and saw that the pillars were made of coral and the ceilings were bedecked with jewels. The walls as well as the arches between the pillars glowed from the decorations of different kinds of sapphires. Throughout the palace there were many canopies made by Viśvakarmā that were decorated with strings of pearls. The chairs and other furniture were made of ivory, bedecked with gold and diamonds, and jeweled lamps dissipated the darkness within the palace. There was so much incense and flavored gum burning that the scented fumes were coming out of the windows. The peacocks sitting on the steps became illusioned by the fumes, mistaking them for clouds, and began dancing jubilantly. There were many maidservants, all of whom were decorated with gold necklaces, bangles and beautiful saris. There were also many male servants, who were nicely dressed in cloaks and turbans and jeweled earrings. Beautiful as they were, the servants were all engaged in different household duties.

Nārada saw that Lord Kṛṣṇa was sitting with Rukmiṇīdevī, the mistress of that particular palace, who was bearing the rod of a *cāmara* whisk. Even though there were many thousands of maidservants who were equally beautiful and qualified, and who were of the same age, Rukmiṇīdevī personally was engaged in fanning Lord Kṛṣṇa. Kṛṣṇa is the Supreme Personality of Godhead, worshiped even by Nārada, but still, as soon as He saw Nārada enter the palace, Kṛṣṇa got down immediately from Rukmiṇī's bedstead and stood up to honor him. Lord Kṛṣṇa is the teacher of the whole world, and in order to instruct everyone how to respect a saintly person like Nārada Muni, Kṛṣṇa bowed down, touching His helmet to the ground. Not only did Kṛṣṇa bow down, but He also touched the feet of Nārada and with folded hands requested him to sit on His chair. Lord Kṛṣṇa is the Supreme Personality worshiped by all devotees. He is the most worshiped spiritual master of everyone. The Ganges water which emanates from His feet sanctifies the three worlds. All qualified *brāhmaṇas* worship Him, and therefore He is called *brahmaṇya-deva.*

Brahmaṇya means one who fully possesses the brahminical qualifications, which are said to be as follows: truthfulness, self-control, purity, mastery of the senses, simplicity, full knowledge by practical application, and engagement in devotional service. Lord Kṛṣṇa personally possesses all these qualities, and He is worshiped by persons who themselves possess such qualities. There are thousands and millions of names of Lord Kṛṣṇa—

Viṣṇu-sahasra-nāma—and all of them are given to Him because of His transcendental qualities.

Lord Kṛṣṇa in Dvārakā enjoyed the pastimes of a perfect human being. When, therefore, He washed the feet of the sage Nārada and took the water on His head, Nārada did not object, knowing well that the Lord did so to teach everyone how to respect saintly persons. The Supreme Personality of Godhead, Kṛṣṇa, who is the original Nārāyaṇa and eternal friend of all living entities, thus worshiped the sage Nārada according to Vedic regulative principles. Welcoming him with sweet nectarean words, He addressed Nārada as *bhagavān,* or one who is self-sufficient, possessing all kinds of knowledge, renunciation, strength, fame, beauty, and similar other opulences. He particularly asked Nārada, "What can I do in your service?"

Nārada replied, "My dear Lord, this kind of behavior by Your Lordship is not at all astonishing because You are the Supreme Personality of Godhead and master of all species of living entities. You are the supreme friend of all living entities, but at the same time You are the supreme chastiser of the miscreants and the envious. I know that Your Lordship has descended on this earth for the proper maintenance of the whole universe. Your appearance, therefore, is not forced by any other agency. By Your sweet will only, You agree to appear and disappear. It is my great fortune that I have been able to see Your lotus feet today. Anyone who becomes attached to Your lotus feet is elevated to the supreme position of neutrality and is uncontaminated by the material modes of nature. My Lord, You are unlimited; there is no limit to Your opulences. Great demigods like Lord Brahmā and Lord Śiva are always busy placing You within their hearts and meditating upon You. The conditioned souls who have now been put into the blind well of material existence can get out of this eternal captivity only by accepting Your lotus feet. Thus, You are the only shelter of all conditioned souls. My dear Lord, You have very kindly asked what You can do for me. In answer to this I simply request that I may not forget Your lotus feet at any time. I do not care where I may be, but I pray that I may be allowed to constantly remember Your lotus feet."

The benediction which the sage Nārada asked from the Lord is the ideal prayer of all pure devotees. A pure devotee never asks for any kind of material or spiritual benediction from the Lord, but his only prayer is that he may not forget the lotus feet of the Lord in any condition of life. A pure devotee does not care whether he is put in heaven or hell; he is satisfied anywhere, provided he can constantly remember the lotus feet of the Lord. Lord Caitanya also taught this same process of prayer in His

Śikṣāṣṭaka, in which He clearly stated that all He wanted was devotional service, birth after birth. A pure devotee does not even want to stop the repetition of birth and death. To a pure devotee, it does not matter whether he has to take birth again in the various species of life. His only ambition is that he may not forget the lotus feet of the Lord in any condition of life.

After departing from the palace of Rukmiṇī, Nāradajī wanted to see the activities of Lord Kṛṣṇa's internal potency, *yogamāyā;* thus he entered the palace of another queen. There he saw Lord Kṛṣṇa engaged in playing chess, along with His dear wife and Uddhava. The Lord immediately got up from His seat and invited Nārada Muni to sit on His personal seat. The Lord again worshiped him with as much paraphernalia for reception as He had in the palace of Rukmiṇī. After worshiping him properly, Lord Kṛṣṇa acted as if He did not know what had happened in the palace of Rukmiṇī. He therefore told Nārada, "My dear sage, when your holiness comes here, you are full in yourself. Although we are householders and are always in need, you don't require anyone's help because you are self-satisfied. Under the circumstances, what reception can we offer you, and what can we possibly give you? Yet, since your holiness is a *brāhmaṇa,* it is our duty to offer you something as far as possible. Therefore, I beg your pleasure to order Me. What can I do for you?"

Nāradajī knew everything about the pastimes of the Lord, so without any further discussion, he simply left the palace silently, in great astonishment over the Lord's activities. He then entered another palace. This time Nāradajī saw that Lord Kṛṣṇa was engaged as an affectionate father petting His small children. From there he entered another palace and saw Lord Kṛṣṇa preparing to take His bath. In this way, Saint Nārada entered each and every one of the sixteen thousand residential palaces of the queens of Lord Kṛṣṇa, and in each of them he found Kṛṣṇa engaged in different ways.

In one place he found Kṛṣṇa engaged in offering oblations to the sacrificial fire and performing the ritualistic ceremonies of the *Vedas* as enjoined for householders. In another palace, Kṛṣṇa was found performing the *pañca-yajña* sacrifice, which is compulsory for a householder. This *yajña* is also known as *pañca-śūna*. Knowingly or unknowingly, everyone, specifically the householder, is committing five kinds of sinful activities. When we receive water from a water pitcher, we kill many germs that are in it. Similarly, when we use a grinding machine or take foodstuff, we kill many germs. When sweeping a floor or igniting a fire we kill many germs, and when we walk on the street we kill manv ants and other insects.

Consciously or unconsciously, in all our different activities, we are killing. Therefore, it is incumbent upon every householder to perform the *pañca-śūna* sacrifice to rid himself of the reactions to such sinful activities.

In one palace Lord Kṛṣṇa was found engaged in feeding *brāhmaṇas* after performing ritualistic *yajñas.* In another palace, Nārada found Kṛṣṇa engaged in silently chanting the Gāyatrī *mantra,* and in a third he found Him practicing fighting with a sword and shield. In some palaces Lord Kṛṣṇa was found riding on horses or elephants or chariots and wandering hither and thither. Elsewhere He was found lying down on His bedstead taking rest, and somewhere else He was found sitting in His chair, being praised by the prayers of His different devotees. In some of the palaces He was found consulting with ministers like Uddhava and others on important matters of business. In one palace He was found surrounded by many young society girls, enjoying in a swimming pool. In another palace He was found engaged in giving well-decorated cows in charity to the *brāhmaṇas,* and in another palace He was found hearing the narrations of the *Purāṇas* or histories, such as the *Mahābhārata,* which are supplementary literatures for disseminating Vedic knowledge to common people by narrating important instances in the history of the universe. Somewhere Lord Kṛṣṇa was found enjoying the company of a particular wife by exchanging joking words with her. Somewhere else He was found engaged along with His wife in religious ritualistic functions. Since it is necessary for householders to increase their financial assets for various expenditures, Kṛṣṇa was found somewhere engaged in matters of economic development. Somewhere else He was found enjoying family life according to the regulative principles of the *śāstras.*

In one palace He was found sitting in meditation as if He were concentrating His mind on the Supreme Personality of Godhead, who is beyond these material universes. Meditation, as recommended in authorized scripture, is meant for concentrating one's mind on the Supreme Personality of Godhead, Viṣṇu. Lord Kṛṣṇa is Himself the original Viṣṇu, but because He played the part of a human being, He taught us definitely by His personal behavior what is meant by meditation. Somewhere Lord Kṛṣṇa was found satisfying elderly superiors by supplying them things which they needed. Somewhere else Nāradajī found that Lord Kṛṣṇa was engaged in discussing topics of fighting, and somewhere else in making peace with enemies. Somewhere Lord Kṛṣṇa was found discussing the ultimate auspicious activity for the entire human society with His elder brother Lord Balarāma. Nārada saw Lord Kṛṣṇa engaged in getting His sons and daughters married with suitable brides and bridegrooms in due course of time, and the marriage ceremonies were being performed with great pomp.

In one palace He was found bidding farewell to His daughters, and in another He was found receiving a daughter-in-law. People throughout the whole city were astonished to see such pomp and ceremonies.

Somewhere the Lord was seen engaged in performing different types of sacrifices to satisfy the demigods, who are only His qualitative expansions. Somewhere He was seen engaged in public welfare activities, establishing deep wells for water supply, rest houses and gardens for unknown guests, and great monastaries and temples for saintly persons. These are some of the duties enjoined in the *Vedas* for householders for fulfillment of their material desires. Somewhere Kṛṣṇa was found as a *kṣatriya* king engaged in hunting animals in the forest and riding on very beautiful *sindhi* horses. According to Vedic regulations, the *kṣatriyas* were allowed to kill prescribed animals on certain occasions, either to maintain peace in the forests or to offer the animals in the sacrificial fire. *Kṣatriyas* are allowed to practice this killing art because they have to kill their enemies mercilessly to maintain peace in society. In one situation the great sage Nārada saw Lord Kṛṣṇa, the Supreme Personality of Godhead and master of mystic powers, acting as a spy by changing His usual dress in order to understand the motives of different citizens in the city and within the palaces.

Saint Nārada saw all these activities of the Lord, who is the Supersoul of all living entities but who played the role of an ordinary human being in order to manifest the activities of His internal potency. He was smiling within himself and began to address the Lord as follows: "My dear Lord of all mystic powers, object of the meditation of great mystics, the extent of Your mystic power is certainly inconceivable, even to mystics like Lord Brahmā and Lord Śiva. But by Your mercy, because of my being always engaged in the transcendental loving service of Your lotus feet, Your Lordship has very kindly revealed to me the actions of Your internal potency. My dear Lord, You are worshipable by all, and demigods and predominating deities of all fourteen planetary systems are completely aware of Your transcendental fame. Now please give me Your blessings so that I may be able to travel all over the universes singing the glories of Your transcendental activities."

The Supreme Personality of Godhead, Lord Kṛṣṇa, replied to Nārada as follows: "My dear Nārada, O sage among the demigods, you know that I am the supreme instructor and perfect follower of all religious principles, as well as the supreme enforcer of such principles. I am therefore personally executing such religious principles in order to teach the whole world how to act. My dear son, it is My desire that you not be bewildered by such demonstrations of My internal energy."

The Supreme Personality of Godhead was engaged in His so-called household affairs in order to teach people how one can sanctify one's household life although he may be attached to the imprisonment of material existence. Actually, one is obliged to continue the term of material existence because of household life. But the Lord, being very kind upon householders, demonstrated the path of sanctifying ordinary household life. Because Kṛṣṇa is the center of all activities, a Kṛṣṇa conscious householder's life is transcendental to Vedic injunctions and is automatically sanctified.

Thus Nārada saw one single Kṛṣṇa living in sixteen thousand palaces by His plenary expansions. Due to His inconceivable energy, He was visible in each and every individual queen's palace. Lord Kṛṣṇa has unlimited power, and Nārada's astonishment was boundless upon observing again and again the demonstration of Lord Kṛṣṇa's internal energy. Lord Kṛṣṇa behaved by His personal example as if He were very much attached to the four principles of civilized life, namely religiousness, economic development, sense gratification and salvation. These four principles of material existence are necessary for the spiritual advancement of human society, and although Lord Kṛṣṇa had no need to do so, He exhibited His household activities so that people might follow in His footsteps for their own interest. Lord Kṛṣṇa satisfied the sage Nārada in every way. Nārada was very much pleased by seeing the Lord's activities in Dvārakā, and thus he departed.

In narrating the activities of Lord Kṛṣṇa in Dvārakā, Śukadeva Gosvāmī explained to King Parīkṣit how Lord Kṛṣṇa, the Supreme Personality of Godhead, descends on this material universe by the agency of His internal potency and personally exhibits the principles which, if followed, can lead one to achieve the ultimate goal of life. All the queens in Dvārakā, more than sixteen thousand in number, engaged their feminine attractive features in the transcendental service of the Lord by smiling and serving, and the Lord was pleased to behave with them exactly as a perfect husband enjoying household life. One should know definitely that such pastimes cannot be performed by anyone but Lord Śrī Kṛṣṇa. Lord Śrī Kṛṣṇa is the original cause of the creation, maintenance and dissolution of the whole cosmic manifestation. Anyone who attentively hears the narrations of the Lord's pastimes in Dvārakā or supports a preacher of the Kṛṣṇa consciousness movement will certainly find it very easy to traverse the path of liberation and taste the nectar of the lotus feet of Lord Kṛṣṇa. And thus he will be engaged in His devotional service.

Thus ends the Bhaktivedanta purport of the Second Volume, Thirty-fourth Chapter of Kṛṣṇa, *"The Great Sage Nārada Visits the Different Homes of Lord Kṛṣṇa."*

Glossary

Ācāryas—spiritual masters who teach by their own personal behavior.
Asura—a demon or nondevotee.
Ātmārāma—a self-satisfied sage.
Avatāra—an incarnation of Godhead who descends from the spiritual world.
Bhagavad-gītā—the book which records the spiritual instructions given by Kṛṣṇa to His friend Arjuna on the Battlefield of Kurukṣetra.
Bhakta—devotee.
Bhakti-yoga—the *yoga* of devotional service to the Lord.
Brahmā—the first created living being in the universe.
Brahmacārī—a celibate student under the guidance of a spiritual master.
Brahmajyoti—the impersonal effulgence that emanates from the body of Kṛṣṇa.
Brahman—the impersonal feature of the Absolute Truth.
Brāhmaṇas—the spiritual order of society whose occupation is the cultivation of Vedic knowledge.
Brahma-saṁhitā—a scripture written by Lord Brahmā in which his authoritative prayers to the Lord are recorded.
Caitanya Mahāprabhu—the incarnation of Kṛṣṇa as His own devotee who comes in this age to teach the process of devotional service by chanting the holy name of God.
Cāmara—a yak-tail whisk.
Deva—a demigod or devotee.
Ekādaśī—a day of celebration which occurs twice a month and which is meant for increasing Kṛṣṇa consciousness.
Gandharvas—celestial denizens of the heavenly planets who sing very beautifully.
Garuḍa—the giant bird-carrier of Viṣṇu.
Gopīs—cowherd girls, specifically the transcendental girl friends of Lord Kṛṣṇa.

Gṛhastha—one who is in the householder order of spiritual life.
Guru—spiritual master.
Jaya—victory.
Jñānī—one who engages in mental speculation in pursuit of knowledge.
Kadamba—a tree which bears a round yellow flower and which is generally seen only in the Vṛndāvana area.
Karma—fruitive activities or their reactions.
Karmī—a fruitive worker.
Kaumudī—an especially fragrant flower found on the bank of the Yamunā River.
Kaustubha—a transcendental jewel worn around the neck of the Supreme Personality of Godhead.
Kṛṣṇa-kathā—narrations spoken by or about Kṛṣṇa.
Kṣatriya—the spiritual order of society whose occupation is governmental administration and military protection of the citizens.
Kuṅkuma—a sweetly flavored reddish powder which is thrown upon the bodies of worshipable persons.
Līlā—pastimes.
Māgadhas—professional singers present at sacrifices.
Mahābhāgavata—a highly advanced devotee.
Mahāmantra—the Hare Kṛṣṇa *mantra:* Hare Kṛṣṇa, Hare Kṛṣṇa, Kṛṣṇa Kṛṣṇa, Hare Hare/Hare Rāma, Hare Rāma, Rāma Rāma, Hare Hare.
Mantra—a transcendental sound vibration.
Māyā (Mahāmāyā)—the external energy of the Supreme Lord, which covers the conditioned soul and does not allow him to understand the Supreme Personality of Godhead.
Māyāvāda—the impersonalist or voidist philosophy.
Māyāvādī—one who adheres to the impersonalist or voidist philosophy and does not accept the eternal existence of the transcendental form of the Lord.
Mukti—liberation.
Mukunda—Lord Kṛṣṇa, who awards liberation and whose smiling face is like a *kunda* flower.
Nirguṇa—literally, without qualities (used to describe the Supreme Lord, who has no material qualities).
Pāṇḍavas—the five sons of King Pāṇḍu (Yudhiṣṭhīra, Arjuna, Bhīma, Nakula and Sahadeva).
Paramahaṁsa—(literally, the supreme swan) a devotee who can appreciate the spiritual essence of life, just as a swan extracts milk from water.
Paramātmā—the expansion of the Supreme Lord who lives in the hearts of all living entities.

Pārijāta–a type of flower found only on the heavenly planets.

Prakṛta sahajiyā–pseudo-devotees of Kṛṣṇa who fail to understand His absolute, transcendental position.

Prāṇāyāma–the yogic breathing exercises.

Prasadam–food first offered to the Supreme Lord and then distributed.

Rasa–a transcendental mellow relationship between the individual soul and the Supreme Lord.

Rāsa-līlā–Lord Kṛṣṇa's transcendental pastime of dancing with the *gopīs.*

Samādhi–trance, absorption in meditation upon the Supreme.

Saṅkīrtana yajña–the chanting of the holy names of God, which is the recommended sacrifice for this age.

Sannyāsī–one who is in the renounced order of spiritual life.

Śāstras–revealed scriptures.

Sāyujya-mukti–the liberation of merging into the existence of the Supreme Lord.

Siddhi–a mystic yogic perfection.

Śiva–the demigod in charge of annihilation and the mode of ignorance.

Śrīmad-Bhāgavatam–the authoritative Vedic scripture that deals exclusively with the pastimes of the Personality of Godhead and His devotees.

Sudarśana–the wheel which is the personal weapon of Viṣṇu or Kṛṣṇa.

Śūdra–the spiritual order of society who are not very intelligent and are unqualified for any work other than menial service.

Śyāmasundara–a name of Kṛṣṇa. *Śyāma* means blackish, and *sundara* means very beautiful.

Tapasya–austerity.

Tilaka–a clay mark that decorates the faces of Kṛṣṇa and His devotees.

Tulasī–a great devotee in the form of a plant who is very dear to Lord Kṛṣṇa.

Vaiṣṇava–a devotee of the Supreme Lord Viṣṇu or Kṛṣṇa.

Vaiśya–the agricultural community in Vedic culture, who protect cows and cultivate crops.

Viṣṇu–an all-pervasive, fully empowered expansion of Lord Kṛṣṇa, qualified by full truth, full knowledge and full bliss.

Yajña–sacrifice.

Yoga–the process of linking with the Supreme.

Yogamāyā–the principal internal (spiritual) potency of the Supreme Lord.

Yogī–one who practices *yoga*

The vowels are pronounced almost as in Italian. The sound of the short *a* is like the *u* in b*u*t, the long *a* is like the *a* in f*a*r and held twice as long as the short *a*, and *e* is like the *a* in ev*a*de. Long *ī* is like the *i* in p*i*que. The vowel *ṛ* is pronounced like the *re* in the English word fib*re*. The *c* is pronounced as in the English word *ch*air, and the aspirated consonants (*ch, jh, dh,* etc.) are pronounced as in staun*ch*-*h*eart, he*dge*-*h*og, re*d*-*h*ot, etc. The two spirants *ś* and *ṣ* are pronounced like the English *sh*; *s* is pronounced as in *s*un.